The Bed & Breakfast Directory

1992-1993 Edition

Edited by Robyn Martins

A BARBOUR BOOK

How To Use This Book

Have you dreamed of spending a few days in a rustic cabin in Alaska? Would you like to stay in an urban town house while taking care of some business in the city? Would your family like to spend a weekend on a midwestern farm feeding the pigs and gathering eggs? Maybe a romantic Victorian mansion in San Francisco or an antebellum plantation in Mississippi is what you've been looking for. No matter what your needs may be, whether you are traveling for business or pleasure, you will find a variety of choices in the 1992 edition of *The Christian Bed & Breakfast Directory*.

In the pages of this guide, you will find nearly 800 bed and breakfasts, small inns, and homestays. All of the information has been updated from last year's edition, and many entries are listed for the first time. Although every establishment is not owned or operated by Christians, each host has expressed a desire to welcome Christian travelers.

The directory is designed for easy reference. At a glance, you can determine the number of rooms available at each establishment and how many rooms have private (PB) and shared (SB) baths. You will find the name of the host or hosts, the price range for two people sharing one room, the kind of breakfast that is served, and what credit cards are accepted. There is also a "Notes" section to let you know important information that may not be included in the description. These notes correspond to the list at the bottom of each page. The descriptions have been written by the hosts. The publisher has not visited these bed and breakfasts and is not responsible for inaccuracies.

It is recommended that you make reservations in advance. Many bed and breakfasts have small staffs or are run single-handedly and cannot easily accommodate surprises. Also, ask about taxes, as city and state taxes vary. Remember to ask for directions, and if your special dietary needs can be met, and confirm check-in and check-out times.

Whether you're planning a honeymoon (first or second!), family vacation, or business trip, *The Christian Bed & Breakfast Directory* will make any outing out of the ordinary.

Robyn Martins, editor

Barbour Books would like to hear about your adventures—both memorable and forgettable—so our next edition will better serve your needs. Just drop a line to the attention of *The Christian Bed & Breakfast Directory*, Barbour & Company, Inc., P.O. Box 719, Uhrichsville, Ohio 44683. We appreciate your help!

© 1992 by Barbour and Company, Inc. All Rights Reserved.
Printed in the United States of America. ISBN 1-55748-289-6
Photograph on front cover courtesy of Oak Square Plantation,
Port Gibson, Mississippi, and used by permission.

Alabama

LEEDS

Bed and Breakfast Birmingham
Route 2, Box 275, 35094
(205) 699-9841

This is a reservation service for the state of Alabama with bed and breakfasts in Anniston, Decatur, Fort Payne, Huntsville, Birgmingham, Arab, Franklin, Spanish Fort, and Muscle Shoals. Meals vary. Kay Rice, coordinator.

MOBILE

Stickney's Hollow
1604 Springhill Road, 36604
(205) 456-4556

The guest house of this Victorian home is nestled in the shade of ancient oak trees and surrounded by azaleas. The original structure dates back to 1805. In 1905, the house was converted from a Creole cottage to a Victorian town house. A private two-bedroom apartment includes livingroom, dining room, and kitchen. The refrigerator is stocked for your convenience and privacy. Rented to one party only.

Host: N. Jack Stallworth
Rooms: 2 (SB) $50-90
Continental Breakfast
Credit Cards: None

Stickney's Hollow

NOTES: Credit cards accepted: A Master Card; B Visa; C American Express; D Discover Card; E Diners Club; F Other; 2 Personal checks accepted; 3 Lunch available; 4 Dinner available; 5 Open all year; 6 Pets welcome; 7 Children welcome; 8 Tennis nearby; 9 Swimming nearby; 10 Golf nearby; 11 Skiing nearby; 12 May be booked through travel agent

Alaska

ANCHORAGE—SEE ALSO EAGLE RIVER

Alaska Bed and Breakfast
320 East 12th Avenue, 99501
(907) 279-3200

This cozy home in downtown Anchorage is within easy walking distance of downtown shops, restaurants, museum, and other points of interest. A large, fenced-in back yard offers flowers and picnic table for a restful place to relax. Kitchen and laundry privileges are available. A longtime Alaskan, your hostess can provide information about the beautiful state of Alaska.

Host: Joy Young
Rooms: 3 (1 PB; 2 SB) $45-60
Continental Breakfast
Credit Cards: A, B, C, D
Notes: 2, 5, 7, 11

Green Bough Bed and Breakfast
3832 Young Street, 99508
(907) 562-4636

Established in 1981 to practice the art of Christian hospitality, Green Bough is Anchorage's oldest independent bed and breakfast home. We have remodeled the kitchen and baths. Slip into freshly ironed sheets, and awaken to freshly brewed coffee and home-baked breads. Amiable felines are available for petting. Your hosts are 25-year Alaskan residents and are involved in evangelical ministries. We offer rates for families and missionaries.

Hosts: Jerry and Phyllis Jost
Rooms: 5 (2 PB; 3 SB) $45-60
Continental Breakfast
Credit Cards: None
Notes: 2, 5, 7, 8, 9, 10, 11, 12

Hillcrest Haven Bed and Breakfast
1449 Hillcrest Drive, 99503
(907) 274-3086; FAX (907) 276-8411

The recipient of several awards for exceptional service from Anchorage's visitors bureau, this European-style guest house is blessed with the finest views of Anchorage, Denali Cook Inlet, and spectacular sunsets. Located in a secluded wilderness setting, it is convenient to downtown, buses, restaurants, shopping, and airport.

NOTES: Credit cards accepted: A Master Card; B Visa; C American Express; D Discover Card; E Diners Club; F Other; 2 Personal checks accepted; 3 Lunch available; 4 Dinner available; 5 Open all

Host: Linda M. Smith
Rooms: 5 (2 PB; 3 SB) $56-68
Continental Breakfast
Credit Cards: A , B, C, D, E
Notes: 2, 5, 8, 9, 11

A Homestay at Homesteads

Mailing address: Box 771283
Eagle River, 99577
(907) 272-8644; (907) 694-8644

Enjoy a breathtaking view surrounded by wilderness, yet close to Anchorage. We know where to hike, pick berries, and fish. Let us make all your Alaska travel arrangements. The wilderness trailhead across the creek can be seen from our flower-lined porch in the summer and is perfect for cross-country skiing in the winter. Breakfast is served with a view of two glaciers or Denali.

Host: Sharon Kelly
Rooms: 3 (1 PB; 2 SB)
Full Breakfast
Credit Cards: None
Notes: 2, 5, 9, 10, 11, 12

DOUGLAS

Windsock Inn Bed and Breakfast

P. O. Box 240223, 99824
(907) 364-2431

Only three families have owned and occupied this historic home built in 1912 in the heart of Douglas, five minutes from downtown Juneau. Pioneer hosts are now retired and spend a portion of the winter south but return each spring to share their Alaskan experience and hospitality with bed and breakfast clientele from all over the world.

Hosts: Julie and Bob Isaac
Room: 2 (SB) $45-50
Full Breakfast
Credit Cards: None
Notes: 2, 7, 8, 9, 10, 11, 12

Alaska's 7 Gables Bed and Breakfast

FAIRBANKS

Alaska's 7 Gables Bed and Breakfast

P. O. Box 80890, 99708
(907) 479-0751

Historically, Alaska's 7 Gables was a fraternity house. It is within walking distance of the University of Alaska, Fairbanks campus, yet near the river and airport. The spacious 10,000-square-foot Tudor-style home features a floral solarium, a foyer with antique stained-glass and an indoor waterfall, cathedral ceilings, wedding chapel, conference room, and dormers. A gourmet breakfast is served daily. Other amenities include cable TV and phones, library, laundry facilities, Jacuzzis, bikes, canoes, and skis. Suites are available.

Hosts: Paul and Leicha Welton
Rooms: 9 (4 PB; 4 SB) $45
Full Breakfast
Credit Cards: A, B, D, E
Notes: 2, 5, 7, 9, 10, 11, 12

Hillside Bed and Breakfast
310 Rambling Road, 99712
(907) 457-2664

Experience authentic Alaskan decor and hospitality in contemporary comfort with a beautiful, wooded location. Spacious rooms, full sourdough breakfasts, laundry facilities, in-room TVs, private kitchenette. Only seven minutes from downtown and close to popular attractions. The hosts have lived several years in the Alaskan bush, as well as in Fairbanks. No smoking.

Hosts: Tim and Deb Vanasse
Rooms: 2 (SB) $45-55
Full Breakfast
Credit Cards: None
Notes: 2, 5, 6, 7, 11, 12

HOMER

Patchwork Farm Bed and Breakfast
36170 Sunshine Drive, 99603
(907) 235-7368

This established bed and breakfast home is in a peaceful, rural setting with fishing and sightseeing just minutes away. This is the perfect place for a long-needed rest or a quiet hike on our nature trail. A children's dream. With so much to explore, they will keep busy for hours. During the winter months, enjoy cross-country skiing on a groomed 15-kilometer ski trail. Afterwards, enjoy conversation beside a toasty fire with a cup of steaming coffee, tea, or cider.

Hosts: Robert and Kim Avera
Rooms: 3 (2 PB; 1 SB) $60-80
Full Breakfast
Credit Cards: None
Notes: 2, 5, 7, 11

MATANUSKA

Yukon Don's
HC 31 5086, 99654
(907) 376-7472

This 10,000-square-foot converted cow barn is one of Alaska's finest bed and breakfast inns and has been selected as one of the top 50 inns in America by *Inn Times* in 1991. Located near the old town site of Matanuska and just 40 minutes from Anchorage, we offer the finest view in the Matanuska Valley. Each of our rooms is theme decorated. A full-color brochure is available on request.

Hosts: Diane and Art Mongeau
Rooms: 5 (1 PB; 4 SB) $50-70

NOTES: Credit cards accepted: A Master Card; B Visa; C American Express; D Discover Card; E Diners Club; F Other; 2 Personal checks accepted; 3 Lunch available; 4 Dinner available; 5 Open all

Continental Breakfast
Credit Cards: None
Notes: 2, 7, 10, 11

SEWARD

Swiss Chalet Bed and Breakfast
P. O. Box 1734, 99664
(907) 224-3939

See Seward and stay one block from the Seward highway at Mile .1 on the road to Exit Glacier where a clean, cozy chalet offers comfortable beds and a tasty breakfast. From Swiss Chalet, it is a short ride to the boat harbor where charters for fishing and Kenai Fjords tours are available in magnificent Resurrection Bay and beyond. Swiss Chalet is located within a short walk of Le Barn Appetit, a delightful, natural food restaurant and bakery.

Hosts: Stan Jones and Charlotte Freeman-Jones
Rooms: 4 (2 PB; 2 SB) $50

Full Breakfast
Credit Cards: A, B
Notes: 2, 12

SITKA

Karras Bed and Breakfast
230 Kegwonton Street, 99835
(907) 747-3985

A warm welcome will be yours at our bed and breakfast overlooking Sitka Sound, the picturesque fishing fleet, and the Pacific Ocean. You can walk to Sitka's main historic attractions, dining, and shopping areas. Bus service is available from the airport or ferry directly to our home. We have a family room for lounging, reading, visiting, and watching the endless marine traffic through a telescope.

Hosts: Pete and Bertha Karras
Rooms: 4 (S2B) $43.20-59.40
Full Breakfast
Credit Cards: C
Notes: 2, 5, 7

---

year; 6 Pets welcome; 7 Children welcome; 8 Tennis nearby; 9 Swimming nearby; 10 Golf nearby; 11 Skiing nearby; 12 May be booked through travel agent

Arizona

BISBEE

Park Place Bed and Breakfast
200 East Vista, 85603
(602) 432-3054 evening
(800) 388-4388 daytime

This pleasant 5,000-square-foot home offers a three-course breakfast, spacious rooms, terraces, early-morning hot coffee. Jogging park, tennis, and golf; close to Mexico.

Hosts: Bob and Janet Watkins
Rooms: 4 (PB; 2 SB) $40-60
Full Breakfast
Credit Cards: A, B
Notes: 2, 5, 8, 10

CORNVILLE

Pumpkinshell Ranch Bed and Breakfast
HC 66, Box 2100, 86325
(602) 634-4797

This new, large solar home is set in the middle of four acres in a secluded country setting. Rooms have private entrances and twin or queen beds. Enjoy the distinguished architecture with luxurious decor, a deck overlooking waterfalls, the pond in the back yard, private library, and restful atmosphere. Indian cliff dwellings are nearby.

Hosts: Kay and Terry Johnson
Rooms: 2 (PB) $65-70
Full Breakfast
Credit Cards: A, B
Notes: 2, 5, 7, 9

TEMPE

Mi Casa Su Casa Bed and Breakfast
P. O. Box 950, 85280-0950
(602) 990-0682; (800) 456-0682 reservations

Our reservation service has more than 130 inspected and approved homestays, guest cottages, ranches, and inns in Arizona, Utah, and New Mexico. Listings include Ajo, Apache Junction, Bisbee, Cave Creek, Cottonwood, Clarkdale, Dragoon, Flagstaff, Mesa, Paradise Valley, Phoenix, Prescott, Scottsdale, Tempe, Tucson, Yuma, and other cities in Arizona; Alburquerque, Carlsbad, Los Cruces, Ramah, Silver

---

NOTES: Credit cards accepted: A Master Card; B Visa; C American Express; D Discover Card; E Diners Club; F Other; 2 Personal checks accepted; 3 Lunch available; 4 Dinner available; 5 Open all

City, and Santa Fe, New Mexico; Moab, Monroe, Monticello, Salt Lake City, Springdale, and St. George, Utah. Private and shared baths ranging from $25 to $125. Full or continental breakfast. Ruth Young, coordinator.

TUCSON

Desert Dream
825 Via Lucitas, 85718
(602) 297-1220

Located in the rolling foothills of the Catalina Mountains, this territorial adobe home offers a spectacular view of the mountains and city. Easy access to the airport and I-10. Guests will find we are always happy to help them plan trips to the many attractions and scenic wonders and to provide information about places to eat, shop, or attend church.

Hosts: Ken and Nell Putnam
Room: 1 (PB) $40
Continental Breakfast

Credit Cards: None
Notes: 2, 5, 10, 11

El Presidio Bed and Breakfast
297 North Main Avenue, 85701
(602) 623-6151

Experience southwestern charm in a desert oasis with the romance of a country inn. Garden courtyards with Old Mexico ambience of lush, floral displays, fountains, and cobblestone surround richly appointed guest houses and suites. Enjoy antique decor, robes, complimentary beverages, fruit, cheese, TVs, and telephones. A Victorian adobe, the award-winning inn is in a historic district close to downtown. Walk to restaurants, museums, and shops.

Hosts. Patti and Jerry Toci
Rooms: 4 (PB) $65-95
Full Breakfast
Credit Cards: None
Notes: 2, 5, 8, 9, 10, 11, 12

---

year; 6 Pets welcome; 7 Children welcome; 8 Tennis nearby; 9 Swimming nearby; 10 Golf nearby; 11 Skiing nearby; 12 May be booked through travel agent

Arkansas

EUREKA SPRINGS

Heart of the Hills
5 Summit, 72632
(501) 253-7468

This historic Victorian home is in a quaint town nestled into the Ozark Mountains. Wake up to a scrumptious breakfast, enjoy a gorgeous four-block walk to shops, museums, and galleries, or catch a trolley for a spin around the area. Rooms have antiques with a Victorian decor. Come, experience a touch of true, southern hospitality.

Host: Jan Jacobs Weber
Rooms: 4 (PB) $60-80
Full Breakfast
Credit Cards: A, B
Notes: 5, 7, 9, 10

The Heartstone Inn and Cottages
35 Kingshighway, 72632
(501) 253-8916

This award-winning, nine-room inn is located in the historic district and has turn-of-the-century charm with all modern conveniences. Two charming cottages are also available. Antiques, fresh flowers, private entrances, air conditioning, cable TV. King, queen, and double beds. "Best breakfast in the Ozarks," the *New York Times*, 1989.

Hosts: Iris and Bill Simantel
Rooms: 9 plus 2 cottages (PB) $58-105
Full Breakfast
Credit Cards: A, B, C
Closed Christmas through January
Notes: 2, 7

Hillside Cottage Bed and Breakfast

Hillside Cottage Bed and Breakfast
23 Hillside Avenue, 72632
(501) 253-8688

NOTES: Credit cards accepted: A Master Card; B Visa; C American Express; D Discover Card; E Diners Club; F Other; 2 Personal checks accepted; 3 Lunch available; 4 Dinner available; 5 Open all

Arkansas 11

This country Victorian bed and breakfast, hidden in the heart of the Ozarks, offers you an escape back in time. Eureka Springs is full of gingerbread homes, wonderful restaurants, and quaint shops. The magnificent statue of the Christ of the Ozarks watches over our entire town, and the famous passion play is open from April through October.

Hosts: Marvin and Barbara Heppner
Rooms: 3 (2 PB; 1 SB) $65-85
Full or Continental Breakfast
Credit Cards: A, B
Notes: 2, 5, 7, 9, 10, 11

Singleton House

Singleton House
11 Singleton, 72632
(501) 253-9111

This old-fashioned Victorian with a touch of magic is whimsically decorated and has an eclectic collection of treasures and antiques. Breakfast is served on the balcony overlooking a fantasy garden and fish pond. Walk to the historic district, shops, and cafes. Passion play and Holy Land tour reservations can be arranged. A guest cottage is also available. An innkeepers' apprenticeship program is also available.

Host: Barbara Bavron
Rooms: 5 (PB) $65-75
Full Breakfast
Credit Cards: A, B, C, D
Notes: 2, 5, 7, 9, 10, 12

Willow Ridge Luxury Lodging
85 Kingshighway, 72632
(501) 253-7737; (800) 467-1737

Enjoy a Victorian aura, a glimpse of the 1920s, or relaxing country charm. Located on 14 wooded acres adjacent to the Eureka Springs chamber of commerce visitors' center, Willow Ridge takes advantage of the natural terrain so that rooms on each story have a ground-level entry and parking. Each upper-story room has a private balcony. Recreational facilities are nearby.

Hosts: Roy and Patricia Manley
Rooms: 7 (PB) $125
Continental Breakfast
Credit Cards: A, B, D
Notes: 5, 12

ROMANCE

Hammons Chapel Farm
271 Hammons Chapel Road, 72136
(501) 849-2819

---

year; 6 Pets welcome; 7 Children welcome; 8 Tennis nearby; 9 Swimming nearby; 10 Golf nearby; 11 Skiing nearby; 12 May be booked through travel agent

This 110-acre Brahman cattle farm in the foothills of the Ozark Mountains is a short distance from 45,000-acre Greers Ferry Lake. John and Susan's white stucco home reflects John's love of reading, writing, painting, and years as a congregational minister, and Susan's interest in cookbooks and gardening. Your stay can be as quiet as a good book by the fire, as scenic as a walk in the fields and woods, or as active as leading the massive yet gentle Brahman bulls in from the pasture.

Hosts: John and Susan Hammons
Rooms: 1 (PB) $55
Full Breakfast
Credit Cards: None
Notes: 2, 4, 6

NOTES: Credit cards accepted: A Master Card; B Visa; C American Express; D Discover Card; E Diners Club; F Other; 2 Personal checks accepted; 3 Lunch available; 4 Dinner available; 5 Open all

California

ANGWIN

Forest Manor
415 Cold Springs Road, 94508
(707) 965-3538

Tucked among the forest and vineyards of famous Napa wine country is this secluded 20-acre English Tudor estate, described as " one of the most romantic country inns. . .a small, exclusive resort." Enjoy the scenic countryside near hot air ballooning, hot springs, lake, and water sports. Fireplaces, verandas, 53-foot pool, spas, spacious suites (one with Jacuzzi), refrigerators, coffee makers, home-baked breakfast. Hosts are former medical missionaries.

Hosts: Harold and Corlene Lambeth
Rooms: 3 (PB) $99-165 off-season; $120-195 in-season
Expanded Continental Breakfast
Credit Cards: A, B
Notes: 2, 5, 8, 9, 10, 12

APTOS

Apple Lane Inn
6265 Soquel Drive, 95003
(408) 475-6868

This secluded 1870s Victorian is set on a hill overlooking acres of gardens, meadows, orchards, a romantic gazebo, and flowering gardens. Each room is unique with period antiques, quilts, and authentic decor. A lavish country breakfast is served in the parlor. Enjoy the game room, darts, croquet, horseshoes, and player piano. Pick apples to feed the horses or gather fresh eggs and produce from the gardens. Walk to the beach. Just minutes from Santa Cruz.

Hosts: Douglas and Diana Groom
Rooms: 5 (3 PB; 2 SB) $70-125
Full Breakfast
Credit Cards: A, B
Notes: 2, 5, 8, 10

Forest Manor

---

year; 6 Pets welcome; 7 Children welcome; 8 Tennis nearby; 9 Swimming nearby; 10 Golf nearby; 11 Skiing nearby; 12 May be booked through travel agent

14 California

AUBURN

Lincoln House Inn
191 Lincoln Way, 95603
(916) 885-8880

Situated in historic Auburn, heart of the gold country, this charming 1933 country inn offers guest rooms decorated with antiques, soft colors, and cozy quilts. Two fireplaces provide the parlor and sitting room with that little extra for quiet evenings and romantic getaways. A sumptuous breakfast is served in the dining room where large windows frame a stunning view of the Sierra Nevada Mountains. The large swimming pool and deck are surrounded by gardens.

Hosts: Leslie and Stan Fronczak
Rooms: 4 (3 PB; 1 SB) $65-95
Full Breakfast
Credit Cards: A, B, C
Notes: 2, 5, 7, 8, 9, 10, 11, 12

Power's Mansion Inn
164 Cleveland Avenue, 95603
(916) 885-1166

This magnificent mansion, which is now known as Power's Mansion Inn, was built from a gold fortune, and no expense was spared to make it an elegant showcase. The legendary, century-old Victorian has been restored to the grandeur of yesteryear with lavishly decorated rooms filled with antique furniture and satin comforters atop high, brass beds. A delicious, full breakfast is served every morning.

Hosts: Tina and Tony Verhaart
Rooms: 11 (PB) $75-160
Full Breakfast
Credit Cards: A, B, C
Notes: 2, 5, 6, 7, 8, 9, 10, 12

The Chalfont House

BISHOP

The Chalfont House
213 Academy, 93514
(619) 872-1790

This 1900 semi-Victorian, two-story house includes country antique furnishings and handmade quilts. There are five rooms and one suite. Tea is served in the afternoon; ice cream sundaes are served in the evenings. Enjoy TV, VCR, and a fireplace in the parlor. Air conditioning and in-room phones. No smoking.

NOTES: Credit cards accepted: A Master Card; B Visa; C American Express; D Discover Card; E Diners Club; F Other; 2 Personal checks accepted; 3 Lunch available; 4 Dinner available; 5 Open all

Hosts: Fred and Sally Manecke
Rooms: 6 (PB) $60-75
Full Breakfast
Credit Cards: C
Notes: 2, 5, 7, 8, 9, 10, 11, 12

CALISTOGA

Foothill House
3037 Foothill Boulevard, 94515
(707) 942-6933

Nestled in the foothills near Mount St. Helens, Foothill House is described as "one of the most romantic inns of the Napa valley," by the *Chicago Tribune*. Foothill House has two suites and one private cottage, all with private baths, fireplaces, queen- or king-size beds, private entrances, and small refrigerators. Decorated with handmade quilts and country antiques.

Hosts: Doris and Gus Beckert
Rooms: 3 (PB) $105-210
Continental Breakfast
Credit Cards: A, B, C
Notes: 2, 5, 8, 9, 10

Hillcrest Bed and Breakfast
3225 Lake County Highway, 94515
(707) 942-6334

My home is your home. Hillcrest offers a million-dollar view of Napa Valley, swimming, hiking, fishing, and a fireplace. The owner's family has been on this piece of land since 1860. Her great, great-grandfather established a winery and vineyards in 1882, which the home overlooks. Rooms have balconies, and the home is filled with heirlooms from the family mansion that burned down in 1964. There is a minimuseum of silver, china, art, and furniture.

Host: Debbie O'Gorman
Rooms: 6 (3 PB; 3 SB) $45-90
Continental Breakfast
Credit Cards: None
Notes: 2, 5, 8, 9, 10, 11, 12

Scarlett's Country Inn
3918 Silverado Trail, 94515
(707) 942-6669

This secluded 1890 farmhouse set in the quiet of green lawns and tall pines that overlook vineyards has three exquisitely appointed suites, one with a fireplace. Breakfast is served in your room or by the woodland swimming pool. Close to wineries and spas, we offer private baths, queen beds, private entrances, air conditioning, and afternoon refreshments.

Hosts: Scarlett and Derek Dwyer
Rooms: 3 (PB) $85-125
Continental Breakfast
Credit Cards: None
Notes: 2, 5, 7, 8, 9, 10

CAMBRIA

The Pickford House Bed and Breakfast
2555 MacLeod Way, 93428
(805) 927-8619

---

year; 6 Pets welcome; 7 Children welcome; 8 Tennis nearby; 9 Swimming nearby; 10 Golf nearby; 11 Skiing nearby; 12 May be booked through travel agent

Enjoy antiques, claw foot tubs with showers, oak pullchain toilets, only seven miles from Hearst Castle. Wine is served at 5:00 P.M. Three rooms have fireplaces; all rooms have in-room TVs and king or queen beds. Near beaches.

Host: Anna Larsen
Rooms: 8 (PB) $85-120
Full Breakfast
Credit Cards: A, B
Notes: 2, 5, 7

CARMEL VALLEY

The Valley Lodge
Carmel Valley Road at Ford Road
Box 93, 93924
(408) 659-2261; (800) 641-4646

A warm Carmel Valley welcome awaits the two of you, a few of you, or a small conference. Relax in a garden patio room or a cozy one- or two-bedroom cottage with fireplace and kitchen. Enjoy a sumptuous continental breakfast, our heated pool, sauna, hot spa, and fitness center. Tennis and golf are nearby. Walk to fine restaurants and quaint shops of Carmel Valley village, or just listen to your beard grow.

Hosts: Peter and Sherry Coakley
Rooms: 31 (PB) $95-125; $150 one-bedroom
    cottage; $225 two-bedroom cottage
Expanded Continental Breakfast
Credit Cards: A, B, C
Notes: 2, 5, 6, 7, 8, 10, 12

CLOVERDALE

Ye Olde' Shelford House
29955 River Road, 95425
(707) 894-5956; (800) 833-6479

This 1885 country Victorian is located in the heart of wine country, with six beautifully decorated rooms with family antiques, fresh flowers, homemade quilts, and porcelain dolls by Ina. A gourmet breakfast is served in our delightful dining room. We will make reservations for you at one of the many good restaurants nearby. Before you retire, you can enjoy the many games in the recreation room, then get into the hot tub to relax after a busy day.

Hosts: Ina and Al Sauder
Rooms: 6 (4 PB; 2 SB) $85-115
Full Breakfast
Closed January
Credit Cards: A, B, C, D
Notes: 2, 7, 8, 9, 10

COLUMBIA

Fallon Hotel
Washington Street, 95310
(209) 532-1470

Since 1857 the Fallon Hotel in the historic Columbia State Park has provided hospitality and comfort to travelers from all over the world. It has been authentically restored to its Victorian grandeur, and many of the antiques and furnish-

---

NOTES: Credit cards accepted: A Master Card; B Visa; C American Express; D Discover Card; E Diners Club; F Other; 2 Personal checks accepted; 3 Lunch available; 4 Dinner available; 5 Open all

ings are original to the hotel. We welcome you to come visit our Fallon Hotel, Fallon Theater, and old-fashioned ice cream parlor for a taste of the Old West.

Host: Tom Bender
Rooms: 14 (13 PB; 1 SB) $50-85
Continental Breakfast
Credit Cards: A, B, C
Notes: 2, 7, 10, 11

"An Elegant Victorian Mansion"

ELK

Elk Cove Inn

6300 South Highway 1, P.O. Box 367, 95432
(707) 877-3321

This 1883 Victorian is nestled atop a bluff overlooking the ocean. Enjoy wide vista views amid the relaxed and romantic setting of a rural village. Behind the main house are four cabins, two with fireplace and skylights. The main house, where a full breakfast is served in the dining rooms, has three large ocean-view rooms, a parlor, and deck. There is access to a drift-wood-strewn beach and numerous scenic trails for hiking and biking nearby.

Host: Hildrun-Uta Triebess
Rooms: 7 (PB) $108-138
Full Breakfast
Credit Cards: None
Notes: 2, 5, 8, 10

EUREKA

"An Elegant Victorian Mansion"

1406 C Street, 95501
(707) 444-3144; (707) 442-5594

This elegant, historic mansion has magnificent woodwork, three fireplaces, and spacious, antique-filled rooms that blend the charm of the past with the comforts of today. A state historic landmark, it is also on the National Register of Historic Places. It features a sauna, croquet, bicycles, antique automobiles, classical music, and spirited and eclectic innkeepers. Near Redwood National Park, fishing, boating, carriage rides, bay cruises, and cultural events.

Hosts: Doug and Lily Vieyra
Rooms: 4 (1 PB; 3 SB) $75-95
Full Breakfast
Credit Cards: A, B
Notes, 2, 3, 5, 8, 10

FERNDALE

The Gingerbread Mansion

400 Berding Street, P. O. Box 40, 95536
(707) 786-4000

Trimmed in gingerbread and surrounded by a formal English garden, the Gingerbread Mansion, circa 1899, is an elegant Queen Anne Eastlake-style Victorian. Completely decorated with antiques, the Victorian theme is carried throughout the four parlors, dining room, and nine guest rooms. The Gingerbread Mansion is located in the state historic landmark village of Ferndale, offering three blocks of shops, galleries, a repertory theater, and museum. The coast, redwoods, hiking trails, and more are nearby.

Host: Ken Torbert
Rooms: 9 (PB) $70-175
Expanded Continental Breakfast
Credit Cards: A,B
Notes: 2, 5, 10, 12

FORT BRAGG

Pudding Creek Inn
700 North Main, 95437
(707) 964-9529; (800) 227-9529

Two lovely 1887 Victorian homes adjoined by a lush garden court offer comfortable and romantic rooms. Your stay includes buffet breakfast in two dining rooms with fresh fruit, juice, main dish, and tantalizing homemade coffee cakes served hot. Antiques, fireplaces, personalized sightseeing assistance. Near scenic Skunk Train excursion through the redwoods, beaches, dining, shops, galleries, hiking, tennis, and golf.

Hosts: Garry and Carole Anloff
Rooms: 10 (PB) $65-115
Full Breakfast
Credit Cards: A, B, C

Closed January
Notes: 2, 5 (by prior arrangement), 7, 8, 9, 10, 12

The Gingerbread Mansion

GEYSERVILLE

Campbell Ranch Inn
1475 Canyon Road, 95441
(707) 857-3476

A 35-acre country setting in the heart of the Sonoma wine country offers a spectacular view, beautiful gardens, tennis court, swimming pool, hot tub, and bicycles. We have five spacious rooms with fresh flowers, fruit, king beds, and balconies. Full breakfast is served on the terrace, and we offer an evening dessert of homemade pie or cake.

Hosts: Mary Jane and Jerry Campbell
Rooms: 5 (PB) $100-145
Full Breakfast
Credit Cards: A, B, D
Notes: 2, 5, 10, 12

NOTES: Credit cards accepted: A Master Card; B Visa; C American Express; D Discover Card; E Diners Club; F Other; 2 Personal checks accepted; 3 Lunch available; 4 Dinner available; 5 Open all

GUALALA

North Coast Country Inn
34591 South Highway 1, 95445
(707) 884-4537

Picturesque redwood buildings on a forested hillside overlook the Pacific Ocean. The large guest suites feature fireplaces, decks, minikitchens, and authentic antique furnishings. Enjoy the romantic hot tub under the pines and the beautiful hilltop garden with gazebo. Near beaches, hiking, golf, tennis, horseback riding, state parks, and restaurants.

Hosts: Loren and Nancy Flanagan
Rooms: 4 (PB) $115
Full Breakfast
Credit Cards: A, B, C
Notes: 2, 5, 8, 10, 12

HEALDSBURG

Frampton House Bed and Breakfast
489 Powell Avenue, 95448
(707) 433-5084

This 1908 Victorian in the heart of wine country offers two large rooms with skylights, queen beds, tubs for two, and views. Also, there is a small, romantic retreat with two skylights, private deck, and fabulous views. The sitting room has a fireplace. Pool, spa, sauna, Ping-Pong, bikes. Privacy and personalized attention with casual ambience.

Host: Paula Bogle
Rooms: 3 (PB) $70-95
Full Breakfast
Credit Cards: A, B
Notes: 2, 5, 7 (over 12), 8, 9, 10

North Coast Country Inn

Healdsburg Inn on the Plaza

110 Matheson Street, 95448
(707) 433-6991; (800) 491-2327

Come to a quiet place in the center of town where history and hospitality meet. Fireplaces, sunrise colors, good things baking, and classical music all add to the special feeling of the little hotel. We have gift shops and a bakery on the street floor. Breakfast is served in the sun-filled solarium.

Host: Genny Jenkins
Rooms: 9 (PB) $75-155
Full Breakfast
Credit Cards: A, B
Notes: 2, 5, 8, 9, 10

HOMEWOOD

Rockwood Lodge

5295 West Lake Boulevard, 96141-0226
(916) 525-5273; FAX (916) 525-5949

Set back in the tall trees on the wooded west shore of Tahoe, the lodge blends in with its surroundings. There is history and elegance in this region. Rockwood is a remnant of the "old Tahoe" and has all the requisites for a special sojourn: knotty-pine walls, huge stone fireplace, sitting room, and an intimate atmosphere. Homey touches add to the enjoyment of a stay at Rockwood. This is the way a mountain chalet ought to be.

Host: Louis Reinkens
Rooms: 4 (2 PB; 2 SB) $100-150

Full Breakfast
Credit Cards: None
Notes: 2, 5, 8, 9, 10, 11, 12

IONE

The Heirloom

214 Shakeley Lane, P.O. Box 322, 95640
(209) 274-4468

Travel down a country lane to a spacious, romantic English garden and a petite Colonial mansion built circa 1863. The house features balconies, fireplaces, and heirloom antiques, along with a gourmet breakfast and gracious hospitality. Located in the historic gold country, close to all major northern California cities. The area abounds with antiques, wineries, and historic sites.

Hosts: Melisande Hubbs and Patricia Cross
Rooms: 6 (4 PB; 2 SB) $50-85
Full Breakfast
Credit Cards: None
Closed Thanksgiving and Christmas
Notes: 2, 5, 10, 11, 12

JACKSON

Gate House Inn

1330 Jackson Gate Road, 95642
(209) 223-3500

The Gate House Inn is a charming turn-of-the-century Victorian in the country on one acre of garden property with a swimming pool. Rooms are decorated with Victorian and country furnishings. One room has a fireplace, and the private cottage has a wood-burning stove.

NOTES: Credit cards accepted: A Master Card; B Visa; C American Express; D Discover Card; E Diners Club; F Other; 2 Personal checks accepted; 3 Lunch available; 4 Dinner available; 5 Open all

Walk to fine restaurants and historic sites. Three-star Mobil rated.

Hosts: Stan and Bev Smith
Rooms: 5 (PB) $75-105
Full Breakfast
Credit Cards: A, B, D
Notes: 2, 5, 7 (over 12), 8, 9, 10, 11, 12

JULIAN

Julian Gold Rush Hotel
2032 Main Street, P.O. Box 1856, 92036
(619) 765-0201; (800) 734-5854

Built almost 100 years ago by a freed slave and his wife, the hotel still reflects the dream and tradition of the genteel hospitality of the Victorian era. The "Queen of the Back Country" has the distinction of being the oldest continuously operating hotel in southern California. Listed on the National Register of Historic Places.

Hosts: Steve and Gig Ballinger
Rooms: 18 (5 PB; 13 SB) $64-145
Full Breakfast
Credit Cards: A, B, C
Notes: 2, 5, 7, 8

KLAMATH

Requa Inn
451 Requa Road, 95548
(707) 482-8205

This historic inn is located in the heart of Redwood National Park on the Klamath River. We are one mile from the ocean and near many hiking trails. This is a quiet place, with no telephones or TVs.

Hosts: Paul and Donna Hamby
Room: 1 (PB) $50-75
Full Breakfast
Credit Cards: A, B, C
Notes: 2, 4

LAGUNA BEACH

The Carriage House
1322 Catalina Street, 92651
(714) 494-8945

This charming New Orleans-style inn is two blocks from the blue Pacific Ocean, convenient for shopping and transportation. All rooms surround a secluded brick courtyard filled with lush plants and flowers. Each suite, decorated with antiques and memorabilia, has a sitting room, bedroom, and private bath. Breakfast is served family style in the courtyard dining room.

Hosts: Vern, Dee, and Tom Taylor
Suites: 6 (PB) $95-150
Continental Breakfast
Credit Cards: None
Notes: 2, 5, 7, 8, 9, 10

LAGUNA BEACH

Eiler's Inn
741 South Coast Highway, 92651
(714) 494-3004

Twelve rooms with private baths and a courtyard with gurgling fountain and colorful, blooming plants are within

---

year; 6 Pets welcome; 7 Children welcome; 8 Tennis nearby; 9 Swimming nearby; 10 Golf nearby; 11 Skiing nearby; 12 May be booked through travel agent

walking distance of town and most restaurants; one-half block from the beach.

Hosts: Henk and Annette Wirtz
Rooms: 12 (PB) $100-130
Full Breakfast
Credit Cards: A, B, C
Notes: 2, 5, 8, 9, 10, 12

LAKE ARROWHEAD

Bluebelle House Bed and Breakfast

263 South State Highway 173
P. O. Box 2177, 92352
(714) 336-3292; (800) 429-BLUE California

The cozy elegance of European decor in an alpine setting welcomes you to Bluebelle House. Guests appreciate immaculate housekeeping, exquisite breakfasts, warm hospitality, and relaxation by the fire or out on the deck. Walk to charming lakeside village, boating, swimming, and restaurants. Private beach club and ice skating are nearby; winter sports 30 minutes away.

Hosts: Rick and Lila Peiffer
Rooms: 5 (3 PB; 2 SB) $75-110
Full Breakfast
Credit Cards: A, B
Notes: 2, 5, 9, 11

LONG BEACH

Lord Mayor's Inn

435 Cedar Avenue, 90802
(310) 436-0324

Our home was built in 1904 by Charles Windham, the first mayor of Long Beach. Edwardian in style with granite pillars flanking the veranda, it has bay windows, and a decorative pediment tops the second story. A grand piano occupies the foyer that is often used for area weddings. Decorated with antiques, such as a carved oak Hawaiian bedstead, guest rooms have access to a sun deck. Near the Queen Mary and World Trade Center. Off-street parking.

Hosts: Laura and Reuben Brasser
Rooms: 5 (PB) $75-85
Full Breakfast
Credit cards: A, B, C
Notes: 2, 5, 7, 8, 9

LOS OSOS

Gerarda's Bed and Breakfast

1056 Bay Oaks Drive, 93402
(805) 528-3973

Gerarda's three-bedroom ranch-style home is comfortably furnished and offers wonderful ocean and mountain views from the elaborate flower gardens in front and back. Gerarda speaks five languages and will welcome you warmly. She cooks a wonderful family-style breakfast. You will be only a few miles from state parks, Morro Bay, Hearst Castle, San Luis Obispo, universities, and a shopping center.

Host: Gerarda Ondang
Rooms: 3 (1 PB; 2 SB) $28-45

NOTES: Credit cards accepted: A Master Card; B Visa; C American Express; D Discover Card; E Diners Club; F Other; 2 Personal checks accepted; 3 Lunch available; 4 Dinner available; 5 Open all

Full Breakfast
Credit Cards: None
Notes: 2, 5, 8, 9, 10

MARIPOSA

Oak Meadows, too Bed and Breakfast

5263 Highway 140 North
P. O. Box 619, 95338
(209) 742-6161

Just a short drive to Yosemite National Park, Oak Meadows, too is located in the historic Gold Rush town of Mariposa. Oak Meadows, too was built with New England architecture and turn-of-the-century charm. A stone fireplace greets you upon arrival in the guest parlor, where a continental-plus breakfast is served each morning. All rooms are furnished with handmade quilts, brass headboards, and charming wallpapers. Air conditioning.

Hosts: Frank Ross and Kaaren Black
Rooms: 6 (PB) $69-79
Expanded Continental Breakfast
Credit Cards: A, B
Notes: 2, 5, 11

MCCLOUD

McCloud Guest House

606 West Colombero Drive
P.O. Box 1510, 90657
(916) 964-3160

This lovely, old country home was built in 1907 and has been restored to its former glory by the owners/hosts. Five large bedrooms are individually decorated. Each has its own bath, three with claw foot tubs. It is situated on parklike grounds with rolling lawns, giant oaks, and flowers stretching around the 16-foot wraparound veranda.

Hosts: Bill and Patti Leigh, Dennis and Pat Abreu
Rooms: 5 (PB) $75-90
Expanded Continental Breakfast
Credit Cards: A, B
Notes: 2, 4, 5, 9, 10, 11

MENDOCINO

The Headlands Inn

Corner of Howard and Albion Streets
P.O. Box 132, 95460
(707) 937-4431

Centrally located within Mendocino's historical preservation district, The Headlands Inn offers four rooms plus a cottage, each with a wood-burning fireplace, bath, and king or queen bed. Full gourmet breakfasts are served to each room, preceded by a San Francisco newspaper. Afternoon tea service includes mineral waters, cookies, and mixed nuts. Other amenities include fresh fruit, flowers, candy, and extra bed pillows.

Hosts: Pat and Rod Stofle
Rooms: 5 (PB) $98-150
Full Breakfast
Credit Cards: None
Notes: 2, 5, 8, 9, 10

---

year; 6 Pets welcome; 7 Children welcome; 8 Tennis nearby; 9 Swimming nearby; 10 Golf nearby; 11 Skiing nearby; 12 May be booked through travel agent

John Dougherty House

John Dougherty House
571 Ukiah Street, P. O. Box 817, 95460
(707) 937-5266

The historic John Dougherty House was built in 1867 and is one of the oldest houses in Mendocino. Located on land bordered by Ukiah and Albion Streets, the inn has some of the best ocean and bay views in the village. Steps away from great restaurants and shopping, but years removed from 20th-century reality. The main house is furnished with period country antiques. Cottages, cabin, and water tower.

Hosts: David and Marion Wells
Rooms: 6 (PB) $95-140
Expanded Continental Breakfast
Credit Cards: None
Notes: 2, 5

Mendocino Village Inn
44860 Main Street, Box 626, 95460
(707) 937-0246

Hummingbirds, Picassos, French-roast coffee, fuchsias, fireplaces, Vivaldi, country breakfasts, Pacific surf, fresh blackberries, four-poster beds, migrating whales--all in a loving, Christian atmosphere.

Hosts: Tom and Sue Allen
Rooms: 12 (10 PB; 2 SB) $59-130
Full Breakfast
Credit Cards: A, B
Notes: 2, 5, 8, 10

MT. SHASTA

Mt. Shasta Ranch Bed and Breakfast
1008 W. A. Barr Road, 96067
(916) 926-3870

The inn is situated in a rural setting with a majestic view of Mt. Shasta and features a main lodge, carriage house, and cottage. Group accommodations are available. Our breakfast room is ideally suited for seminars and retreats with large seating capacity. The game room includes piano, Ping-Pong, pool table, and board games. Guests also enjoy an outdoor Jacuzzi. Nearby recreational facilities include alpine and Nordic skiing, fishing, hiking, mountain bike rentals, surrey rides, and museums. Call for pastor's discount.

Hosts: Bill and Marry Larsen
Rooms: 9 (4 PB; 5 SB) $55-75
Cabin: 1
Full Breakfast
Credit Cards: A, B, C
Notes: 2, 5, 7, 8, 9, 10, 11, 12

NOTES: Credit cards accepted: A Master Card; B Visa; C American Express; D Discover Card; E Diners Club; F Other; 2 Personal checks accepted; 3 Lunch available; 4 Dinner available; 5 Open all

NAPA

Old World Inn
1301 Jefferson Street, 94559
(707) 257-0112

This romantaic 1906 Victorian was built as the private residence of E. W. Doughty, a prominent contractor who virtually built Old Town Napa. This charming home's interior is graced with enchanting wooden pillars, brightly appointed rooms, stenciled walls, and claw foot tubs. In addition to a gourmet breakfast, guests are pampered with afternoon tea and a chocolate lover's dessert buffet. To end a most enjoyable visit, an outdoor Jacuzzi is available.

Host: Diane Dumaine
Rooms: 8 (PB) $85-140
Full Breakfast
Credit Cards: A, B, C, D
Notes: 2, 5, 10, 12

NEWPORT BEACH

The Little Inn on the bay
617 Lido Park Drive, 92663
(714) 673-8880; FAX (714) 673-1500

The Little Inn on the bay, the only inn or hotel on the water in Newport Beach, is centrally located close to all the Orange County attractions, such as Disneyland, Knotts Berry Farm, the Queen Mary, and the Performing Arts Center. It is decorated and furnished in the style of an early 1800s New England inn, and its Irish staff provides a refreshing surprise for the discerning traveler. Amenities include a boat tour of harbor, bicycles, and milk and cookies.

Host: Herrick Hanson
Rooms: 29 (PB) $80-160
Continental Breakfast
Credit Cards: A, B, C, D, E
Notes: 5, 7, 8, 9, 12

Old World Inn

NEVADA CITY

The Parsonage Bed and Breakfast Inn
427 Broad Street, 95959
(916) 265-9478

Gold Rush history comes alive in this 125-year-old home. Located in the town's historic district, the Parsonage Bed and Breakfast Inn is within easy walking distance of many fine restaurants, boutiques, and a diverse and lively nightlife. The parlor, dining and family rooms, as well as the three cozy guest rooms, are lovingly furnished with the innkeeper's own pioneer-family antiques. In every way, the Parsonage evokes a gentler bygone era.

Host: Deborah Dane
Rooms: 3 plus cottage (PB) $65-90
Expanded Continental Breakfast
Credit Cards: A, B
Notes: 2, 5, 9, 10, 11, 12

OAKHURST

Ople's Guest House
41118 Highway 41, 93644
(209) 683-4317

Set on a hill and half hidden by trees is the rambling house where Yosemite travelers make a stop for the night. The easy-going atmosphere, the pleasant accommodations, and affordable rates make Ople's Guest House a favorite in Oakhurst. Families are welcome, and guests may enjoy a fireplace and TV in the livingroom. Off-street parking and wheelchair access.

Host: Ople Smith
Rooms: 3 (SB) $40
Continental Breakfast
Credit Cards: A, B, D, F
Notes: 2, 5, 7, 8, 9, 10, 11, 12

OJAI

Theodore Woolsey House
1484 East Ojai Avenue, 93023
(805) 646-9779

The Theodore Woolsey House is a country bed and breakfast inn for nature lovers with room to roam on seven oak-shaded acres. Guests feel at home in this 5,000-square-foot, two-story farmhouse. The livingroom has a charming, country atmosphere, with its low-beam ceiling and stone fireplace. The dining room is spacious, and the bedrooms are beautifully decorated, some with private baths and fireplaces. Other rooms have balconies overlooking the 50-foot, kidney-shaped pool and nearby mountains.

Host: Ana Cross
Rooms: 5 (4 PB; 1 SB) $50-95
Continental Breakfast
Credit Cards: None
Notes: 2, 5, 7, 9, 10

PACIFIC GROVE

Roserox Country Inn By-The Sea
557 Ocean View Boulevard, 93950
(408) 373-7673

This historic 1904 mansion sits on the edge of the Pacific Ocean shoreline. The charming, four-story inn offers eight guest rooms with ocean views, beautifully decorated with designer linens and high, brass beds. Slippers to take home, imported French water, and a country breakfast will entice you. The famous cheese and wine hour is observed in the parlor around the cozy fireplace. Walk to Monterey Aquarium, John Steinbeck's Cannery Row, swimming, golf, fishing, and whale watching excursions.

NOTES: Credit cards accepted: A Master Card; B Visa; C American Express; D Discover Card; E Diners Club; F Other; 2 Personal checks accepted; 3 Lunch available; 4 Dinner available; 5 Open all

Host: Dawn Yvette Browncroft
Rooms: 8 (SB) $125-205
Full Breakfast
Crediti Cards: None
Notes: 2, 5, 8, 9, 10, 12

Seven Gables Inn

555 Ocean View Boulevard, 93950
(408) 372-4341

This century-old Victorian mansion is situated on a rocky promontory overlooking scenic Monterey Bay and is furnished throughout with elegant, original European and American antiques. Enjoy a panoramic ocean view from every room. Afternoon tea is complimentary. Nearby are Monterey Aquarium, Carmel, Seventeen Mile Drive, Big Sur, beaches, bicycling, and all the many attractions of the Monterey Peninsula.

Host: The Flatley family
Rooms: 14 (PB) $95-185
Full Breakfast
Credit Cards: A, B
Notes: 2, 5, 8, 9, 10

PALM SPRINGS

Casa Cody Bed and Breakfast Country Inn

175 South Cahuilla Road, 92262
(619) 320-9346

A romantic, historic hideaway is nestled against the spectacular San Jacinto mountains in the heart of Palm Springs Village. Completely redecorated in Santa Fe decor, it has 17 ground-level units consisting of hotel rooms, studio suites, and one- and two-bedroom suites with private patios, fireplaces, fully equipped tiled kitchens. Cable TV and private phones; two pools; secluded, tree-shaded whirlpool spa.

Hosts: Therese Hayes and Frank Tysen
Rooms: 17 (PB) $35 summer midweek; $160
        winter weekend
Continental Breakfast
Credit Cards: A, B, C
Notes: 2, 5, 6 (limited), 7 (limited), 8, 9, 10, 11

PALO ALTO

Hotel California

2431 Ash Street, 94306
(415) 322-7666

Hotel California is a 20-room, quaint, European-style inn conveniently located in the California Avenue neighborhood near Stanford University. The cozy and comfortable rooms are furnished in turn-of-the-century furniture. All rooms have color TVs and telephones. Central kitchen and laundry facilities are available. The charming neighborhood has restaurants, unique shops, and bookstores within walking distance of the hotel.

Hosts: Mark and Mary Ann Hite
Rooms: 20 (PB)$ 51-58
Continental Breakfast
Credit Cards: A, B, C, D
Notes: 5, 12

---

year; 6 Pets welcome; 7 Children welcome; 8 Tennis nearby; 9 Swimming nearby; 10 Golf nearby; 11 Skiing nearby; 12 May be booked through travel agent

PLACERVILLE

The Chichester House Bed and Breakfast Inn
800 Spring Street, 95667
(916) 626-1882; (800) 831-4008

This elegant 1892 Victorian home was built by lumber baron D. W. Chichester. Enjoy fireplaces, fretwork, stained glass, antique furnishings, and relaxing hospitality. A special, full breakfast is served in the dining room. Three air-conditioned rooms have private half-baths and robes. The inn is in historic Placerville near Apple Hill, gold discovery site, river rafting, and ballooning.

Hosts: Doreen and Bill Thornhill
Rooms: 3 (SB) $75-80
Full Breakfast
Credit Cards: A, D
Notes: 2, 5, 7, 10, 11, 12

REDDING

Palisades Paradise Bed and Breakfast
1200 Palisades Avenue, 96003
(916) 223-5305

Enjoy a spectacular view of the Sacramento River, mountains, and city lights at night from a spacious, contemporary home on the bluffs in Redding. This private home has two guest rooms, fireplace, garden spa, and air conditioning.

Host: Gail Goetz
Rooms: 2 (SB) $55-80
Full Breakfast
Credit Cards: A, B, C
Notes: 2, 5, 8, 9, 10, 11

The Chichester House
Bed and Breakfast Inn

REDONDO BEACH

Ocean Breeze Bed and Breakfast
122 South Juanita Avenue, 90277
(310) 316-5123

Norris and Betty welcome you to a luxurious and comfortable stay. Our amenities include a refrigerator, microwave, breakfast corner, and king or twin beds. Rooms have good sleeping areas that are quiet and well-ventilated. A separate entrance and TV with remote control are available. Ask Norris about his antique collection. We are five blocks from the beach with 21 miles of bike path. Near Los Angeles, Hollywood, and Disneyland.

Hosts: Betty and Norris Binding
Rooms: 2 (PB) $30-50; weekly rates available
Continental Breakfast
Credit Cards: None
Notes: 2, 5, 7 (over five), 8, 10, 11

NOTES: Credit cards accepted: A Master Card; B Visa; C American Express; D Discover Card; E Diners Club; F Other; 2 Personal checks accepted; 3 Lunch available; 4 Dinner available; 5 Open all

RIVERSIDE

J. H. Pratt House
4561 Orange Grove Avenue, 92501
(714) 683-3246

Located in the Prospect Place historical district, the J. H. Pratt House is a fine, two-story example of the arts and crafts architectural movement. A City Structure of Merit built in 1909, it has always been a single-family home. It is within walking distance of downtown, fine restaurants, and unique shops. Relax in our spa, and enjoy fine antique furniture and decorations.

Host: Nelle Lethers
Rooms: 5 (SB) $35-69
Continental Breakfast
Credit Cards: None
Notes: 2, 5, 8, 10, 11

ST. HELENA

Bartels Ranch and Country Inn
1200 Conn Valley Road, 94574
(707) 963-4001; FAX (707) 963-5100

Situated in the heart of the world-famous Napa Valley wine country is this secluded, romantic, elegant country estate overlooking a "100-acre valley with a 10,000-acre view." Honeymoon "Heart of the Valley" suite has sunken Jacuzzi, sauna, shower, stone fireplace, and silver service. Award-winning accommodations, expansive entertainment room, poolside lounging, tailored itinerary, afternoon refreshments, pool table, fireplace, library and terraces overlooking the vineyard. Nearby wineries, lake, golf, tennis, fishing, boating, and mineral spas.

Host: Jami Bartels
Rooms: 3 (PB) $99-275
Expanded Continental Breakfast
Credit Cards: A, B, C
Notes: 2, 3, 4, 5, 9, 10, 12

Cinnamon Bear Bed and Breakfast
1407 Kearney Street, 94574
(707) 963-4653

Cinnamon Bear is furnished in the style of the 1920s with many fine antiques. Gleaming hardwood floors and Oriental carpets add to its unique elegance. Relax in front of the fireplace in the livingroom, or watch the world go by on the spacious front porch. Puzzles, games, and books are available in the parlor for your enjoyment, or peruse a selection of local menus.

Host: Genny Jenkins
Rooms: 4 (PB) $75-150
Full Breakfast
Credit Cards: A, B
Notes: 2, 5, 8, 9, 10

Erika's Hillside
285 Fawn Park, 94574
(707) 963-2887

---

year; 6 Pets welcome; 7 Children welcome; 8 Tennis nearby; 9 Swimming nearby; 10 Golf nearby; 11 Skiing nearby; 12 May be booked through travel agent

You will be welcomed with warm, European hospitality when you arrive at this hillside chalet that is more than 100 years old. Just two miles from St. Helena, you will find a peaceful and romantic, wooded country setting with a view of vineyards and wineries. The spacious, airy rooms have private entrances and bath, fireplace, and hot tub. Continental breakfast and German specialties are served on the patio or in the garden room.

Host: Erika Cunningham
Rooms: 3 (PB) $65-165
Continental Breakfast
Credit Cards: C
Notes: 2, 5, 7, 8, 9, 10, 12

SAN DIEGO

Heritage Park Bed and Breakfast Inn
2470 Heritage Park Row, 92110
(619) 295-7088

In San Diego's most unique setting on a beautiful, seven-acre Victorian park in historic Old Town, this Queen Anne mansion from 1889 has nine antique-filled rooms, full breakfasts, and exquisite candlelight dinners. It is ten minutes from the airport and zoo. Free off-street parking available.

Hosts: Don and Angela Thiess
Rooms: 9 (5 PB; 4 SB) $85-125
Full Breakfast
Credit Cards: A, B
Notes: 4, 5, 7, 9, 10, 12 (weekday bookings)

SAN FRANCISCO

Amsterdam Hotel
749 Taylor Street, 94108
(415) 673-3277; (800) 637-3444; FAX (415) 673-0453

Originally built in 1909, the hotel reflects the charm of a small European hotel. It is situated on Nob Hill, just two blocks from the cable car.

Host: Orisa
Rooms: 31 (26 PB; 5 SB) $49-70
Continental Breakfast
Credit Cards: A, B, C
Notes: 5, 8, 9, 11

Archbishops Mansion Inn
1000 Fulton Street, 94117
(415) 563-7872

Built in 1904, this inn is a splendid example of old San Francisco wealth. The three-story mansion facing historic Alamo Square has been lovingly restored to its original beauty: rich, polished woodwork, thick carpets, vaulted ceilings, crystal chandeliers, and a lovely stained-glass dome over the staircase. Rooms feature 19th-century French antiques, fine linens, and many have fireplaces or Jacuzzi baths. Limousine service to the nearby opera house or symphony hall is available.

Host: Kathleen Austin
Rooms: 15 (PB) $100-285
Expanded Continental Breakfast
Credit Cards: A, B, C
Notes: 2, 5, 7, 12

NOTES: Credit cards accepted: A Master Card; B Visa; C American Express; D Discover Card; E Diners Club; F Other; 2 Personal checks accepted; 3 Lunch available; 4 Dinner available; 5 Open all

Casa Arguello
225 Arguello Boulevard, 94118
(415) 752-9482

Comfortable rooms in this cheerful, elegant flat are only 15 minutes from the center of town in a desireable, residential neighborhood convenient to Golden Gate Park, the Presidio, Golden Gate Bridge, restaurants, and shops. Public transportation is at the corner.

Hosts: Emma Baires and Marina McKenzie
Rooms: 5 (3 PB; 2 SB) $50-75
Expanded Continental Breakfast
Credit Cards: None
Notes: 2, 5, 7, 8, 9, 10

Casita Blanca
330 Edgehill Way, 94127
(415) 564-9339

Casita Blanca is located high on a hill near Golden Gate Park. It is a delightful studio, nestled in the trees, complete with kitchen and fireplace.

Host: Joan Bard
Room: 1 (PB) $80
Continental Breakfast
Credit Cards: None
Notes: 2, 4, 8, 9, 10

The Chateau Tivoli Bed and Breakfast Inn
1057 Steiner Street, 94115
(415) 776-5462; (800) 228-1647

The chateau is a landmark mansion built in 1892. Guests experience a time travel back to San Francisco's golden age of opulence. Choose from five rooms, two with fireplaces, and two suites; all with phones. Breakfast is served in guest rooms or in the dining room. Near shops, restaurants, opera, and symphony. Reservation deposit required.

Hosts: Rodney, Willard, and Shiobhan
Rooms: 7 (5 PB; 2 SB) $80-200
Full Breakfast; Continental breakfast weekdays
Credit Cards: None
Note: 6

The Monte Cristo
600 Presidio Avenue, 94115
(415) 931-1875

The Monte Cristo has been a part of San Francisco since 1875, located two blocks from the elegantly restored Victorian shops, restaurants, and antique stores on Sacramento Street. There is convenient transportation to downtown San Francisco and to the financial district. Each room is elegantly furnished with authentic period pieces.

Host: George Yuan
Rooms: 14 (11 PB; 3 SB) $63-108
Full Breakfast
Credit Cards: A, B, C, E
Note: 5

SAN GREGORIO

Rancho San Gregorio
Route 1, Box 54, 94074
(415) 747-0810; FAX (415) 747-0184

---

year; 6 Pets welcome; 7 Children welcome; 8 Tennis nearby; 9 Swimming nearby; 10 Golf nearby; 11 Skiing nearby; 12 May be booked through travel agent

Five miles inland from the Pacific Ocean is an idyllic rural valley where Rancho San Gregorio welcomes travelers to share relaxed hospitality. Picnic, hike, or bike in wooded parks or on ocean beaches. Our country breakfast features local specialties. Located 45 minutes from San Francisco, Santa Cruz, and the bay area.

Hosts: Bud and Lee Raynor
Rooms: 4 (PB) $65-135
Full Breakfast
Credit Cards: A, B, C
Notes: 2, 5, 7, 10

SANTA BARBARA

Blue Quail Inn and Cottages

1908 Bath Street, 93101
(800) 676-1622 U.S.A.; (800) 549-1622 California

Cottages and suites in a delightfully relaxing country setting are close to town and beaches. A delectable full breakfast, afternoon light hors d'oeuvres, and evening sweets and hot spiced apple cider are served. Guests have use of our bicycles. Three blocks to Sansum Clinic and Cottage Hospital. Picnic lunches and gift certificates available. Off-season midweek and extended-stay discounts.

Host: Jeanise Suding Eaton
Rooms: 9 (7 PB; 2 SB) $73-165
Full Breakfast
Credit Cards: A, B, C
Notes: 2, 3, 5, 7, 8, 9, 10, 12

Long's Seaview Bed and Breakfast

317 Piedmont Road, 93105
(805) 687-2947

This ranch-style home overlooking Santa Barbara has views of the ocean and Channel Islands. The guest room with private entrance is furnished with antiques and king bed. A huge patio and gardens are available. Near all attractions, beach, and Solvang. Your friendly host will be happy to provide you with maps and information about the area.

Host: LaVerne Long
Room: 1 (PB) $70-75
Full Breakfast
Credit Cards: B
Notes: 2, 7 (over 10), 8, 9, 10

The Old Yacht Club Inn

431 Corona Del Mar Drive, 93103
(805) 962-1277; (800) 549-1676 California
(800) 676-1676 U.S.A.; FAX (805) 962-3989

The inn at the beach! These 1912 California craftsman and 1925 early California-style homes house nine individually decorated guest rooms furnished with antiques. Bicycles, beach chairs, and towels are included, and an evening social hour is provided. Gourmet dinner is available on Saturdays.

Hosts: Nancy, Sandy, and Lu
Rooms: 9 (PB) $75-135
Full Breakfast
Credit Cards: A, B, C, D
Notes: 2, 4 (Saturdays), 7, 9, 10, 12

NOTES: Credit cards accepted: A Master Card; B Visa; C American Express; D Discover Card; E Diners Club; F Other; 2 Personal checks accepted; 3 Lunch available; 4 Dinner available; 5 Open all

Simpson House Inn
121 East Arrellaga, 93101
(805) 963-7067; (800) 676-1280

Secluded on one acre of English gardens, this beautiful Eastlake-style Victorian home, circa 1874, is just a five-minute walk to Santa Barbara's restaurants, theaters, museums, and shops. Lovingly restored, it is elegantly appointed with antiques, English lace, Oriental carpets, large comfortable beds with goose down comforters, fresh flowers, and claw foot tubs. Enjoy fresh California juices and fruits, the finest of coffees and teas, and homemade breads.

Hosts: Gillean Wilson, Linda, and Glyn Davies
Rooms: 6 (PB) $75-150
Full Breakfast
Credit Cards: A, B
Notes: 2, 5, 8, 9

SANTA CRUZ

Babbling Brook Inn
1025 Laurel Street, 95060
(408) 427-2437; (800) 866-1131
FAX (408) 427-2457

The foundations of the inn date back to the 1790s when padres from the local mission built a grist mill to take advantage of the stream to grind corn. In the 19th century, a water wheel generated power for a tannery. A few years later, a rustic log cabin was built, which remains as the heart of the inn. Most of the rooms are chalets in the garden, surrounded by pines and redwoods, cascading waterfalls, and gardens.

Host: Helen King
Rooms: 12 (PB) $85-135
Full Breakfast
Credit Cards: A, B, C, D, E
Notes: 2, 5, 8, 9, 10, 12

The Darling House, A Bed and Breakfast Inn by the Sea
314 West Cliff Drive, 95060
(408) 458-1958; (800) 458-1958

This 1910 oceanside architectural masterpiece designed by William Weeks is lighted by the rising sun through beveled glass and Tiffany lamps. The spacious lawns, rose gardens, citrus orchard, towering palms, and expansive ocean-view verandas create colorful California splendor in an atmosphere of peaceful elegance. Stroll to secluded beaches, lighthouse, wharf, and boardwalk. Complimentary gourmet dinner weekdays except holidays.

Hosts: Darrell and Karen Darling
Rooms: 8 (2 PB; 6 SB) $85-225
Continental Breakfast
Credit Cards: A, B, C, D
Notes: 2, 4, 5, 7, 8, 9, 10, 12

SANTA ROSA

Pygmalion House
331 Orange Street, 95407
(707) 526-3407

One of Santa Rosa's historical landmarks, Pygmalion House is a fine example of Queen Anne Victorian archi-

---

year; 6 Pets welcome; 7 Children welcome; 8 Tennis nearby; 9 Swimming nearby; 10 Golf nearby; 11 Skiing nearby; 12 May be booked through travel agent

tecture. This charming home was built in the 1800s on land owned by one of the city's leading developers, Thomas Ludwig. The house withstood the great earthquake and fire of 1906 and is within walking distance of Railroad Square, popular for its specialty shops and fine restaurants.

Host: Lola Wright
Rooms: 5 (PB) $50-70
Full Breakfast
Credit Cards: A, B, C
Notes: 2, 5, 8, 10, 12

Willow Springs Country Inn

SEAL BEACH

The Seal Beach Inn and Gardens
212 Fifth Street, 90740
(310) 493-2416

Just outside Los Angeles and 20 miles from Disneyland, nestled in a charming beachside community is The Seal Beach Inn, French Mediterranean in style. Our Old World inn is surrounded by wrought iron balconies and lush gardens. The rooms vary, but all are furnished with antiques, hand-painted tiles, and lace comforters. Sit by the fireplace in our library, or listen to the fountains. Suites and all the services of a fine hotel are available.

Hosts: Marjorie Bettenhausen and Harty Schmaehl
Rooms: 23 (PB) $98-135
Full Breakfast
Credit Cards: A, B, C, D, F
Notes: 3, 5, 6 (by arrangement), 8, 9, 10, 11, 12

SOULSBYVILLE

Willow Springs Country Inn
20599 Kings Court, 95370
(209) 533-2030; (800) 643-8731

Built by the town's founder, this homey, 1800s ranch house provides a perfect year-round hideaway in a peaceful, country setting below winter's snow and above summer's heat. Enjoy breakfast, evening refreshments, horseshoes, tennis, hot tub, fireplaces, books, or VCR. Air conditioned.

Host: William
Rooms: 4 (PB) $50-80
Full Breakfast
Credit Cards: None
Notes: 2, 5, 7, 8, 9, 10, 11, 12

SUMMERLAND

Summerland Inn
2161 Ortega Hill Road, P. O. Box 1209, 93067
(805) 969-5225

NOTES: Credit cards accepted: A Master Card; B Visa; C American Express; D Discover Card; E Diners Club; F Other; 2 Personal checks accepted; 3 Lunch available; 4 Dinner available; 5 Open all

Located minutes from beautiful Santa Barbara, this newly built New England-style bed and breakfast is a must for southern California travelers. Enjoy ocean views, fireplace rooms, brass and four-poster beds, country folk art, biblical quotations, and Christian motifs. Christian reading material is available. All rooms include cable TV and free local calls.

Host: James Farnet
Rooms: 10 (PB) $55-120 (10% discount to Christian Bed and Breakfast Directory patrons)
Continental Breakfast
Credit Cards: A, B, C, E
Notes: 2, 5, 7, 8, 9, 10

SUSANVILLE

The Roseberry House
609 North Street, 96130
(916) 257-5675

The Roseberry House was built in 1902. It has unique Victorian styling and spacious upstairs rooms. Breakfast is served in the large, formal dining room, while early-morning coffee is available in the upstairs hall. Chocolates and other treats are served in the evening, and bicycles are available for guests to use. We have warm summer days, spectacular autumn colors, and often a white Christmas.

Hosts: Bill and Maxine Ashmore
Rooms: 4 (PB) $50-70
Full Breakfast
Credit Cards: A, B, C
Notes: 2, 5, 8, 9

SUTTER CREEK

Sutter Creek Inn
75 Main Street, P.O. Box 385, 95685
(209) 267-5606; (209) 267-0642

The inn is known for its fireplaces, hanging beds, and private patios. All rooms have private baths and electric blankets. All guests gather 'round the kitchen fireplace to enjoy a hot breakfast. A large library in the livingroom invites guests to while away the time before afternoon refreshments.

Host: Jane Way
Rooms: 19 (PB) $45-135
Full Breakfast
Credit Cards: None
Notes: 2, 5, 7, 8, 9, 10, 11, 12

The Roseberry House

TRINIDAD

Trinidad Bed and Breakfast
560 Edwards Street, P. O. Box 849, 95570
(707) 677-0840

---

year; 6 Pets welcome; 7 Children welcome; 8 Tennis nearby; 9 Swimming nearby; 10 Golf nearby; 11 Skiing nearby; 12 May be booked through travel agent

Our Cape Cod-style home overlooks beautiful Trinidad Bay and offers spectacular views of the rugged coastline and fishing harbor below. Two suites, one with fireplace, and two upstairs bedrooms are available. We are surrounded by dozens of beaches, trails, and Redwood National Park; within walking distance of restaurants and shops. Breakfast is delivered to guests staying in suites, while a family-style breakfast is served to guests in rooms. Closed Monday and Tuesday, November 1 to February 28.

Hosts: Paul and Carol Kirk
Rooms: 4 (PB) $105-145
Expanded Continental Breakfast
Credit Cards: A, B, D
Notes: 2, 5

Trinidad Bed and Breakfast

UKIAH

Vichy Springs Resort and Inn
2605 Vichy Springs Road, 95482
(707) 462-9515

Vichy Springs is a delightful two-hour drive north of San Francisco. Historic cottages and rooms await with delightful vistas from all locations. Vichy Springs features naturally sparkling 90-degree mineral baths, a communal 104-degree pool, and Olympic-size pool, along with 700 private acres with trails and roads for hiking, jogging, picnicking, and mountain bicycling. Vichy's idyllic setting is a quiet, healing environment.

Hosts: Gilbert and Marjorie Ashoff
Rooms: 14 (PB) $105-150
Full Breakfast
Credit Cards: A, B, C, D, E, F
Notes: 2, 3, 4, 5, 7, 8, 9, 10, 12

VENTURA

La Mer
411 Poli Street, 93001
(805) 643-3600

Built in 1890, this is a romantic European getaway in a Victorian Cape Cod home. A historic landmark nestled on a green hillside overlooking the spectacular California coastline. The distinctive guest rooms, all with private entrances, are each a European adventure, furnished in European antiques to capture the feeling of a specific country. Bavarian buffet-style breakfast and complimentary refreshments; midweek packages; horse carriage rides.

Host: Gisela Flender Baida
Rooms: 5 (PB) $105-155
Full Breakfast
Credit Cards: A, B
Notes: 2, 5, 8, 9, 10, 12

NOTES: Credit cards accepted: A Master Card; B Visa; C American Express; D Discover Card; E Diners Club; F Other; 2 Personal checks accepted; 3 Lunch available; 4 Dinner available; 5 Open all

WESTPORT

Howard Creek Ranch
P. O. Box 121, 95488
(707) 964-6725

Howard Creek Ranch is a historic 1867 oceanfront farm bordered by miles of beach and mountains in a wilderness area. Flower gardens, antiques, fireplaces, redwoods, a 75-foot swinging foot bridge over Howard Creek, cabins, hot tub, sauna, cold pool, and nearby horseback riding are combined with comfort, hospitality, and good food.

Hosts: Charles and Sally Grigg
Rooms: 6 (3 PB; 3 SB) $50-110
Full Breakfast
Credit Cards: A, B
Notes: 2, 5, 6 (by arrangement), 7 (by arrangement)

WHITTIER

Coleen's California Casa
P. O. Box 9302, 90608
(310) 699-8427

Coleen's California Casa is located less than five minutes from the freeway in a quiet, residential area. There is a lovely view of the city from the front deck. After a day's outing, enjoy hors d'oeuvres. Dinner is also available if requested in advance. Children are welcome here, and the house is convenient to Disneyland, Knott's Berry Farm, and most Los Angeles attractions.

Host: Coleen Davis
Rooms: 3 (PB) $60-85
Full Breakfast
Credit Cards: None
Notes: 2, 3, 4, 5, 7, 8, 9, 10

YOUNTVILLE

Bordeaux House
6600 Washington Street, 94599
(707) 944-2855

The formal red brick building is nestled in lush gardens like a building half-English, half-French. Bordeaux House is well off the main Napa Valley highway but quickly accessible to it, and is only a little more than one hour from San Francisco. In the spacious rooms, ornamentation has been kept to a minimum. Individual patios provide leisurely views across the sea of vines.

Rooms: 6 (PB) $95-120
Continental Breakfast
Credit Cards: A, B, C, D, E
Notes: 5, 12

---

year; 6 Pets welcome; 7 Children welcome; 8 Tennis nearby; 9 Swimming nearby; 10 Golf nearby; 11 Skiing nearby; 12 May be booked through travel agent

Colorado

ARVADA

On Golden Pond Bed and Breakfast
7831 Eldridge, 80005
(303) 424-2296

For European hospitality and a relaxing blend of country comfort, join us at our secluded ten-acre retreat located only 15 miles west of downtown Denver. Enjoy dramatic views of mountains, prairies, and downtown Denver, and an extensive breakfast on the deck or indoors. Each room has a large sliding door that opens on to the spacious deck. Two suites have large Jacuzzis; outdoor swimming pool, hot tub, nearby horseback riding, golf, bicycles, tennis.

Host: Kathy Kula
Rooms: 5 (PB) $50-80
Full Breakfast
Credit Cards: A, B, D
Notes: 2, 5, 6, 8, 9, 10, 11, 12

ASPEN

Christmas Inn
232 West Main Street, 81611
(800) 521-4055

Attractive rooms have private baths, cable TV, and telephones. Full breakfast, off-street parking, Jacuzzi, sauna, daily maid service, sun deck with panoramic view of Aspen Mountain, free ski buses to four mountains. Within walking distance of shops and restaurants and summer music festival tent. Near bike trails and walking path.

Host: Janine Zanecki
Rooms: 22 (PB) $40 off-season; $96 in-season
Full Breakfast
Credit Cards: A, B
Notes: 2 (for advance booking), 5, 7, 10, 11, 12

Little Red Ski Haus
118 East Cooper, 81611
(303) 925-3333

We are a quaint historic lodge that has had only one owner for 30 years. The 100-year-old Victorian house has additional rooms for a total of 21 bedrooms. Christian hosts look forward to welcoming Christian groups. Rates vary depending on number of guests and whether baths are private or shared.

Hosts: Marge Babcock Rily and Irene Zydek
Rooms: 21 (4 PB; 17 SB) $70-100
Continental Breakfast in summer/fall

NOTES: Credit cards accepted: A Master Card; B Visa; C American Express; D Discover Card; E Diners Club; F Other; 2 Personal checks accepted; 3 Lunch available; 4 Dinner available; 5 Open all

Full Breakfast in winter/spring
Credit Cards: A, B, C
Notes: 7, 8, 9, 10, 11

BOULDER

Sandy Point Inn
6485 Twin Lakes Road, 80301
(303) 530-2939; (800) 322-2939

Homey, quiet, clean, comfortable, warm, and friendly. These spacious studio suites with minikitchens are set in a residential neighborhood with lots of open space. There are also free skiing, complimentary use of the health club, great dining discounts, and laundry rooms. A breakfast buffet is provided, and lunch and dinner may be catered.

Host: Juaneta Miller
Suites: 30 (PB) $59-150
Continental Breakfast
Credit Cards: A, B, D, E
Notes: 2, 5, 6, 7, 9, 10, 11, 12

CARBONDALE

The Van Horn House
0318 Lions Ridge Road, 81623
(303) 963-3605

A warm and cozy country home filled with antiques and family heirlooms. Each guest room has a beautiful view of the mountains and valley. Your hosts desire to make you feel at home and offer you the warmth and hospitality you deserve. Located between Aspen and Glenwood Springs for year-round activities. Easy access to Highway 82.

Hosts: Jack and Jane E. Van Horn
Rooms: 4 (2 PB; 2 SB) $50-65
Full Breakfast
Credit Cards: A, B
Notes: 2, 5, 7 (over 12), 8, 9, 10, 11

COLORADO SPRINGS

Holden House—1902 Bed and Breakfast Inn
1102 West Pikes Peak Avenue, 80904
(719) 471-3980

This historic 1902 storybook Victorian and 1906 carriage house are filled with antiques and family treasures. Five lovely guest rooms (three suites) boast feather pillows, individual decor, period furnishings, and queen beds. Honeymoon suites are available. Centrally located just one mile west of downtown near the historic district, shopping, restaurants, and attractions, the inn is in a quiet, residential area. The romance of the past with the comforts of today.

Hosts: Sallie and Welling Clark
Rooms: 5 (PB) $57-85
Full Breakfast
Credit Cards: A, B, C, D
Notes: 2, 5, 8, 9, 10, 11

DENVER

Queen Anne Inn
2147 Tremont Place, 80205
(303) 296-6666; (800) 432-INNS

---

year; 6 Pets welcome; 7 Children welcome; 8 Tennis nearby; 9 Swimming nearby; 10 Golf nearby; 11 Skiing nearby; 12 May be booked through travel agent

This award-winning Queen Anne has been honored 16 times for excellence and featured in more than 180 publications. In a *Bridal Guide* cover story, it was named one of "America's top ten" sites for a honeymoon.

Hosts: Ann and Chuck Hillestad
Rooms: 10 (PB) $64-124
Expanded Continental Breakfast
Credit Cards: A, B, C, D, F
Notes: 2, 5, 8, 9, 10, 11, 12

DURANGO

Country Sunshine Bed and Breakfast
35130 Highway, 550 North, 81301
(303) 247-2853; (800) 383-2853

This spacious ranch home on the Animas River has Ponderosa pines, quilts, and an informal atmosphere. It is a safe place for children and adults. An ample guest kitchen, washer, and drier are available, and there are plenty of common areas.

Hosts: Jim and Jill Anderson
Rooms: 7 (4 PB; 3 SB) $50-70
Full Breakfast
Credit Cards: A, B
Notes: 2, 7, 10, 12

Logwood Bed and Breakfast— The Verheyden Inn
35060 U. S. Highway 550, 81301
(303) 259-4396

Built in 1988, this western red-cedar log structure was designed as a home and a bed and breakfast. Large windows allow the natural beauty of the Upper Animas Valley to be with you indoors. Guest rooms are uniquely decorated. Handmade comforters cover the beds. The mood of these rooms is western in contrast to the understated elegance of the living and dining areas. Pamper yourselves; come home to Logwood.

Host: Debby and Greg Verheyden
Rooms: 5 (PB) $65-75
Full Breakfast
Credit Cards: A, B
Notes: 2, 5, 7 (over six), 9, 11, 12

Penney's Place
1041 County Road 307, 81301
(303) 247-8928

Penney's Place is located on 26 acres in the quiet, rolling countryside overlooking the spectacular La Plata Mountains. There is a gabled-ceiling room with a king bed and private entrance, deck, kitchenette, and washer and drier. A spiral staircase joins this room to the common room that has a hot tub, satellite TV, and wood-burning stove.

Host: Penny O'Keefe
Rooms: 3 (1 PB; 2 SB) $45-75
Full Breakfast
Credit Cards: A, B
Notes: 2, 5, 8, 10, 11, 12

NOTES: Credit cards accepted: A Master Card; B Visa; C American Express; D Discover Card; E Diners Club; F Other; 2 Personal checks accepted; 3 Lunch available; 4 Dinner available; 5 Open all

EATON

The Victorian Veranda
515 Cheyene Avenue, P.O. Box 361, 80615
(303) 454-3890

This two-story, Queen Anne-style home has a wraparound porch to view the Rocky Mountains. All rooms are furnished from the late 1800s with casablanca fans. Built in 1894, the home has a beautiful oak staircase and a baby grand player piano.

Hosts: Nadine and Dick White
Rooms: 3 (1 PB; 2 SB) $40-55
Full Breakfast
Credit Cards: None
Notes: 2, 5, 7, 10, 11

FRISCO

The Lark Bed and Breakfast
109 Granite at First Avenue
P. O. Box 1646, 80443
(303) 668-5237

The Lark is a large two-story home influenced by European design. It is central to Breckenridge, Copper Mountain, Keystone, and Vail. The bike path and summit shuttle stop are one block away. Rates include a full breakfast, and there is an outdoor hot tub for guests' enjoyment.

Hosts: Mark and Roberta Fish
Rooms: 3 (PB) $50-90
Full Breakfast
Credit Cards: A, B, C
Notes: 2, 5, 8, 9, 10, 11, 12

GEORGETOWN

The Hardy House Bed and Breakfast Inn
605 Brownell, P. O. Box 0156, 80444
(303) 569-3388

The Hardy House with its late-19th-century charm invites you to relax in the parlor by the pot-bellied stove, sleep under feather comforters, and enjoy a savory breakfast. Georgetown is only 55 minutes from Denver and the airport. Surrounded by mountains, it boasts unique shopping, wonderful restaurants, and close proximity to seven ski areas.

Host: Sarah Schmidt
Rooms: 4 (PB) $45-72
Full Breakfast
Credit Cards: A, B
Notes: 2, 5, 7 (over 7), 11

NATHROP

Deer Valley Ranch
16825 C.R. 162, Box BB, 81236
(719) 395-2353

Colorado's Christian family guest ranch welcomes you to the heart of the Rocky Mountains. The hosting ranch family provides the best of western hospitality in a unique Christian atmosphere. In summer, enjoy horseback riding, whitewater rafting, hiking, tennis, hot springs pools, four wheel drives, fishing, golf, and evening entertainment. In winter, enjoy snowmobiling, Nordic and alpine skiing. Off-season rates available.

---

year; 6 Pets welcome; 7 Children welcome; 8 Tennis nearby; 9 Swimming nearby; 10 Golf nearby; 11 Skiing nearby; 12 May be booked through travel agent

Hosts: Harold DeWalt and John Woomington
Rooms: 10 plus cottages (PB) $75
Full Breakfast
Credit Cards: None
Notes: 2, 3, 4, 7, 8, 9, 10, 11

The Damn Yankee Bed and Breakfast Inn

OURAY

The Damn Yankee Bed and Breakfast Inn
100 Sixth Avenue, 81427
(800) 845-7512

Get off life's fast track and discover the intimate charm and cozy comfort of Old Colorado. Eight uniquely appointed rooms with private entrances and queen beds await you. Relax in our hot tub, in front of your favorite movie on cable TV, or with friends and music around our baby grand piano. Complimentary fresh fruit and afternoon snacks served in the third-story lounge and a hearty breakfast keep you fueled for adventure.

Hosts: Mike and Joyce Manley
Rooms: 8 (PB) $58-145
Full Breakfast
Credit Cards: A, B
Notes: 2, 8, 9, 10, 11, 12

Ouray 1898 House
322 Main Street, P. O. Box 641, 81427
(303) 325-4871

This 90-year-old house has been completely renovated and combines the elegance of the 19th century with the comfortable amenities of the 20th century. Each room features a TV and a spectacular view of the San Juan Mountains from its deck. Eat a health-conscious, full breakfast on antique china. Jeep rides, horseback riding, and the city's hot spring pool are a few of the local diversions.

Hosts: Lee and Kathy Bates
Rooms: 4 (PB) $48-68
Full Breakfast
Credit Cards: A, B
Notes: 2, 7, 9

PAGOSA SPRINGS

Davidson's Country Inn
Box 87, 81147
(303) 264-5863

Davidson's Country Inn is a three-story log house located at the foot of the Rocky Mountains on 32 acres. The inn provides a library, a playroom, a game room, and some outdoor activities. A two-bedroom cabin is also available. The inn is tastefully decorated with family heirlooms and antiques, with a warm country touch to make you feel at home. Two miles east of Highway 160.

Hosts: Gilbert and Evelyn Davidson
Rooms: 7 (4 PB; 3 SB) $38-62
Full Breakfast

NOTES: Credit cards accepted: A Master Card; B Visa; C American Express; D Discover Card; E Diners Club; F Other; 2 Personal checks accepted; 3 Lunch available; 4 Dinner available; 5 Open all

Credit Cards: A, B
Notes: 2, 6, 7, 8, 9, 10, 11

PAONIA

Agape Inn
206 Rio Grande Avenue, P. O. Box 640, 81428
(303) 527-4004

This completely remodeled 1906 Victorian is in the heart of the Colorado Rocky Mountain fruit land. Excellent hunting, fishing, and snowmobiling are close by. Three bedrooms, two and one-half baths. No smoking or drinking.

Host: Jim and Norma Shutts
Rooms: 3 (1 PB; 1 SB) $40
Full Breakfast
Credit Cards: None
Notes: 2, 5, 7, 10

PINE

Meadow Creek Bed and Breakfast Inn
13438 Highway 285, 80470
(303) 838-4167

Nestled in pines and aspens on 35 acres and restored in 1988, this 1929 mountain bed and breakfast offers a relaxing, romantic, friendly getaway. There are six bedrooms, common room with fireplace, Jacuzzi, sauna, decks, gazebo, and good home cooking. Family-owned and operated, we are pleased to share our little piece of "God's country."

Hosts: Pat and Dennis Carnahan; Judy and Don Otis
Rooms: 6 (PB) $69-99
Full Breakfast
Credit Cards: A, B
Notes: 2, 4, 5, 10, 12

PUEBLO

Abriendo Inn
300 West Abriendo Avenue, 81004
(719) 544-2703

A classic bed and breakfast on the National Register of Historic Places and in the heart of Pueblo. Enjoy the comfort, style, and luxury of the past in rooms delightfully furnished with antiques, crocheted bedspreads, and brass and four-poster beds. Breakfast is always hearty and served in the oak wainscoted dining room or on one of the picturesque porches. Restaurants, shops, and galleries are minutes away.

Hosts: Kerrelyn and Chuck Trent
Rooms: 7 (PB) $48-85
Full Breakfast
Credit Cards: A, B, C, E
Notes: 2, 5, 7 (over 7), 8, 9, 10, 11, 12

Abriendo Inn

year; 6 Pets welcome; 7 Children welcome; 8 Tennis nearby; 9 Swimming nearby; 10 Golf nearby; 11 Skiing nearby; 12 May be booked through travel agent

SILVERTON

Christopher House Bed and Breakfast
821 Empire Street, P. O. Box 241, 81433
(303) 387-5857 June-September;
(904) 567-7549 October-May

This charming 1894 Victorian home has the original, golden oak woodwork, parlor fireplace, and antiques throughout. All bedrooms offer comfortable mattresses, wall-to-wall carpeting, and a mountain view. Guests are warmly welcomed with mints and fresh wildflowers. A full breakfast is served to Christian and Irish music. Conveniently located only four blocks from the town's narrow-gauge train depot, Old West shops, restaurants, and riding stables. Guest transportation to and from the train depot is available.

Hosts: Howard and Eileen Swonger
Rooms: 4 (1 PB; 3 SB) $42-52
Full Breakfast
Credit Cards: None
Notes: 2, 7, 8, 10, 12

STEAMBOAT SPRINGS

Oak Street Bed and Breakfast
702 Oak Street, Box 772434, 80477
(303) 870-0484

We pamper you with modern goodness and southern charm. We are located in downtown Steamboat Springs in the heart of "Ski Town USA." The rooms are decorated with unique antiques, dried flower arrangements, and old-fashioned quilts. Each morning, enjoy a full breakfast that includes homemade breads, fruits, souffles, and quiches.

Rooms: 13 (11 PB; 1 SB) $45-75 summer; $70-100 winter
Full Breakfast
Credit Cards: A, B
Notes: 2, 7 (over five), 8, 9, 10, 11, 12

Scandinavian Lodge
2883 Burgess Creek Road
P. O. Box 774484, 80477
(800) 233-8102

Tucked away among the clouds, you will find the European setting of the Scandinavian Lodge. With lovely views of the distant Flat Top Mountains and a location near the Steamboat ski areas, this lodge provides romantic seclusion while maintaining accessibility to the numerous recreational activities in the area. Our European breakfast buffet, plus Sunday brunch, and gourmet Swedish restaurant add a special taste to our charming atmosphere.

Hosts: The Olsson family
Rooms: 34 (30 PB; 4 SB) $34-98
Full Breakfast
Credit Cards: None
Notes: 2, 4, 5, 6, 7, 8, 9, 10, 11

NOTES: Credit cards accepted: A Master Card; B Visa; C American Express; D Discover Card; E Diners Club; F Other; 2 Personal checks accepted; 3 Lunch available; 4 Dinner available; 5 Open all

Connecticut

CLINTON

Captain Dibbell House
21 Commerce Street, 06413
(203) 669-1646

Our 1886 Victorian, just two blocks from the shore, features a wisteria-covered, century-old footbridge and gazebo on our one-half acre of lawn and gardens. Spacious livingroom and bedrooms are comfortably furnished with antiques and family heirlooms, fresh flowers, fruit baskets, home-baked treats. There are bicycles, nearby beaches, and marinas to enjoy.

Hosts: Helen and Ellis Adams
Rooms: 4 (PB) $65-85
Full Breakfast
Credit Cards: A, B, C
Notes: 2, 8, 9, 10

COLCHESTER

The Chalet
46 Cemetery Road, 06415
(203) 267-0793

Come and stay in a chalet, situated in the rolling hills of southeastern Connecticut. Convenient to New York City; Boston, Massachusetts; Rhode Island; and Connecticut beaches, state parks, and historic places. One room is contemporary in decor with twin beds, a sitting area, and a private balcony. The other room is Victorian with antique accents and a queen bed. We also have housekeeping by the week that includes both rooms with a fully equipped kitchenette, private entrance, bath, and air conditioning.

Hosts: Richard and Gail Sonnichsen
Rooms: 2 (SB) $45; $150 per week
Full Breakfast
Credit Cards: None
Notes: 2, 5, 7 (over 11), 9, 10

Captain Dibbell House

---

year; 6 Pets welcome; 7 Children welcome; 8 Tennis nearby; 9 Swimming nearby; 10 Golf nearby; 11 Skiing nearby; 12 May be booked through travel agent

CORNWALL BRIDGE

The Cornwall Inn
Route 7, 06754
(203) 672-6884; (800) 786-6884

The Cornwall Inn is a charming, country inn dating back to 1810. Rooms are decorated with antiques and king or queen beds. Enjoy fine, country dining in a relaxed candlelit atmosphere or on the terrace in-season overlooking the pool. The inn is located in the northwest corner of Connecticut with the Housatonic River nearby for fly fishing, canoeing, and tubing. Hiking, biking, antiqueing, skiing, auto racing, and foliage bring many travelers.

Hosts: Lois, Emily, Robyn, Ron, and Brian
Rooms: 13 (12 PB; 1 SB) $50-100
Full Breakfast
Credit Cards: A, B, C, D
Notes: 2, 3, 4, 5, 6, 7, 8, 9, 10, 11, 12

GLASTONBURY

Butternut farm
1654 Main Street, 06033
(203) 633-7197

This 18th-century architectural jewel is furnished with period antiques. Prize-winning dairy goats, pigeons, and chickens roam in an estate setting with trees and herb gardens. The farm is located ten minutes from Hartford by expressway; one and one-half hours to any place in Connecticut.

Host: Don Reid
Rooms: 4 (2 PB; 2 SB) $65-83
Full Breakfast
Credit Cards: A, B, C
Notes: 2, 5, 7, 8, 9

NEW HAVEN

Bed and Breakfast, Limited
P. O. Box 216, 06513
(203) 469-3260 September to June, call after 5:00 P.M. or weekends

Bed and Breakfast, Limited is a reservation service covering the entire state of Connecticut and some listings in Rhode Island. We feature 125 bed and breakfasts statewide from elegantly simple to simply elegant. We offer a unique variety of host homes and customize our service to meet your needs and budget. A quick call assures up-to-the-minute descriptions and availability. Rates range from $55 to 75. Jack M. Argenio, coordinator.

NEW MILFORD

The Heritage Inn of Litchfield County
34 Bridge Street, 06776
(203) 354-8883; FAX (203) 350-5543

Located in the center of the village of New Milford, the Heritage Inn is a painstakingly restored 1800s tobacco barn, which the region is famous for. All 20 rooms are tastefully designed in a rich, traditional decor with color cable TV and telephone. It is within walking distance of shops, restaurants, movies,

---

NOTES: Credit cards accepted: A Master Card; B Visa; C American Express; D Discover Card; E Diners Club; F Other; 2 Personal checks accepted; 3 Lunch available; 4 Dinner available; 5 Open all

and the historic town green. Come, relax in this beautiful building, enjoy our hearty breakfast in the morning, and unwind in the Litchfield hills.

Host: Tricia Rockhill
Rooms: 20 (PB) $69-94
Full or Continental Breakfast
Credit Cards: A, B, C
Notes: 2, 5, 6, 7, 8, 9, 10, 12

SOMERSVILLE

The Old Mill Inn
63 Maple Street, P.O. Box 443, 06072
(203) 763-1473

This gracious, old New England home has twin or double beds, cable TV, phone, refrigerator, stereo, fireplace, and books everywhere. The beautiful muraled dining room with a glass wall overlooks the lawn and its surrounding gardens, flowering trees, and shrubs. It is convenient to shopping, restaurants, airport, and many other attractions.

Hosts: Ralph and Phyllis Lumb
Rooms: 4 (2 PB; 2 SB) $54-60
Expanded Continental Breakfast
Credit Cards: None
Notes: 2, 5, 8, 9, 10

OLD MYSTIC

Red Brook Inn
P. O. Box 237, 06372
(203) 572-0349

Nestled on seven acres of New England wooded countryside, bed and breakfast lodging is provided in two historic buildings: the Haley Tavern, circa 1740, is a restored center-chimney Colonial tavern. The Crary Homestead, circa 1770, is a Colonial built by sea captain Nathaniel Crary. Each room is appointed with period furnishings, including canopy beds, and there are many working fireplaces throughout the inn. A hearty breakfast is served family style in the ancient keeping room. Enjoy a quiet, colonial atmosphere near Mystic Seaport Museum, antique shops, and aquarium. Colonial dinner weekends are also available.

Host: Ruth Keyes
Rooms: 11 (PB) $95-169
Full Breakfast
Credit Cards: A, B
Notes: 5, 7, 8, 9, 10

RIDGEFEILD

West Lane Inn
22 West Lane, 06877
(203) 438-7323

Enjoy cozy, oversized rooms, beautiful grounds and gardens, and lovely countryside with swimming, tennis, and golf nearby. Museums, shopping, and antiquing are nearby. The inn has the prestigious four-diamond award from AAA.

Host: M. M. Mayer
Rooms: 20 (PB) $95-165
Continental Breakfast
Credit Cards: A, B, C, E
Notes: 3, 5,7, 8, 9, 10, 11

---

year; 6 Pets welcome; 7 Children welcome; 8 Tennis nearby; 9 Swimming nearby; 10 Golf nearby; 11 Skiing nearby; 12 May be booked through travel agent

WETHERSFIELD

Chester Bulkley House Bed and Breakfast
184 Main Street, 06109
(203) 563-4236

Hosts: Frank and Sophie Bottaro
Rooms: 5 (3 PB; 2 SB) $65-75
Full Breakfast
Credit Cards: A, B
Notes: 2, 5, 8, 9, 10, 11, 12

Nestled in the historic village of Old Wethersfield, this classic Greek Revival house has been lovingly restored by innkeepers Frank and Sophie Bottaro to provide a warm and gracious New England welcome to the vacationer, traveler, or businessperson. Built in 1830, the house boasts five delightfully airy guest rooms, each with a unique character and decorated with period antiques and vintage design details.

Chester Bulkley House Bed and Breakfast

NOTES: Credit cards accepted: A Master Card; B Visa; C American Express; D Discover Card; E Diners Club; F Other; 2 Personal checks accepted; 3 Lunch available; 4 Dinner available; 5 Open all

Delaware

DOVER

Inn at Meeting House Square

305 South Governors Avenue, 19901
(302) 678-1242

This Victorian home built in 1849 is located in the historic district. Four guest rooms have air conditioning, cable TV, antiques, and travel memorabilia. Walk to shopping and fine dining. Close to old state building, John Dickenson mansion, and wildlife preserve.

Hosts: Sherry and Carolyn DeZwarte
Rooms: 4 (PB) $42-58
Full Breakfast
Credti Cards: A, B, C, D
Notes: 2, 5, 7, 10, 12

NEW CASTLE

William Penn Guest House

206 Delaware Street, 19720
(302) 328-7736

Visit historic New Castle and stay in a charmingly restored home, circa 1692, close to museums and major highways.

Hosts: Richard and Irma Burwell
Rooms: 3 (1 PB; 2 SB) $40
Continental Breakfast
Credit Cards: None
Notes: 2, 7, 8

O'Connor's Bed and Breakfast

REHOBOTH BEACH

O'Connor's Bed and Breakfast

20 Delaware Avenue, 19971
Winter address: 1700 Taylor Avenue
Fort Washington, MD 20744
(302) 227-2419

O'Connor's Bed and Breakfast is a remodeled Victorian home located just one-half block from the ocean beach

---

year; 6 Pets welcome; 7 Children welcome; 8 Tennis nearby; 9 Swimming nearby; 10 Golf nearby; 11 Skiing nearby; 12 May be booked through travel agent

and boardwalk, convenient to shopping and restaurants. Each room is individually air conditioned, and parking is available for compact cars. We are family-owned and operated. Also available is a one-bedroom apartment that is tiny but sleeps four and is rented on a weekly basis.

Host: Patricia O'Connor
Rooms: 6 (S4B) $50-75
Apartment: $595 weekly
Continental Breakfast
Credit Cards: None
Notes: 2, 8, 9, 10

WILMINGTON

A Small Wonder Bed and Breakfast Homestay

213 West Crest Road, 19803
(302) 764-0789; (800) 373-0781

Enjoy award-winning hospitality and landscaping in this gracious, non-historic home convenient to chateau country, businesses, and historic attractions. Double and king beds, air conditioning, spa, pool, TV/VCR, phone, use of entire home and garden. One-half mile north of I-95, Exit 9. See Winterthur, Longwood, Nemours, Hagley, Bellevue, Rockwood, historic New Castle, Wyeth Museum, Odessa, and much more.

Hosts: Dot and Art Brill
Rooms: 2 (PB) $60-65
Full Breakfast
Credit Cards: A, B, C
Notes: 2, 5, 8, 9, 10, 12

NOTES: Credit cards accepted: A Master Card; B Visa; C American Express; D Discover Card; E Diners Club; F Other; 2 Personal checks accepted; 3 Lunch available; 4 Dinner available; 5 Open all

District of Columbia

Adams Inn
1744 Lanier Place Northwest, 20009
(202) 745-3600

This turn-of-the-century town house is in a neighborhood with many ethnic restaurants and has comfortable, homestyle furnishings. Near transportation, convention sites, government buildings, and tourist attractions.

Hosts: Gene and Nancy Thompson
Rooms: 25 (12 PB; 13 SB) $45-90
Expanded Continental Breakfast
Credit cards: A, B, C, E, F
Notes: 2, 7

The Reeds
P. O. Box 12011, 20005
(202) 328-3510

Built in the late 1800s, this large Victorian home features original wood panelng, including a unique oak staircase, stained glass, chandeliers, Victorian-style lattice porch, and art nouveau and Victorian antiques and decorations. The house has been featured in the *Washington Post* and the *Philadelphia Inquirer* and as part of Christmas at the Smithsonian. It is located ten blocks from the White House at historic Logan Circle.

Hosts: Charles and Jackie Reed
Rooms: 6 (1 PB; 5 SB) $55-85
Expanded Continental Breakfast
Credit Cards: A, B, C, E
Notes: 2 (two weeks in advance only), 5, 7, 8, 9

The Reeds

---

year; 6 Pets welcome; 7 Children welcome; 8 Tennis nearby; 9 Swimming nearby; 10 Golf nearby; 11 Skiing nearby; 12 May be booked through travel agent

Florida

AMELIA ISLAND

Elizabeth Pointe Lodge
98 South Fletcher, P. O. Box 1210, 32034
(904) 277-4851

The main house of the lodge is constructed in an 1890s Nantucket shingle style with a strong maritime theme, broad porches, rockers, sunshine, and lemonade. Located prominently by the Atlantic Ocean, the inn is only steps from often deserted beaches. Suites are available for families. A newspaper is delivered to your room in the morning, and breakfast is served overlooking the ocean.

Hosts: David and Susan Caples
Rooms: 20 (PB) $85-105
Full Breakfast
Credit Cards: A, B, C
Notes: 2, 3, 4, 5, 7, 8, 9, 10, 12

COLEMAN

The Son's Shady Brook Bed and Breakfast
P. O. Box 551, 33521
(904) 748-7867

Come for a refreshing change in a rural setting that is easy to find. This modern house on 21 secluded, wooded acres overlooking a springfed creek offers solitude with tranquility and therapeutic, picturesque surroundings. This is a relaxing retreat for the elderly, newlyweds, handicapped, and others. The bedrooms are beautifully decorated. Enjoy the piano, library, fireplace, and more. Within one hour of Orlando and Tampa.

Host: Jean Lake Martin
Rooms: 4 (PB) $40-60
Full Breakfast
Credit Cards: A, B, C
Notes: 2, 3 (by arrangement), 4 (by arrangement), 5, 8, 9, 10

Elizabeth Pointe Lodge

NOTES: Credit cards accepted: A Master Card; B Visa; C American Express; D Discover Card; E Diners Club; F Other; 2 Personal checks accepted; 3 Lunch available; 4 Dinner available; 5 Open all

DAYTONA BEACH

Captain's Quarters Inn
3711 South Atlantic Avenue, 32127
(904) 767-3119; (800) 332-3119

Daytona's first bed and breakfast directly on the Atlantic Ocean has oceanfront suites in a quiet section of Daytona. "Your home away from home" is our motto. Enjoy private balconies, complete kitchens, guest laundry, daily newspapers, unique gift shop, pool heated to 80 degrees, fishing pier next door. Close to shopping.

Host: Becky Sue Morgan and family
Rooms: 26 (PB) $75-195
Full Breakfast
Credit Cards: A, B, C, D
Notes: 2, 3, 5, 7, 8, 9, 10, 12

DELRAY BEACH

Hutch's Haven
811 Northwest Third Avenue, 33444
(407) 276-7390

This artist's studio/home/bed and breakfast is in a beautiful vacation town on Florida's east coast, one and one-half miles from the beach. From the beautiful tropical yard, guests may pick their own breakfast fruit and enjoy homemade jellies and jams made from the fruit grown here. Full use of the house, bicycles, beach umbrellas. Breakfast served on the screened porch is a treat.

Host: Jean Hutchison
Rooms: 2 (PB) $55
Full Breakfast
Credit Cards: None
Closed August
Notes: 2, 8, 9, 10

FORT MYERS

Embe's Hobby House and Art Gallery
5570-4 Woodrose Court, 33907
(813) 936-6378

This town house-type home is designed to be your home away from home. The spacious accommodation includes a bright and cheery suite with a large, private bath and dressing area. Located 15 minutes from the beaches, Sanibel and Captiva islands, fine shopping, good restaurants, and the University of Florida. Resident cat.

Hosts: Embe Burdick
Room: 1 (PB) $55
Continental Breakfast
Credit Cards: None
Notes: 2, 8, 9, 10

LAKELAND

Sunset Motel
2301 New Tampa Highway, 33801
(813) 683-6464

This resort motel with pool and recreation room is central to Cyprus Gardens, Disneyworld, Sea World, Universal Studios, Busch Gardens, and more. Walk to banks and shopping. TV and refrigerator in all rooms; microwaves and grills available; kitchenettes.

---

year; 6 Pets welcome; 7 Children welcome; 8 Tennis nearby; 9 Swimming nearby; 10 Golf nearby; 11 Skiing nearby; 12 May be booked through travel agent

Hosts: Eunice, John, Will, and Bill
Rooms: 14 (PB) $50
Continental Breakfast
Credit Cards: A, B
Notes: 2, 5, 6, 7, 9, 10, 12

LAKE WALES

Chalet Suzanne Country Inn and Restaurant
P.O. Drawer AC, 33859
(813) 676-6011; (800) 288-6011

Listed on the National Register of Historic Places, Chalet Suzanne has been family-owned and operated since 1931. It is on 100 acres in a fairy tale setting. Thirty guest rooms have all the amenities. Our four-star restaurant serves breakfast, lunch, and dinner. We also have gift shops, a ceramic studio, swimming pool, soup cannery, and lighted airstrip. We are proud to say that our soups accompanied Jim Irwin on Apollo 15. Ask about our minivacation for two.

Hosts: Carl and Vita Hinshaw
Rooms: 30 (PB) $85-185
Full Breakfast
Credit Cards: A, B, C, D, E, F
Notes: 2, 3, 4, 6, 7, 8, 9, 10

MARATHON

Hopp-Inn Guest House
5 Man-O-War Drive, 33050
(305) 743-4118; FAX (305) 743-9220

Established in 1981, this guest house is located in the heart of the Florida Keys and looks out on the ocean. Breakfast often includes homemade muffins or banana bread. We are convenient to Key West, Dolphin Research Center, and all water activities. We also have charter fishing packages available aboard the *Sea Wolf*.

Hosts: Joe and Joan Hopp
Rooms: 4 (PB) $45-70
Full Breakfast
Credit Cards: A, B

MICANOPY

Herlong Mansion
P. O. Box 667, 32667
(904) 466-3322

The Herlong Mansion was originally a two-story farmhouse with detached kitchen and of wood construction, circa 1845. In 1910, a Greek Revival mansion of brick was constructed over the old farmhouse with four Corinthian columns. The inside has ten fireplaces, six different kinds of wood, and period antiques. Nearby are 20 antique shops, Payne's Prairie, a state park, Margorie Kennan Rawlings House, a wonderful restaurant, and the University of Florida.

Host: H. C. (Sonny) Howard, Jr.
Rooms: 6 (PB) $75-125
Full Breakfast; Continental weekdays
Credit Cards: A, B, D
Notes: 2, 5, 7, 12

NEW SMYRNA BEACH

The Riverview Hotel
103 Flagler Avenue, 32169
(904) 428-5858

NOTES: Credit cards accepted: A Master Card; B Visa; C American Express; D Discover Card; E Diners Club; F Other; 2 Personal checks accepted; 3 Lunch available; 4 Dinner available; 5 Open all

Florida 55

A charming, elegantly restored 1885 hotel adjoins the award-winning Riverview Charlie's Restaurant. We are located on the Intracoastal Waterway and just a short walk to the area's finest beach. Breakfast is served in your room.

Hosts: Jim and Christa Kelsey
Rooms: 18 (PB) $63-150
Expanded Continental Breakfast
Credit Cards: A, B, C, D, E, F
Notes: 3, 4, 5, 7, 8, 9, 10, 12

The Courtyard at Lake Lucerne

ORLANDO

The Courtyard at Lake Lucerne
211 North Lucerne Circle, East, 32801
(407) 648-5188; (800) 444-5289

A unique property made up of three historic buildings furnished with antiques and surrounding a tropically landscaped brick courtyard, this establishment is located in the historic district on the southern edge of downtown Orlando, convenient to everything central Florida has to offer. Rooms have phones and cable TV; two suites have double Jacuzzis and steam showers.

Hosts: Charles and Paula Meiner
Rooms: 22 (PB) $65-150
Expanded Continental Breakfast
Credit Cards: A, B, C
Notes: 2, 5, 6, 7, 8, 9, 12

The Rio Pinar House
532 Pinar Drive, 32825
(407) 277-4903

Located in the quiet Rio Pinar golf community 30 minutes from Disney World, Sea World, and Universal Studios, the Rio Pinar House features comfortable rooms. A full breakfast is served in the formal dining room or on the screened-in porch overlooking the yard.

Hosts: Victor and Delores Freudenburg
Rooms: 3 (PB) $45055
Full Breakfast
Credit Cards: None
Notes: 2, 5, 7, 8, 10, 12

PENSACOLA

Liechty's Homestead Inn
7830 Pine Forest Road, 32526
(904) 944-4816

This modern Victorian home is located in northwest Florida off I-10. Six guest rooms are individually appointed and have TV and phone. Two rooms have fireplaces, and one features a garden tub. Attractions include beaches, Navy museum, tennis, golf, and deep-sea fishing. A full six-course breakfast includes Amish waffles with fresh fruit and homemade toppings and quiche. A full-

---

year; 6 Pets welcome; 7 Children welcome; 8 Tennis nearby; 9 Swimming nearby; 10 Golf nearby; 11 Skiing nearby; 12 May be booked through travel agent

service restaurant will be available beginning April 1992. No smoking.

Hosts: Neil and Jeanne Liechty
Rooms: 6 (PB) $59-79
Full Breakfast
Credit Cards: A, B, C
Notes: 2, 5

ST. AUGUSTINE

Old Powder House Inn
38 Cordova Street, 32084
(800) 447-4149

Towering pecan and oak trees shade verandas with large rockers to watch the passing horse and buggies. An introduction to a romantic escape in the charming turn-of-the-century Victorian inn. Amenities include, high tea, hors d'oeuvres, Jacuzzi, cable TV, parking, bicycles, family hospitality, picnics, special honeymoon packages, anniversaries, and birthdays.

Rooms: 9 (PB) $59-98
Full Breakfast
Credit Cards: A, B
Notes: 2, 4, 5, 7, 8, 9, 10, 12

SARASOTA

Crescent House Bed and Breakfast
459 Beach Road, 34242
(813 346-0857

This lovely home, more than 170 years old, has been fully restored and furnished with comfortable antiques. Sun bathe on a spacious wood deck, or step across the street to a white sandy beach and cool off in the Gulf of Mexico. The house is located within a short walk of Siesta Village and Pavilion, with its many restaurants, quaint shops, tennis courts, and public beach. Your hosts specialize in European service and hospitality.

Hosts: Bob and Paulette Flaherty
Rooms: 3 (2 PB; 1 SB) $40-95
Continental Breakfast
Credit Cards: None
Notes: 2, 5, 7, 8, 9, 10, 12

VENICE

The Banyan House
519 South Harbor Drive, 34285
(813) 484-1385

Experience the Old World charm of one of Venice's historic Mediterranean homes, circa 1926, on the gulf coast. Relax in the peaceful atmosphere of our lovely courtyard dominated by a huge banyan tree. This provides an unusual setting for the garden patio, pool, and Jacuzzi. Central to shopping, beaches, restaurants, and golf. Complimentary bicycles.

Hosts: Chuck and Susan McCormick
Rooms: 9 (7 PB; 2 SB) $49-89
Continental Breakfast
Credit Cards: None
Notes: 2, 5, 7 (over 12), 9

NOTES: Credit cards accepted: A Master Card; B Visa; C American Express; D Discover Card; E Diners Club; F Other; 2 Personal checks accepted; 3 Lunch available; 4 Dinner available; 5 Open all

Georgia

AMERICUS

Morris Manor
425 Timberlane Drive, 31709
(912) 924-4884

This stately, contemporary Georgian Colonial inn is surrounded by Georgia pines and spacious grounds. In season, delicious nuts and fruit await guests in the adjacent orchards. Enjoy the quiet surroundings of the country, yet be close to restaurants and shopping. Visit nearby Plains, hometown of President Jimmy Carter, Andersonville National Park, Georgia Southwestern College, Providence Canyon, and Westville.

Hosts: Troy and Betsey Morris
Rooms: 5 (3 PB; 2 SB) $55
Full Breakfast
Credit Cards: A,B
Notes: 2, 5, 7 (over 11), 10, 12

ATLANTA

Bed and Breakfast Atlanta
1801 Piedmont Avenue, Northeast
Suite 208, 30324
(404) 875-0525

This is a professional reservation service that carefully screens bed and breakfast homestays and inns in the metropolitan Atlanta area. All accommodations offer at least one private bedroom and bath. Baths are shared only when parties are traveling together. Accommodations include a 1920s Tudor home, a carriage house adjacent to an 1830s farmhouse, a ranch-style house, a pool house, 1930s bungalow, and many others. Breakfast is usually continental. $40-100.

Beverly Hills Inn

Beverly Hills Inn
65 Sheridan Drive, Northeast, 30305
(404) 233-8520

---

year; 6 Pets welcome; 7 Children welcome; 8 Tennis nearby; 9 Swimming nearby; 10 Golf nearby; 11 Skiing nearby; 12 May be booked through travel agent

A charming European-style hotel with 18 suites uniquely decorated with period furnishings offers fresh flowers, continental breakfast, and the little things that count. We're a morning star, not a constellation; a solitary path, not a highway. Only some will understand, but then, we don't have room for everybody!

Hosts: Bonnie and Lyle Klienhans
Rooms: 18 (PB) $68-90
Continental Breakfast
Credit Cards: A, B, C, E
Notes: 2, 5, 6 (by arrangement), 7, 8, 9

Shellmont Bed and Breakfast Lodge

Shellmont Bed and Breakfast Lodge

821 Piedmont Avenue, Northeast, 30308
(404) 872-9290

Built in 1891, Shellmont is on the National Register of Historic Places and is a City of Atlanta Landmark Building. A true Victorian treasure of carved woodwork, stained and leaded glass, and unique architecture located in midtown, Atlanta's restaurant, theater, and cultural district, one mile from downtown. It is furnished entirely with antiques.

Hosts: Ed and Debbie McCord
Rooms: 4 (PB) $65-90
Continental Breakfast
Credit Cards: A, B, C
Notes: 2, 7 (limited), 8, 9, 10

CLARKESVILLE

Habersham Hollow Country Inn and Cabins

Route 6, Box 6208, 30523
(404) 754-5147
(706) 754-5147 after May 1992

This peaceful oasis of solitude and serenity is nestled in the northeast Georgia mountains. A five-minute drive from Alpine Helen, it is a place of quiet, simple pleasures and genuine warmth and charm. The elegant country bed and breakfast has secluded, cozy cabins with fireplaces. The relaxed, casual, friendly atmosphere will make you feel as though you were in the country home of old friends.

Hosts: C. J. and Maryann Gibbons
Rooms: 4 (PB) $60-95
Full Breakfast
Credit Cards: A, B
Notes: 2, 5, 6, 7, 8, 9, 10, 11

CLEVELAND

Tyson Homestead

Route 5, Box 5130, 30528
(404) 865-6914

NOTES: Credit cards accepted: A Master Card; B Visa; C American Express; D Discover Card; E Diners Club; F Other; 2 Personal checks accepted; 3 Lunch available; 4 Dinner available; 5 Open all

A warm, distinctive, and Christian atmosphere awaits you at this secluded, 12-acre, one-dwelling, nine-year-old Colonial homestead situated on a private lake. Families are welcome. Located in the hills of northeast Georgia, gateway to the Blue Ridge Mountains. Less than ten minutes from Alpine Helen and five minutes from Cleveland, home of Babyland General.

Hosts: J. T. and Mary Tyson
Rooms: 5 (1 PB; 4 SB) $40-65
Continental Breakfast
Credit Cards: None

COMMERCE

The Pittman House
103 Homer Street, 30529
(404) 335-3823

A gracious, white Colonial built around 1890 is completely furnished with period antiques. If our furnishings are inspiring, visit our antique shop next door. Also, you may enjoy one of Tom's hand-carved Old World Santas. A discount shopping mall is only five minutes away.

Hosts: Tom and Dot Tomberlin
Rooms: 4 (2 PB; 2 SB) $50-55
Full Breakfast
Credit Cards: A, B
Notes: 2, 5, 7, 8, 9, 10, 12

HAMILTON

Wedgwood Bed and Breakfast
Highway 27 and Mobley, P.O. Box 115, 31811
(404) 628-5659

Wedgwood is located six miles south of world-famous Callaway Gardens, 20 miles from Roosevelt's Little White House in Warm Springs, and 20 miles from Columbus. This 1850 home radiates the warmth, friendliness, and enthusiasm of your hostess. The inside is Wedgwood blue with white stenciling. Spacious rooms are comfortably furnished with period antiques. Personalized service and complimentary refreshments. No smoking.

Host: Janice Neuffer
Rooms: 3 (1 PB; 2 SB) $55-70
Full Breakfast
Credit Cards: None
Notes: 2, 5, 7, 8, 9, 10

HELEN

Hofbrauhaus Inn
1 Main Street, 30545
(404) 878-2248; (800) 257-8528

Bavarian decor. All rooms have one queen bed, telephone, color cable TV, VCR. Two rooms have private balconies overlooking the Chattahoochee

River. Breakfast is served in your room, and we have a full service lounge and dining room downstairs. Walk to Alpine Village, shopping, entertainment, fishing, and Octoberfest.

Host: Chris Hammersen
Rooms: 4 (PB) $35-95
Continental Breakfast
Credit Cards: A, B, C, D, E, F
Notes: 2, 3, 4, 5, 6, 8, 9, 10, 12

LAKEMONT

Lake Rabun Hotel

Lake Rabun Road, P. O. Box 10, 30552
(404) 782-4946

This historic, quaint hotel on Lake Rabun has been in operation since 1922. It has antique furnishings and a rustic and charming atmosphere, including a huge stone fireplace in the great room downstairs and beautiful rock work. A honeymooon couple's paradise.

Hosts: Jan and Bill Pettys
Rooms: 16 (2 PB; 14SB) $50
Continental Breakfast
Credit Cards: A, B
Notes: 2, 5, 7, 8, 9, 10, 11, 12

MOUNTAIN CITY

York House, Inc.

P. O. Box 126, 30562
(404) 746-2068

This lovely 1896 bed and breakfast inn has a country flair and is listed on the National Register of Historic Places. It is nestled among the beautiful north Georgia mountains and is close to recreational activities. Completely renovated, the 13 guest rooms are decorated with period antiques and offer cable color TV. Guests begin their day with a continental breakfast served on a silver tray.

Hosts: Phyllis and Jimmy Smith; Tim and Kim Cook
Rooms: 13 (PB) $60-75
Continental Breakfast
Credit Cards: A, B
Notes: 2, 5, 7, 8, 9, 10, 11, 12

SAVANNAH

Bed & Breakfast Inn

117 West Gordon at Chatham Square, 31401
(912) 238-0518

The inn is a wonderful 1853 Federalist town house overlooking the square in the heart of the historic district. The home is furnished with antiques and period reproductions, Oriental carpets, Chinese fine porcelains, and artwork. Books are in every room. Near River Street, restaurants, and shopping.

Host: Bob McAlister
Rooms: 13 (5 PB; 8 SB) $42-75
Full Breakfast
Credit Cards: A, B, C, D
Notes: 2, 5, 7

Eliza Thompson House

5 West Jones Street, 31401
(912) 236-3620

Nestled in a tranquil, residential neighborhood in the heart of one of the larg-

---

NOTES: Credit cards accepted: A Master Card; B Visa; C American Express; D Discover Card; E Diners Club; F Other; 2 Personal checks accepted; 3 Lunch available; 4 Dinner available; 5 Open all

est national historic districts in the United States is The Eliza Thompson House. Built in 1847, this regally restored mansion is now Savannah's most charming and comfortable inn. You will enjoy the rich elegance of heart-of-pine floors and period furnishings and still have a phone and color TV.

Host: Lee Smith
Roomts: 24 (PB) $68-108
Expanded Continental Breakfast
Credit Cards: A, B, C
Notes: 2, 5, 7, 8, 10

President's Quarters
225 East President Street, 31401
(912) 233-1600; FAX (912) 238-0849

This premier historic inn, circa 1855 offers suites with Jacuzzi baths, fireplaces, TV/VCR, and period reproductions. Amenities include fruit, afternoon high tea, and nightly turndown. Balconies overlook the secluded courtyard with Jacuzzi pool. Private off-street parking is available. Four-diamond award 1988-1992.

Host: Muril Broy
Rooms: 16 (PB) from $97
Expanded Continental Breakfast
Credit Cards: A, B, C, D, E
Notes: 2, 5, 8

Pulaski Square Inn
203 West Charlton Street, 31403
(912) 232-8055; (800) 227-0650

The Pulaski Square Inn is a historic town house built in 1853. It is located in downtown Savannah within walking distance of the river and historical places of interest. It is beautifully restored with the original pine flooring, marble mantels, and chandeliers. It is furnished with Oriental rugs, antiques, and traditional furniture.

Host: J. B. Smith
Rooms: 9 (6 PB; 2 SB) $48-88
Continental Breakfast
Credit Cards: A, B, C
Notes: 2, 5, 7, 8, 9, 10

SENOIA

The Culpepper House Bed and Breakfast
P. O. Box 462, 30276
(404) 599-8182

Treat yourself to a whimsical Victorian adventure in this restored, hospitable home located in a picturesque country town. Just 20 minutes from the Atlanta airport.

Host: Mary Brown
Rooms: 4 (2 PB; 2 SB) $50-60
Full Breakfast
Credit Cards: None
Notes: 2, 7 (infants and over 10), 8, 9

SWAINSBORO

The Coleman House Bed and Breakfast
323 North Main Street, 30401
(912) 237-2822

---

year; 6 Pets welcome; 7 Children welcome; 8 Tennis nearby; 9 Swimming nearby; 10 Golf nearby; 11 Skiing nearby; 12 May be booked through travel agent

The Coleman House was built between 1902 and 1904. This Victorian-era mansion exhibits 12-foot ceilings, large pocket doors and bay windows, a veranda surrounding three and one-half sides of the house, and 11 fireplaces with bric-a-brac mantels. All this is set on three acres with 23 pecan trees.

Hosts: Ron and Karen Horvath
Rooms: 10 (PB) $65-95
Full Breakfast
Credit Cards: A, B, C, E
Notes: 2, 5, 7, 8, 10

THOMASVILLE

Quail Country Bed and Breakfast, Ltd.
1104 Old Monticello Road, 31792
(912) 226-7218; (912) 226-6882

Whether you choose to stay on a plantation, in a registered historic home downtown, or in a guest cottage with private pool, we can arrange your accommodations in Thomasville. Countless activities of interest include historic restorations, plantation tours, Pebble Hill Plantation Museum, and nearby hunting preserves.

Coordinators: Mercer Watt and Kathy Lanigan
Houses: 10 (PB) $30-65
Continental Breakfast
Credit Cards: None
Notes: 2, 5, 7, 8, 9

TOCCOA

The Simmons-Bond Inn
130 West Tugalo Street, 30577
(404) 886-8411; (800) 533-7693

This Victorian mansion on the National Register of Historic Places is located on Stephens County's courthouse square. Built in 1903 for lumber baron James B. Simmons, the home has nine original fireplaces, dozens of interior oak columns, handsome oak paneling, woodwork with hand-carved trim, and specially crafted bay windows with stained and beveled glass. Accented with chandeliers, the house represents turn-of-the-century craftsmanship.

Hosts: Joni and Don Ferguson
Rooms: 3 (PB) $45-48
Continental Breakfast
Credit Cards: A, B, C
Notes: 2, 3, 4, 5, 6, 7, 8, 9, 10, 12

The Simmons-Bond Inn

NOTES: Credit cards accepted: A Master Card; B Visa; C American Express; D Discover Card; E Diners Club; F Other; 2 Personal checks accepted; 3 Lunch available; 4 Dinner available; 5 Open all

Hawaii

HAWAII—HILO

Hale Kai
111 Honolii Pali, 96720
(808) 935-6330

Christian hosts offer their beautiful, modern bed and breakfast on the bluff facing the ocean, surfing beach, and Hilo Bay, just two miles from downtown Hilo. Guests are treated as family. We were recently selected as one of the 100 top bed and breakfasts in the United States and Canada. Explore the entire island from this location: Rainbow Falls, three miles away; botanical gardens, three miles away; National Volcanoes Park, 30 miles away; Waipo Valley, 32 miles away; fish auction, three miles away; snorkeling, 4 miles away. Also available is a cottage with livingroom, bedroom, kitchen, and bath.

Host: Evonne Bjornen
Rooms: 5 plus cottage (PB) $85-95
Full Breakfast
Credit Cards: None
Notes: 2, 5, 7 (over 12), 8, 9, 10, 12

HAWAII—VOLCANO

Volcano Bed and Breakfast
P. O. Box 22, 96785
(808) 967-7779

The 1912 renovated, three-story home offers a peaceful setting and safe haven that draws visitors from all over the world. All three guest rooms look out onto tree ferns, fragrant ginger, and surrounding native ohia forest. Various activities nearby include Hawaii Volcanoes National Park's hiking trails and spectacular lava flows. Christian hosts Jim and Sandy, a Hawaii native, Pedersen provide an abundance of information and great breakfasts.

Hosts: Jim and Sandy Pederson
Rooms: 3 (SB) $50-55
Full Breakfast
Credit Cards: A, B
Notes: 2, 5, 7, 8, 9, 10, 12

---

year; 6 Pets welcome; 7 Children welcome; 8 Tennis nearby; 9 Swimming nearby; 10 Golf nearby; 11 Skiing nearby; 12 May be booked through travel agent

Volcano Heart Chalet
P. O. Box 404, Hana, 96713
(808) 248-7725

Located on the Big Island of Hawaii near Volcanoes National Park, this new cedar chalet has three keyed rooms, a lounge, laundry, and light cooking privileges. Cool nights, tropical natural flora, and parking by the house. Your hostess lives nearby. Two-night minimum in advance. No smoking or drinking.

Hosts: John and JoLoyce Kaia
Rooms: 3 (PB) $50
Continental Breakfast
Credit Cards: None
Notes: 2 (in advance), 5, 10

Poipu Bed and Breakfast Inn

KAUAI—KOLOA

Poipu Bed and Breakfast Inn
2720 Hoonani Road, 96756
(808) 742-1146; (800) 552-0095

This award-winning, renovated 1933 plantation inn is in a garden setting one block from the water. Just a few doors away, our new oceanfront inn offers spectacular ocean views. Rooms or suites have TV/VCR and ceiling fans; some have whirlpool tubs, kitchenettes, and air conditioning. One is handicapped accessible. Amenities include free videos, popcorn, games, barbecue, laundry facilities, free tennis and pool at nearby club. Walk to shops, restaurants, and beaches. Weekly discounts available.

Hosts: Dotti Cichon and B. Young
Rooms: 8 (PB) $50-195
Expanded Continental Breakfast
Credit Cards: A, B, C, D, E, F
Notes: 2, 5, 7, 8, 9, 10, 12

KAUAI—PRINCEVILLE

Hale 'Aha
3875 Kamehameha Drive
P. O. Box 3370, 96722
(808) 826-6733; (800) 826-6733
FAX (808) 826-6733

Newly built on the golf course, overlooking the ocean and lush mountains of Kauai, beautiful Hale 'Aha offers private entries and decks to each bedroom. Honeymoon and 1,000-square-foot penthouse suites have whirlpool bath, panoramic view, and Christian library. The resort community of Princeville is on the Garden Isle.

Hosts: Herb and Ruth Bockelman
Rooms: 4 (PB) $80; $190 suites
Continental Breakfast
Credit Cards: A, B
Notes: 2, 5, 8, 9, 10, 12

NOTES: Credit cards accepted: A Master Card; B Visa; C American Express; D Discover Card; E Diners Club; F Other; 2 Personal checks accepted; 3 Lunch available; 4 Dinner available; 5 Open all

MAUI—HANA

Kaia Ranch and Company
Ulaino Road, P. O. Box 404, 96713
(808) 248-7725

Located on Maui Island, drive 52 spectacular miles from Kahului Airport to Hana. This flower and fruit farm is quiet and private. With no electricity, it uses modern gas appliances and kerosene lamps. Choose from a cottage with private bath or half of a farmhouse with shared bath. Walk in the garden or picnic in the pavillion. The real Hawaii at its best.

Hosts: John and JoLoyce Kaia
Rooms: Cottage and studio (1 PB; 1 SB) $50-100
Continental Breakfast
Credit Cards: None
Notes: 5, 8, 9

OAHU—KANEOHE

Hawaii Host
1349 Manu-Aloha Street, 96734
(808) 261-2478

Located in the heart of the tropical winward side of Oahu, overlooking the Koolau Mountain Range, is a beautifully decorated cottage suite and guest rooms. The cottage suite has a private entrance, full kitchen, king bed, and TV/VCR. We are near Kailua beach, modern shopping, theater, and restaurants. Swimming, snorkling, sailing, windsurfing, diving, deep-sea fishing, golf, tennis, hospital, and churches are nearby. The friendly and gracious hosts have inside information about where to go and what to see.

Hosts: Jerry and Carolyn Farris
Rooms: 3 (2 PB; 1 SB) $40-60
Continental Breakfast
Credit Cards: None
Notes: 2, 5, 7, 8, 9, 10, 12

OAHU—KANEOHE

Emma's Guest Rooms
47-600 Hui Ulili Street, 96744
(808) 239-7248; FAX (808) 239-7224

Located in beautiful Temple Valley on Oahu's lush windward shore. The valley is guarded by mountains filled with singing birds, peace, and tranquility. Emma's is centrally located and convenient to Oahu's finest beaches, visitor attractions, modern shopping mall, and numerous restaurants. Guest kitchenette, dining, and TV lounge.

Hosts: Emma and Stan Sargeant
Rooms: 3 (PB) $45
Continental Breakfast
Credit Cards: A, B, C, D
Notes: 2, 5, 8, 9, 10

---

year; 6 Pets welcome; 7 Children welcome; 8 Tennis nearby; 9 Swimming nearby; 10 Golf nearby; 11 Skiing nearby; 12 May be booked through travel agent

Idaho

COEUR D'ALENE

Cricket on the Hearth
1521 Lakeside Avenue, 83814
(208) 664-6926

Cricket on the Hearth, Coeur d'Alene's first bed and breakfast inn, has a touch of country that gives the inn a "down home" aura. Each of the five guest rooms is furnished in theme, from romantic to unique. After a relaxing weekend around the inn with its two cozy fireplaces and delicious full breakfast, guests are sure to find staying at Cricket on the Hearth habit forming.

Hosts: Al and Karen Hutson
Rooms: 5 (3 PB; 2 SB) $45-75
Full Breakfast
Credit Cards: None
Notes: 2, 5, 8, 9, 10, 11

Katie's Wild Rose Inn
5150 Highway 90 East, 83814
(208) 765-9474; (800) 328-9474

Looking through the pine trees to Lake Coeur d'Alene, Katie's Wild Rose Inn is a haven for the weary traveler. Only 600 feet from the public dock and beach road, the inn has four cozy rooms, one with its own Jacuzzi. Guests can relax in the family room beside the fireplace or enjoy the old player piano. A full breakfast is served on the deck or in the dining room where you can admire the view.

Hosts: Joisse and Lee Knowles
Rooms: 4 (2 PB; 2 SB) $45-85
Full Breakfast
Credit Cards: None
Notes: 2, 5, 10, 11

Katie's Wild Rose Inn

NOTES: Credit cards accepted: A Master Card; B Visa; C American Express; D Discover Card; E Diners Club; F Other; 2 Personal checks accepted; 3 Lunch available; 4 Dinner available; 5 Open all

Sleeping Place of the Wheels
3308 Lodgepole Road, 83814
(208) 765-3435

We are located five minutes from downtown and the lake shore, close to a lovely golf course and one hour from downhill skiing. Handmade quilts cover our beds, and the hostess can be persuaded to construct one especially for you. Children will enjoy the sandbox, playhouse, swings, and toys. High chair and crib are also available. Breakfasts are full, unless you prefer something lighter. We try to meet any of our guests' dietary requests.

Host: Donna Bedord
Rooms: 2 (SB) $22.50-35
Full Breakfast
Credit Cards: A, B
Notes: 2, 4, 5, 7, 8, 9, 10, 11

Illinois

BARRINGTON

Barbara B's Bed and Breakfast
P. O. Box 1415, 60010
(708) 526-8876

Barbara B's Bed and Breakfast features a warm and inviting atmosphere in a country setting overlooking a conservation area. Breakfast is served on a screened-in porch or in the dining room. Guests can relax by a roaring fire amid antiques or walk to a nearby lake.

Hosts: Les and Barbara Ayres
Room: 1 (PB) $45
Full Breakfast
Credit Cards: None
Notes: 2, 5, 7, 8, 9, 11, 12

CARLYLE

Country Haus
1191 Franklin, 62231
(618) 594-8313

Country Haus is a comfortable 1890s Eastlake-style home. Located one mile from Carlyle Lake, there are a number of outdoor activities to choose from such as sailing, boating, skiing, fishing, and hiking. A museum and specialty shop are within walking distance. A gift shop is located on the premises, and lunch and dinner are available by advance reservation. Each room is individually decorated, and TV and stereo are ready for our guests to use in the downstairs library. A Jacuzzi is located on the first floor.

Hosts: Ron and Vickie Cook
Rooms: 4 (PB) $45-55
Full Breakfast
Credit Cards: A, B, C
Notes: 2, 3, 4, 5, 7, 8, 9, 10, 11

CHAMPAIGN

Aunt Zelma's Country Guest House
1074 Country Road 800 North, Tolono, 61880
(217) 485-5101

This lovely home near Tolono on the outskirts of Champaign is furnished with family antiques and quilts. Located 15 minutes from the University of Illinois and three miles from the airport. Watch the sun set as you stroll down the country road, or just sit a spell.

NOTES: Credit cards accepted: A Master Card; B Visa; C American Express; D Discover Card; E Diners Club; F Other; 2 Personal checks accepted; 3 Lunch available; 4 Dinner available; 5 Open all

Host: Zelma Weibel
Rooms: 3 (1 PB; 2 SB) $40-45
Full Breakfast
Credit Cards: None
Notes: 2, 7, 10

EVANSTON

The Margarita European Inn
1566 Oak Avenue, 60201
(708) 869-2273

The romantic at heart will truly enjoy this modest and charming European-style inn in Evanston, the home of Northwestern University. Relax in the grand parlor with the morning paper or in the roof garden at sunset. Explore the numerous antique and specialty shops nearby. On rainy days, curl up with a novel from our wood-paneled English library, or indulge in a culinary creation from our critically acclaimed northern Italian restaurant, Va Pensiero.

Hosts: Barbara and Tim Gorham
Rooms: 34 (5 PB; 29 SB) $50-55
Continental Breakfast
Credit Cards: None
Notes: 2, 4, 5, 7, 8, 9, 10, 12

GALENA

Avery Guest House
606 South Prospect Street, 61036
(815) 777-3883

This pre-Civil War home located near Galena's main shopping and historic buildings is a homey refuge after a day of exploring. Enjoy the view from our porch swing, feel free to play the piano, watch TV, or join a table game. Sleep soundly on comfortable queen beds, then enjoy our hearty continental breakfast in the sunny dining room with bay window. Mississippi river boats nearby.

Hosts: Flo and Roger Jensen
Rooms: 4 (S2B) $45-60
Expanded Continental Breakfast
Credit Cards: A, B, C, D
Notes: 2, 5, 7, 8, 9, 10, 11, 12

The Margarita European Inn

Belle Aire Mansion
11410 Route 20 West, 61036
(815) 777-0893

Belle Aire Mansion guest house is a pre-Civil War Federal home surrounded by 16 well-groomed acres that include extensive lawns, flowers, and a block-long, tree-lined driveway. We do our best to make our guests feel they are special friends.

---

year; 6 Pets welcome; 7 Children welcome; 8 Tennis nearby; 9 Swimming nearby; 10 Golf nearby; 11 Skiing nearby; 12 May be booked through travel agent

Hosts: Jan and Lorraine Svec
Rooms: 4 (PB) $65-85
Full Breakfast
Credit Cards: A, B, C
Notes: 2, 7, 8, 10, 11

Brierwreath Manor Bed and Breakfast
216 North Bench Street, 61036
(815) 777-0608

Brierwreath Manor, circa 1884, is just one block from Galena's Main Street and has a dramatic and inviting wraparound porch that beckons to you after a hard day. The house is furnished with an eclectic blend of antique and Early American furniture. You'll not only relax but feel right at home. Central air conditioning, ceiling fans, and cable TV add to your enjoyment.

Hosts: Mike and Lyn Cook
Rooms: 3 (PB) $70-80
Full Breakfast
Credit Cards: None
Notes: 2, 5, 8, 9, 10, 11

Brierwreath Manor Bed and Breakfast

Colonial Guest House
1004 Park Avenue, 61036
(815) 777-0336

Built in 1826, this 21-room mansion has 11 outside doors, five large porches, one four-room penthouse that overlooks the city, and three rooms with kitchens. It is one block off Main Street. This house is loaded with antiques and has operated as a guest house for 33 years.

Host: Mary Keller
Rooms: 6 (PB) $50-60
Continental Breakfast
Credit Cards: None
Notes: 2, 5, 7 (small), 8, 9, 10, 11, 12

NAPERVILLE

Harrison House Bed and Breakfast
26 North Eagle Street, 60540
(708) 420-1117

Harrison House Bed and Breakfast, circa 1911, is a warm and friendly guest house 25 miles west of Chicago. Five antique-filled guest rooms, all with central air conditioning, one with a Jacuzzi. Walk to the train, great shops, wonderful restaurants, and historic sites. Receive homemade chocolate chip cookies on arrival, and enjoy a scrumptious breakfast. Prepare to be pampered.

Hosts: Neal and Lynn Harrison; Dawn Dall
Rooms: 5 (3 PB; 2 SB) $35-108
Full Breakfast on weekends; continental breakfast on weekdays
Credit Cards: A, B, C
Notes: 2, 8, 9, 10, 11

NOTES: Credit cards accepted: A Master Card; B Visa; C American Express; D Discover Card; E Diners Club; F Other; 2 Personal checks accepted; 3 Lunch available; 4 Dinner available; 5 Open all

NAUVOO

Mississippi Memories
Rural Route 1, Box 291, 62354
(217) 453-2771

Located on the banks of the Mississippi River, this gracious home offers lodging and elegantly served full breakfasts. In quiet, wooded surroundings, it is just two miles from historic Nauvoo, with its dozens of restored Mormon-era homes and shops. Two decks offer spectacular sunsets, drifting barges, and bald eagle watching.

Hosts: Marge and Dean Starr
Rooms: 5 (2 PB; 3 SB) $45-59
Full Breakfast
Credit Cards: A, B
Notes: 2, 5, 7, 8, 9. 10

Parley Lane Bed and Breakfast
Rural Route 1, Box 220, 62354
(217) 453-2277

This secluded, mid-1800s restored farmhouse is situated on 80 peaceful acres of timber and pastures. Enjoy rooms furnished with antiques, and wake up to a delightful continental breakfast. Stroll down Parley's wooded lane or ride complimentary bicycles into historic Nauvoo. Visit the visitor's center, restaurants, antique shops, and many specialty shops. Let this home be your home, and experience a memorable stay in rural Illinois.

Hosts: Ben and Hazel Appeldorn
Rooms: 4 (1 PB; 3 SB) $35
Continental Breakfast
Credit Cards: A, B
Notes: 2, 5, 6, 7, 8, 9, 10

OAK PARK

Toad Hall
301 North Scoville Avenue, 60302
(708) 386-8623

A 1909 brick Colonial is located in the Frank Lloyd Wright historic district with Old World atmosphere and services. Antiques, Oriental rugs, Laura Ashley furnishings, television, phones, and air conditioning. Walk to 25 Wright masterpieces, Ernest Hemingway museum, lovely shops and restaurants, and public transportation to Chicago. No smoking.

Host: Cynthia Mungerson
Rooms: 3 (PB) $55-65
Full Breakfast
Credit Cards: None
Notes: 2, 8

QUINCY

The Kaufmann House
1641 Hampshire, 62301
(217) 223-2502

The Kaufmann House, built 100 years ago, is situated amid Quincy's beautiful historic district, which boasts of tree-lined streets and gorgeous architectural gems. The guests are served breakfast in the ancestor's room or on the stone-terraced patio. They are invited to browse through the antique-filled rooms, play the piano, watch TV, read, or enjoy popcorn by the fire.

Hosts: Emory and Bettie Kaufmann
Rooms: 3 (1 PB; 2 SB) $40-60
Expanded Continental Breakfast
Credit Cards: None
Notes: 2, 5, 7, 8, 9, 10

PEORIA

Ruth's Bed and Breakfast
1506 West Alta Road, 61615
(309) 243-5977

Guest rooms share a bath in this private home. Enjoy family atmosphere. Children are welcome. There are four acres to roam near family restaurants and within 20 minutes of city attractions. Reservations required.

Hosts: Ruth and William Giles
Rooms: 3 (SB) $30
Continental Breakfast
Credit Cards: None
Notes: 2, 5, 7, 10

NOTES: Credit cards accepted: A Master Card; B Visa; C American Express; D Discover Card; E Diners Club; F Other; 2 Personal checks accepted; 3 Lunch available; 4 Dinner available; 5 Open all

Indiana

BEVERLY SHORES

Dunes Shore Inn
33 Lakeshore County Road, Box 807, 46301
(219) 879-9029

A bed and breakfast in the Gasthof tradition, Dunes Shores Inn is quiet and informal. It is located one block from Lake Michigan and its national and state park beaches and is a four-season oasis for those who wish to relax in the natural beauty of the Indiana Dunes. An ideal inn for stopping off to explore this unique area.

Hosts: Rosemary and Fred Braun
Rooms: 12 summer, 10 winter (SB) $42-50
Expanded Continental Breakfast
Credit Cards: A, B
Notes: 2, 5, 7, 8, 9, 10, 11

CORYDON

The Kintner House Inn
101 South Capitol Street, 47112
(812) 738-2020

This completely restored inn, circa 1873, is on the National Register of Historic Places and is furnished with Victorian and country antiques. It features five fireplaces and serves a full breakfast in the dining room. The staff prides itself on personal attention and guests' comfort.

Host: Mary Jane Bridgwater
Rooms: 16 (PB) $47-94
Full Breakfast
Credit Cards: A, B, C, D
Notes: 2, 5, 8, 9, 10, 11, 12

HAGERSTOWN

The Teetor House
300 West Main Street, 47346
(317) 489-4422

This elegant, historic mansion on ten landscaped acres in a quaint, small town caters to travelers for business or pleasure. Affordable luxury. Fine restaurants and many antique stores are nearby. The house is fully air conditioned and offers many unique amenities. Five miles north of I-70 in east-central Indiana, a one-hour drive from Dayton, Ohio and Indianapolis.

Hosts: Jack and JoAnne Warmoth
Rooms: 4 (PB) $70-85
Full Breakfast
Credit Cards: A, B
Notes: 2, 4 (by arrangement), 5, 7, 8, 9, 10

---

year; 6 Pets welcome; 7 Children welcome; 8 Tennis nearby; 9 Swimming nearby; 10 Golf nearby; 11 Skiing nearby; 12 May be booked through travel agent

HUNTINGTON

Purviance House
326 South Jefferson, 46750
(219) 356-4218; (219) 356-9215

Built in 1859, this beautiful home is on the National Register of Historic Places. It features winding cherry staircase, ornate ceilings, unique fireplaces, and parquet floors. It has been lovingly restored and decorated with antiques and period furnishings to create a warm, inviting atmosphere. Amenities include TV in rooms, snacks, beverages, kitchen privileges, and library. Near recreational areas with swimming, boating, hiking, and bicycling. Historic tours available. One-half hour from Fort Wayne; two hours from Indianapolis.

Hosts: Bob and Jean Gernand
Rooms: 4 (2 PB; 2 SB) $40-60
Full Breakfast
Credit Cards: None
Notes: 2, 5, 7, 8, 9, 10

LAGRANGE

The 1886 Inn
P. O. Box 5, 46761
(219) 463-4227

The 1886 Inn bed and breakfast is filled with historic charm and elegance. Every room is aglow with old-fashioned beauty. It is the finest lodging in the area, yet affordable. Ten minutes from Shipshewana flea market.

Hosts: Duane and Gloria Billman
Rooms: 5 (3 PB; 2 SB) $69-89
Expanded Continental Breakfast
Credit Cards: A, B
Notes: 2, 5, 8, 10

METAMORA

The Thorpe House Country Inn
Clayborne Street, P.O. Box 36, 47030
(317) 932-2365; (317) 647-5425

Visit the Thorpe House in historic Metamora where the steam engine still brings passenger cars and the grist mill still grinds cornmeal. Spend a relaxing evening in this 1840 canal town home. Rooms are tastefully furnished with antiques and country accessories. Enjoy a hearty breakfast before visiting more than 100 shops in this quaint village. Our family-style dining room is also open to the public.

Hosts: Mike and Jean Owens
Rooms: 4 plus two-room suite (PB) $60-100
Full Breakfast
Credit Cards: A, B, D
Notes: 2, 3, 4, 6, 7, 10, 12

MIDDLEBURY

Bee Hive Bed and Breakfast
Box 1191, 46540
(219) 825-5023

NOTES: Credit cards accepted: A Master Card; B Visa; C American Express; D Discover Card; E Diners Club; F Other; 2 Personal checks accepted; 3 Lunch available; 4 Dinner available; 5 Open all

Come visit Amish country and enjoy Hoosier hospitality. The Bee Hive is a two-story, open floor plan with exposed hand-sawed red oak beams and a loft. Enjoy our collection of antique farm machinery and other collectibles. Snuggle under handmade quilts and wake to the smell of freshly baked muffins.

Hosts: Herb and Treva Swarm
Rooms: 3 (SB) $49.50-60
Full Breakfast
Credit Cards: A, B
Notes: 2, 5, 7, 10, 11

The Lookout Bed and Breakfast
14544 CR 12, 46540
(219) 825-9809

Located in the Amish country of northeast Indiana. Near the Menno-Hof (Amish-Mennonite Information Center); Shipshewana auction and flea market; antique, craft, and gift shops; famous restaurants; and the 1832 Bonneyville mill. Enjoy the spectacular view with a country-style breakfast in the sunroom. Swim in the private pool, or walk the wooded trails.

Hosts: Mary-Lou and Jim Wolfe
Rooms: 5 (3 PB; 2 SB) $50-70
Full Breakfast
Credit Cards: A, B
Notes: 2, 5, 7, 9, 11, 12

Patchwork Quilt Country Inn
11748 CR2, 46540
(219) 825-2417

Relax and enjoy the simple grace and charm of our 100-year-old farmhouse. Sample our country cooking with homemade breads and desserts. Tour our back roads, and meet our Amish friends. Buy handmade articles, then return to the inn and rest in our quaint guest rooms.

Host: Maxine Zook
Rooms: 9 (SB) $50.95-95
Full Breakfast
Credit Cards: A, B
Closed first two weeks of January, holidays, and Sundays
Notes: 2, 3, 4, 8, 10, 11

PAOLI

Braxtan House Inn Bed and Breakfast
210 North Gospel Street, 47454
(812) 723-4677

This inn is an 1893 Queen Anne Victorian with 21 rooms and listed on the National Register of Historic Places. The Braxtan family converted it into a hotel in the 1920s, and it has been restored and furnished with antiques by your hosts. Ski Paoli Peaks, enjoy Patoka Lake, and explore the nearby cave and canoeing country.

---

year; 6 Pets welcome; 7 Children welcome; 8 Tennis nearby; 9 Swimming nearby; 10 Golf nearby; 11 Skiing nearby; 12 May be booked through travel agent

Hosts: Terry and Brenda Cornwell
Rooms: 6 (PB) $40-70
Full Breakfast
Credit Cards: A, B, D
Notes: 2, 5, 8, 9, 10, 11

ROCHESTER

Minnow Creek Farm Bed and Breakfast
Rural Route 3, Box 381, 46975
(219) 223-7240

Minnow Creek Farm is an irrigated grain and pasture farm. The clapboard house, built in 1915, has been remodeled to provide the comforts of today's lifestyle. Joanne's great-grandparents came to Fulton County in 1867, and her home is filled with family antiques. She would enjoy sharing their history with you. Located less than one mile east of U.S. 31, this bed and breakfast is easily accessible to travelers. Reservations required.

Host: Joanne Newcomb Bendall
Rooms: 3 (1 PB; 2 SB) $35-45
Continental Breakfast
Credit Cards: None
Open May to October
Note: 2

SHIPSHEWANA

Morton Street Bed and Breakfast
140 Morton Street, P. O. Box 775, 46565
(219) 768-4391

Remember when beds were made of white iron and were piled high with homemade quilts? You'll enjoy the attention you receive from the staff as they give you that "welcome home" feeling! Located within easy walking distance of all shops, the flea market, and the Buggy Wheel Restaurant.

Hosts: Joel and Kim Mishler and Esther Mishler
Rooms: 10 (PB)
Full Breakfast
Credit Cards: A, B, D
Notes: 2, 5, 7

SOUTH BEND

Home Bed and Breakfast
21166 Clover Hill Court, 46614
(219) 291-0535

A warm, homelike environment awaits you at our Home Bed and Breakfast in the European tradition. Located south of the city on a quiet, residential court overlooking a pond, the guest rooms are the "empty nest" rooms. Eight miles south of Notre Dame; one mile west of U.S. 31 south off Kern and Lilac roads; a one-hour drive from Amish communities and Lake Michigan beaches. Advanced reservations only.

Hosts: Mark and Joyce Funderburg
Rooms: 3 (1 PB; 2 SB) $45-60
Full Breakfast
Credit Cards: None
Notes: 2, 5, 7, 8, 9, 10

NOTES: Credit cards accepted: A Master Card; B Visa; C American Express; D Discover Card; E Diners Club; F Other; 2 Personal checks accepted; 3 Lunch available; 4 Dinner available; 5 Open all

Indiana

Bessinger's Hillfarm Wildlife Refuge
Bed and Breakfast

TIPPECANOE

Bessinger's Hillfarm Wildlife Refuge Bed and Breakfast
4588 State Road 110, 46570
(219) 223-3288

This cozy log home overlooks 143 acres of rolling hills, woods, pasture fields, and marsh with 41 islands. It is ideal for geese and deer year-round. This farm features hiking trails with beautiful views, picnic areas, and benches tucked away in a quiet area. Varied seasons make it possible to canoe, swim, fish, bird-watch, hike, and cross-country ski. Start with a country breakfast, and be ready for an unforgettable experience.

Hosts: Wayne and Betty Bessinger
Rooms: 2 (PB) $45
Full Breakfast
Credit Cards: None
Notes: 2, 4, 5, 9

WALKERTON

Koontz House Bed and Breakfast
Rural Route 3, Box 592, 46574
(219) 586-7090

Come enjoy the beautiful home Sam Koontz built, circa 1880, on the west edge of 387-acre Koontz Lake with swimming area and boat dock. The house features large, airy bedrooms with color TV. A lakeside restaurant, marina, boat rental, and antique shops are all within walking distance. Potato Creek State Park is 12 miles away, Christmas shop and paraplanes are 60 miles away.

Hosts: Les and Jan Davison
Rooms: 4 (SB) $30-50
Full Breakfast
Credit Cards: None
Notes: 2, 5, 7, 8, 9, 10, 11, 12

WARSAW

White Hill Manor
2513 East Center Street, 46580
(219) 269-6933

This restored English Tudor mansion has hand-hewn oak beams and leaded-glass windows. Eight elegant bedrooms have phone, TV, and air conditioning. A conference room and a luxurious suite with spa bath are also available. Breakfast is served on the dining porch that is furnished with wicker. Adjacent to Wagon Wheel Theatre and Restau-

---

year; 6 Pets welcome; 7 Children welcome; 8 Tennis nearby; 9 Swimming nearby; 10 Golf nearby; 11 Skiing nearby; 12 May be booked through travel agent

rant. Lake recreation and wonderful antique shops are nearby. Corporate discount.

Host: Gladys Deloe
Rooms: 8 (PB) $75-112
Full Breakfast
Credit Cards: A, B, C
Notes: 2, 5, 7, 8, 9, 10

WESTFIELD

Country Roads Guesthouse
2731 West 146th Street, 46074-9611
(317) 846-2376

This 100-year-old farmhouse and barn are set on four acres nine miles north of Indianapolis. The air-conditioned home has high ceilings, kitchen with fireplace, and antique furniture. Guests may use the swimming pool and basketball court. Good location for biking and jogging; close to Conner Prairie and the historic village of Zionsville.

Host: N. A. Litz
Rooms: 2 (SB) $40-80
Continental Breakfast
Credit Cards: None
Notes: 2, 7, 10

NOTES: Credit cards accepted: A Master Card; B Visa; C American Express; D Discover Card; E Diners Club; F Other; 2 Personal checks accepted; 3 Lunch available; 4 Dinner available; 5 Open all

Iowa

AMANA COLONIES

Die Heimat Country Inn
Main Street, Homestead, 52236
(319) 622-3937

Die Heimat Country Inn is located in the historic Amana Colonies. It was built in 1854 and is listed on the National Register of Historic Places. The inn is decorated with locally handcrafted walnut and cherry furniture, with many homemade quilts and antiques throughout.

Hosts: Don and Sheila Janda
Rooms: 19 (PB) $36-65
Full Breakfast
Credit Cards: A, B, D
Notes: 2, 5, 6, 7, 8, 9, 10, 11

CALMAR

Calmar Guesthouse
Rural Route 1, Box 206, 52132
(319) 562-3851

Newly remodeled, this century-old Victorian home was built by attorney John B. Kaye and has stained glass, antiques, and upstairs and downstairs sitting rooms with cable TV. It is located close to Bily Clocks in Spillville, the smallest church, Spook Cave, Niagara Cave, Lake Meyer, bike trails, golf courses, a community college, Norwegian museum, and Luther College in Decorah. Breakfast is served in the formal dining room.

Hosts: Art and Lucille Kruse
Rooms: 5 (SB) $35-45
Full Breakfast
Credit Cards: A, B
Notes: 2, 5, 7, 8, 9, 10, 11

Die Heimat Country Inn

CLERMONT

Mill Street Bed and Breakfast
505 Mill Street, P. O. Box 34, 52135
(319) 423-5531

---

year; 6 Pets welcome; 7 Children welcome; 8 Tennis nearby; 9 Swimming nearby; 10 Golf nearby; 11 Skiing nearby; 12 May be booked through travel agent

Mill Street Bed and Breakfast is a ranch-style home with central air conditioning. Near excellent restaurant and gift shops. Enjoy Montauk, canoeing, and fishing.

Hosts: Roger and Lois Amundson
Rooms: 2 (PB) $35
Full Breakfast
Credit Cards: None
Notes: 2, 5, 7, 8

DUBUQUE

Another World— Paradise Valley Inn
16338 Paradise Valley Road, Durango, 52039
(319) 552-1034

An ideal getaway awaits you in a contemporary log inn nestled in the majestic hills of Paradise Valley. Ideally located within minutes of the Mississippi River and riverboat rides, two miles from Heritage Nature Trail, and five miles from a ski area. Amenities include a hilltop location with picturesque view, fully equipped kitchenette, spacious great room with cathedral ceilings, and an open loft. The unique interior resembles a ski chalet. Very inviting!

Hosts: Karen and Gene Parker
Rooms: 4 (3 PB; 1 SB) $55-85
Full Breakfast
Credit Cards: A, B
Notes: 2, 5, 7, 11, 12

The Mandolin Inn
199 Loras Boulevard, 52001
(319) 556-0069

This unusual 1908 Victorian has original oil paintings on the dining room walls and an Italian tile fireplace. Ideally located in the historic section of Dubuque, it is surrounded by magnificent turn-of-the-century churches, private homes, and historically significant government buildings.

Host: Jan Oswald
Rooms: 7 (5 PB; 2 SB) $65-85
Full Breakfast
Credit Cards: A, B, D
Notes: 2, 5, 7, 9, 10, 11, 12

LEIGHTON

Leighton-Pella Heritage House
1345 Highway 163-48MM, 50143
(515) 626-3092

This lovely redecorated farm home has TVs and central air conditioning. The Victorian room is filled with antique furniture and an old pump organ. Located near Pella, famous for Tulip Time the second week of May, historical tours are available to experience a touch of Holland. Dutch shops and a gourmet restaurant are nearby. Near Rock Dam recreation areas. Hunters are welcome; lots of pheasant and quail, facilities to dress game, and freezer space for storage.

Host: Iola Vander Wilt
Rooms: 3 (1 PB; 2 SB) $35-50
Full Breakfast
Credit Cards: None
Closed January and February
Notes: 2, 6, 7, 8, 9, 10, 11

NOTES: Credit cards accepted: A Master Card; B Visa; C American Express; D Discover Card; E Diners Club; F Other; 2 Personal checks accepted; 3 Lunch available; 4 Dinner available; 5 Open all

MARENGO

Loy's Bed and Breakfast
Rural Route 1, Box 82, 52301
(319) 642-7787

This beautiful, modern home is on a working grain and hog farm with quiet and pleasant views of rolling countryside. A farm tour is offered with friendly hospitality. The large recreation room includes a pool table, table tennis, and shuffleboard. Swing set and sand pile are in the large yard. Close to the Amana Colonies, Kalona, Iowa City, West Branch, and Cedar Rapids. I-80, Exit 216 north one mile.

Host: Loy and Robert Walker
Rooms: 3 (1 PB; 2 SB) $45-60
Full Breakfast
Credit Cards: None
Notes: 2, 4 (by arrangement), 5, 6 (caged), 7, 8, 9, 10, 11, 12

STRATFORD

Hooks Point Farmstead
Rural Route 3495, Hooks Point Drive, 50249
(515) 838-2781; (800) 383-7062

One hour north of Des Moines, 20 minutes west of I-35, near Boone and Scenic Valley RR, is this inviting 1904 homestay with old-fashioned warmth and modern comforts. Featherbeds, full breakfast, and opportunities for on-premises gourmet dining, backwood picnics, bicycling, canoeing, and antiquing. This is a working grain farm.

Hosts: Marvin and Mary Jo Johnson
Rooms: 3 (2 PB; 1 SB) $45-90
Full Breakfast
Credit Cards: None
Notes: 2, 4, 5, 7, 8, 9, 10, 11, 12

Roses and Lace Bed and Breakfast

WASHINGTON

Roses and Lace Bed and Breakfast
821 North Second Avenue, 52353
(319) 653-2462

Step back in time and return to the charm of yesteryear in this restored 1893 Queen Anne Victorian. Capture the ambience of an early-1890s family residence with antique period furniture and decor. The home boasts beautiful Eastlake woodwork, oak floors, beaded spandrells, sliding pocket doors, original chandeliers, and stained glass. Guests can gather at the dining room table to talk, enjoy lemonade on the porch, or relax in front of the parlor fireplace.

---

year; 6 Pets welcome; 7 Children welcome; 8 Tennis nearby; 9 Swimming nearby; 10 Golf nearby; 11 Skiing nearby; 12 May be booked through travel agent

Hosts: Milt and Judi Wildebuer
Rooms: 2 (PB) $45
Full Breakfast
Credit Cards: None
Notes: 2, 5, 8, 9, 10, 11

WEBSTER CITY

Centennial Farm Bed and Breakfast
1091 220th Street, 50595
(515) 832-3050

Centennial Farm is a bed and breakfast homestay located on a working farm that has been in the family since 1869. Guests may gather their own eggs and take a ride in a 1929 Model A pickup truck, if desired. In a quiet location near several good antique shops. Member of Iowa Bed and Breakfast Innkeepers Association, Inc. Air conditioned. Twenty-two miles west of I-35 at Exit 142 or Exit 144.

Hosts: Tom and Shirley Yungclas
Rooms: 2 (SB) $35
Full Breakfast
Credit Cards: None
Notes: 2, 5, 7, 8, 10, 11

NOTES: Credit cards accepted: A Master Card; B Visa; C American Express; D Discover Card; E Diners Club; F Other; 2 Personal checks accepted; 3 Lunch available; 4 Dinner available; 5 Open all

Kansas

ABILENE

Victorian Reflections
303 North Cedar, 67410
(913) 263-7774

This 100-year-old Victorian inn offers comfortable elegance in the heart of Abilene. Four bedrooms are furnished with antiques, a parlor is available for relaxation, and a full breakfast is served in the dining room. All guest rooms have half baths. Located within walking distance of Abilene's many attractions, two mansions, and Eisenhower Center.

Hosts: Don and Diana McBride
Rooms: 4 (SB) $40
Full Breakfast
Credit Cards: A, B
Notes: 2, 5

ATWOOD

Goodnite at Irenes'
703 South Sixth, 67730
(913) 626-3521

Enjoy old-fashioned hospitality in a clean comfortable home. Relax on an outdoor deck, hearing the birds sing while viewing the country pasture. Guests are welcome to enjoy the patio, large back yard, and the family room with TV and phone. We specialize in homemade continental or country-style breakfast. Hunters welcome, but no hunting privileges. Non-smokers preferred.

Host: Irene E. Holste
Rooms: 2 (1 PB; 1 SB) $35
Full or Continental Breakfast
Credit Cards: None
Notes: 7, 9, 10

HALSTEAD

Heritage Inn
300 Main Street, Box 43, 67056
(316) 835-2118

The Heritage Inn offers the charm of the 1920s with the conveniences of the 1990s. Each room is beautifully decorated and has cable TV, refrigerator, individual heating and air conditioning. Breakfast is served in our cozy hotel cafe. While enjoying a leisurely breakfast, you can swap stories with other guests, or get acquainted with local business people.

---

year; 6 Pets welcome; 7 Children welcome; 8 Tennis nearby; 9 Swimming nearby; 10 Golf nearby; 11 Skiing nearby; 12 May be booked through travel agent

84 Kansas

Hosts: Jim and Heri Hartong
Rooms: 5 (PB) $28
Full Breakfast
Credit Cards: A, B
Notes: 2, 3, 4, 5, 7, 9, 10, 11

LENEXA

Bed and Breakfast Kansas City
P. O. Box 14781, 66285
(913) 888-3636

This reservation service can arrange your accommodations in Kansas City or the St. Louis, Missouri area. From an 1857 plantation mansion on the river to a geodesic dome in the woods with hot tub, there is a price and style for everyone. Victorian, turn-of-the-century, English Tudor, and contemporary are available. Double, queen, or king beds, most with private baths. The service represents 35 inns and homes. $40-125.

LINDSBORG

Swedish Country Inn
112 West Lincoln, 67456
(913) 227-2985

The Swedish Country Inn is an authentic Swedish bed and breakfast. There are 19 rooms furnished with Swedish-pine imported furniture and handmade quilts. Each room has a TV and phone. A full buffet Scandinavian breakfast is served. Use of sauna and bicycles is included. We have a small gift shop just off the lobby and are only one-half block off Main Street where there are wonderful shops and art galleries.

Host: Virginia Brusell
Rooms: 19 (PB) $40-70
Full Breakfast
Credit Cards: A, B
Notes: 2, 5, 7, 8, 9, 10

VALLEY FALLS

The Barn Bed and Breakfast Inn
Rural Route 2, Box 87, 66088
(913) 945-3225

In the rolling hills of northeast Kansas, this 100-year-old barn has been converted into a bed and breakfast. Sitting high on a hill with a beautiful view, it has a large, indoor heated pool, fitness room, three livingrooms, king and queen beds in all rooms. We serve you supper, as well as a full breakfast, and have three large meeting rooms available.

Hosts: Tom and Marcella Ryan
Rooms: 18 (PB) $53-68
Full Breakfast
Credit Cards: A, B, C, D, E
Notes: 2, 3, 4, 5, 7, 8, 9, 10, 12

WAKEFIELD

Bed 'N Breakfast— Still Country
206 Sixth Street, 67487
(913) 461-5596

NOTES: Credit cards accepted: A Master Card; B Visa; C American Express; D Discover Card; E Diners Club; F Other; 2 Personal checks accepted; 3 Lunch available; 4 Dinner available; 5 Open all

Wakefield, a town of 900, is in the heart of God's farming country—an excellent getaway. For more than 30 years our home has offered comfort and privacy. We boast a modern, unique museum, an arboretum of 193 wooded exotic acres with trails and birds, a 75-acre county park with camper facilities, a pool, and beaches on the 23-mile-long Milford Lake. Our farm is three miles from town. Nearby are antiques and the attractions of Abilene.

Host: Pearl Thurlow
Rooms: 2 (SB) $35
Full Breakfast
Credit Cards: None
Notes: 2, 5, 7, 8, 9, 10

Kentucky

GEORGETOWN

Log Cabin Bed and Breakfast
350 North Broadway, 40324
(502) 863-3514

This authentic log cabin has two bedrooms, fireplace, kitchen/family room, air conditioning. Georgetown is a quiet, historic town five miles north of Kentucky Horse Park and 12 miles north of Lexington. Facilities are completely private.

Hosts: Clay and Janis McKnight
Cabin: 1 (PB) $64
Expanded Continental Breakfast
Credit Cards: None
Notes: 2, 5, 6, 7

MIDDLESBORO

The RidgeRunner Bed and Breakfast
208 Arthur Heights, 40965
(606) 248-4299

This 1891 Victorian home is furnished with authentic antiques and nestled in the Cumberland Gap Mountains. A picturesque view is enjoyed from a 60-foot front porch. A relaxed, peaceful atmosphere; you will be treated like a special person. Five minutes from Cumberland Gap National Historical Park, 12 miles from Pine Mountain State Park, 50 miles from Knoxville, Tennessee.

Host: Susan Richards
Rooms: 5 (2 PB; 3 SB) $40-45
Full Breakfast
Credit Cards: A, B
Notes: 2, 5

PADUCAH

Ehrhardt's Bed and Breakfast
285 Springwell Lane, 42001
(502) 554-0644

Our brick Colonial ranch home is located just one mile off I-24, which is noted for its lovely scenery. We hope to make you feel at home in antique-filled bedrooms and a cozy den with a fireplace. Nearby are the beautiful Kentucky and Barkley lakes and the famous Land Between the Lakes area.

Hosts: Eileen and Phil Ehrhardt
Rooms: 2 (SB) $35

NOTES: Credit cards accepted: A Master Card; B Visa; C American Express; D Discover Card; E Diners Club; F Other; 2 Personal checks accepted; 3 Lunch available; 4 Dinner available; 5 Open all

Full Breakfast
Credit Cards: None
Notes: 2, 7 (over 12), 8, 9, 10

SPRINGFIELD

Maple Hill Manor Bed and Breakfast
Route 3B, Box 20
Perryville Road (150 E), 40069
(606) 336-3075

Listed on the National Register of Historic Places, we are located on 14 tranquil acres in the scenic Bluegrass region. The home, circa 1851, took three years to build, has ten-foot doors, thirteen and one-half-foot ceilings, nine-foot windows, cherry spiral staircase, stenciling in the foyer, three brass and crystal chandeliers, and nine fireplaces. The honeymoon hideaway has a canopy bed and Jacuzzi. One hour from Louisville and Lexington. No smoking.

Hosts: Kay and Bob Carroll
Rooms: 7 (PB) $60-80
Full Breakfast
Credit Cards: A, B
Notes: 2, 5, 7, 8, 9, 10, 12

Maple Hill Manor Bed and Breakfast

Louisiana

NEW ORLEANS

Bougainvillea House
841 Bourbon Street, 70116
(504) 525-3983

From this location in the heart of the French Quarter, walk to antique shops, paddle wheelers, and jazz clubs. It's just a street car ride to the zoo. This elegant town house has 12-foot ceilings, balcony, and fireplace. The royal canopy suite offers antique furniture, magnificent canopy bed, and modern marble bath. Free off-street parking and convenient to convention center. Church listings available.

Host: Flo Cairo
Rooms: 3 (PB) $75-125
Continental Breakfast
Credit Cards: B, C
Note: 5

New Orleans Bed and Breakfast and Accommodations
P. O. Box 70182, 70182
(504) 838-0071

This reservation service has approximately 100 units throughout the city of New Orleans. We have accommodations in historic sections, such as the French Quarter and Garden District, as well as the newer condominiums on the riverfront in the Warehouse District. These units are convenient to the convention center. We are celebrating our "lucky" 13th year. Owner Sarah Margaret Brown is always pleased to assist guests. $40-200.

St. Charles Guest House
1748 Prytania Street, 70130
(504) 523-6556

A simple, cozy, and affordable pension in the Lower Garden District on the streetcar line is ten minutes to downtown and the French Quarter. Breakfast is served overlooking a charming pool and patio complete with banana tree. Tours are available from our lobby.

Hosts: Joanne and Dennis Hilton
Rooms: 30 (26 PB; 4 SB) $30
Continental Breakfast
Credit Cards: None
Notes: 2 (in advance), 5, 7, 8, 9

NOTES: Credit cards accepted: A Master Card; B Visa; C American Express; D Discover Card; E Diners Club; F Other; 2 Personal checks accepted; 3 Lunch available; 4 Dinner available; 5 Open all

PORT VINCENT

Tree House in the Park
Mailing address: 16520 Airport Road, Prairieville, 70769
(504) 622-2850; (504) 335-8942

Tree House in the Park is a Cajun cabin in the swamp. A large bedroom has a double Jacuzzi and queen waterbed. A private hot tub is on the sun deck; a heated pool is on the lower deck. Boat slip, fishing dock, double kayak float trip on Amite River. Rates include breakfast and supper. No smoking.

Hosts: Fran Schmieder
Rooms: 2 (PB) $100
Full Breakfast
Credit Cards: A, B
Notes: 2, 4 (included), 5, 9, 12

SHREVEPORT

Fairfield Place Bed and Breakfast
2221 Fairfield Avenue, 71104
(318) 222-0048

Fairfield Place Bed and Breakfast was built before the turn of the century and has been beautifully restored. Conveniently located near downtown, I-20, the medical centers, and Louisiana Downs, it is within walking distance of fine restaurants and unique shops. Our rooms are individually decorated with European and American antiques. Relax in our oversized tubs and enjoy the quiet, casually elegant atmosphere.

Host: Janie Lipscomb
Rooms: 6 (PB) $79-135
Full Breakfast
Credit Cards: A, B, C
Notes: 2, 5, 10

WHITE CASTLE

Nottoway Plantation Inn and Restaurant
Louisiana Highway 1, P.O. Box 160, 70788
(504) 545-2730; (504) 545-9167

Built in 1859 by John Randolph, a wealthy sugar cane planter, Nottoway is a blend of Italianate and Greek Revival styles. Nottoway is the largest remaining plantation home in the South. Its guest rooms are individually decorated with period furnishings.

Hosts: Cindy Hidalgo and Faye Russell
Rooms: 13 (PB) $125-150
Full Breakfast
Credit Cards: A, B, C, D
Closed Christmas Day
Notes: 2, 3, 4, 5, 8, 9, 10, 12

Maine

BAR HARBOR

Black Friar Inn
10 Summer Street, 04609
(207) 288-5091

Black Friar Inn is a completely rebuilt and restored inn incorporating beautiful woodwork, mantels, windows, and bookcases from old mansions and churches on Mount Desert Island. Gourmet breakfast includes homemade breads, pastry, and muffins. Afternoon refreshments are provided. All rooms have queen beds. Within easy walking distance of the waterfront, restaurants, and shops, with ample parking available. Short drive to Acadia National Park.

Hosts: Barbara and Jim Kelly
Rooms: 6 (PB) $85-98
Full Breakfast
Credit Cards: A, B
Closed winter months
Notes: 2, 7 (over 11), 8, 9, 10

Canterbury Cottage
12 Roberts Avenue, 04609
(207) 288-2112

Canterbury Cottage offers guests a cozy and comfortable alternative to the big inns. Our location is on a quiet side street two blocks from the many village and harbor activities. We are only five minutes from Acadia National Park and the Nova Scotia ferry terminal.

Hosts: Michele and Rick Suydam
Rooms: 4 (2 PB; 2 SB) $65-85
Expanded Continental Breakfast
Credit Cards: None
Closed November to June
Notes: 2, 8, 9, 10

Hearthside Bed and Breakfast
7 High Street, 04609
(207) 288-4533

Built in 1907 as a private residence, the inn features a blend of country and Victorian furnishings. All rooms have queen beds, some have a private porch or fireplace. We serve a homemade full breakfast, afternoon tea and homemade cookies, and evening refreshments. Located on a quiet side street in town, we are five minutes from Acadia National Park.

NOTES: Credit cards accepted: A Master Card; B Visa; C American Express; D Discover Card; E Diners Club; F Other; 2 Personal checks accepted; 3 Lunch available; 4 Dinner available; 5 Open all

Hosts: Susan and Barry Schwartz
Rooms: 9 (PB) $55-70 in winter; $75-110 in-season
Full Breakfast
Credit Cards: A, B
Notes: 2, 5, 8, 9, 10, 11

BATH

Fairhaven Inn
Rural Route 2, North Bath Road
Box 85, 04530
(207) 443-4391

A 1790 Colonial nestled on the hillside overlooking the Kennebec River on 20 acres of country sights and sounds. Beaches, golf, and maritime museum nearby, plus cross-country ski trails and wood fires. Gourmet breakfast is served year-round. Candlelight dinners available in winter.

Hosts: Sallie and George Pollard
Rooms: 6 (4 PB; 2 SB) $45-70
Full Breakfast
Credit Cards: A, B, C
Notes: 2, 3 (box), 4 (weekend package), 5, 6 (by arrangement), 7 (by arrangement), 8, 9, 10, 11

BELFAST

The Jeweled Turret Inn
16 Pearl Street, 04915
(207) 338-2304

This grand lady of the Victorian era, circa 1898, offers many unique architectural features and is on the National Register of Historic Places. The inn is named for the grand staircase that winds up the turret, lighted by stained- and leaded-glass panels with jewellike embellishments. Each guest room is filled with Victoriana and has its own bath. A gourmet breakfast is served. Shops, restaurants, and waterfront are a stroll away.

Hosts: Carl and Cathy Heffentrager
Rooms: 7 (PB) $55-75
Full Breakfast
Credit Cards: None
Notes: 2, 5, 8, 9, 10, 11, 12

The Jeweled Turret Inn

Northport House Inn Bed and Breakfast
197 Northport Avenue, 04915
(207) 338-1422; (800) 338-1422 U.S. and Canada; (800) 339-1422 Maine

The Northport House Inn, a wonderfully restored Victorian house, circa 1873, is in a coastal community near Camden and Searsport. At one time it was an overnight stop on the Portland Bar Harbor Road. In the morning, enjoy our full breakfast of Belgian waffles, pancakes, French toast, eggs, omelets, muffins, biscuits, fresh fruit, and coffee or tea served in our common room.

Hosts: Peter and Mary Lou Mankevetch
Rooms: 8 (4 PB; 4 SB) $53
Full Breakfast
Credit Cards: A, B
Notes: 2, 5, 7, 8, 9, 10, 11

Northport House Inn Bed and Breakfast

BRUNSWICK

Harborgate Bed and Breakfast
Rural Delivery 2, #2260, 04011
(207) 725-5894

This contemporary redwood home is 40 feet from the ocean. Flower gardens and wooded landscape provide gracious relaxation. Two ocean-facing, first-floor bedrooms are separated by a guest livingroom with patio. Dock for swimming and sunbathing. Close to Bowdoin College, L. L. Bean, and sandy beaches.

Wide selection of stores, gift shops, and steak and seafood restaurants. Summer theater, college art museum, Perry McMillan Museum, and historical society buildings and events.

Host: Carolyn Bolles
Rooms: 2 (SB) $50-60
Continental Breakfast
Credit Cards: None
Closed November - April
Notes: 2, 9

CAPE NEDDICK

The Cape Neddick House
1300 Route 1, P.O. Box 70, 03902
(207) 363-2500

Nestled in the historic, coastal community of York, this 100-year-old restored Victorian farmhouse offers guests a true taste of Maine. After a restful night's sleep in antique beds, snuggled under handmade quilts, guests awake to smells of baked blueberry muffins, peach pancakes, and cinnamon popovers with wild raspberry jam. Beaches, boutiques, antique shops, boat cruises, wildlife sanctuaries, factory outlets, historical and cultural opportunities abound. Relaxing in a rocker on the front porch, watching the world go by is a favorite pastime.

Hosts: Dianne and John Goodwin
Rooms: 6 (SB) $55-70
Full Breakfast
Credit Cards: None
Notes: 2, 5, 8, 9

NOTES: Credit cards accepted: A Master Card; B Visa; C American Express; D Discover Card; E Diners Club; F Other; 2 Personal checks accepted; 3 Lunch available; 4 Dinner available; 5 Open all

CLARK ISLAND

Craignair Inn
Clark Island Road, 04859
(207) 594-7644; (800) 524-ROOM

Located on the water, the inn is near great hiking trails along the shore or through the forests. The inn was formerly a boarding house for stonecutters from the nearby quarries that provide great swimming. The annex was once the village chapel. A peaceful and secluded setting.

Host: Terry Smith
Rooms: 22 (8 PB; 14 SB) $57-87
Full Breakfast
Credit Cards: A, B, C
Notes: 2, 4, 6, 7, 8, 9, 10, 11, 12

DAMARISCOTTA

Brannon-Bunker Inn
HCR 64, Box 045B, 04543
(207) 563-5941

Brannon-Bunker Inn is an intimate and relaxed country bed and breakfast situated minutes from sandy beach, lighthouse, and historic fort in Maine's mid-coastal region. Located in a 1920s Cape, converted barn, and carriage house, the guest rooms are furnished in themes reflecting the charm of yesterday and the comforts of today. Antique shops, too!

Hosts: Jeanne and Joe Hovance
Rooms: 7 (4 PB; 3 SB) $50-60
Expanded Continental Breakfast
Credit Cards: A, B, C
Closed Christmas week
Notes: 2, 5, 7, 8, 9, 10

Down Easter Inn at Damariscotta
Bristol Road, Routes 129 and 130, 04543
(207) 563-5332; (201) 540-0500 winter

The Down Easter Inn, one mile from downtown Damariscotta, is in the heart of the rocky coast of Maine. On the National Register of Historic Places, it features a two-story porch framed by Corinthian columns. Minutes from golfing, lakes, and the ocean. Nearby are lobster wharfs for local fare and boat trips around Muscongus Bay and to Monhegan Island. The inn features 22 lovely rooms with TVs.

Hosts: Mary and Robert Colquhoun
Rooms: 22 (PB) $65-75
Continental Breakfast
Credit Cards: A, B
Notes: 2, 9, 10

EAST BOOTHBAY

Five Gables Inn
Murray Hill Road, 04544
(207) 633-4551; (800) 451-5048

The Five Gables Inn is an elegantly restored 125-year-old bed and breakfast located on Linekin Bay. The inn has 15 rooms, all with a water view and some with working fireplaces. It is located away from the busy Boothbay Harbor area on a quiet street in East

Boothbay. Swimming, boating, golfing, or just relaxing on the veranda are available. No smoking.

Hosts: Ellen and Paul Morissette
Rooms: 15 (PB) $80-120
Full Breakfast
Credit Cards: A, B
Closed December-April
Notes: 2, 7

EASTPORT

Todd House
Todd's Head, 04631
(207) 853-2328

Large, center-chimney Cape, circa 1775, overlooking Passamadoddy Bay. Barbecue facilities, deck, library with items of local history. In 1801, men formed a Masonic order in what is now a guest room. Beautiful sunrises and sunsets!

Host: Ruth M. McInnis
Rooms: 5 (2 PB; 3 SB) $40-75
Expanded Continental Breakfast
Credit Cards: None
Notes: 2, 5, 6, 7

ELIOT

High Meadows
Route 101, 03903
(207) 439-0590

Located only four and one-half miles on Route 101 from Route 1 (turn at Kittery Trading Post), this Colonial house, circa 1736, is in a country setting, but only minutes away from historic Portsmouth, New Hampshire. Fine dining, theater, discount outlets, beaches, and mountain regions. We have single, double, and queen beds with private or shared bath.

Host: Elaine Raymond
Rooms: 5 (3 PB; 2 SB) $50-60
Full Breakfast
Credit Cards: None
Notes: 2, 9, 10

High Meadows

FREEPORT

Captain Josiah Mitchell House
188 Main Street, 04032
(207) 865-3289

Two blocks from L. L. Bean, this house is a five-minute walk past centuries-old sea captains' homes and shady trees to all shops in town. After exploring, relax on our beautiful, peaceful veranda with antique wicker furniture and "remember when" porch swing. State inspected and approved. Family owned and operated.

NOTES: Credit cards accepted: A Master Card; B Visa; C American Express; D Discover Card; E Diners Club; F Other; 2 Personal checks accepted; 3 Lunch available; 4 Dinner available; 5 Open all

Hosts: Loretta and Alan Bradley
Rooms: 6 (PB) $55-78
Full Breakfast
Credit Cards: A, B
Notes: 2, 5, 9, 10, 11, 12

Country at Heart Bed and Breakfast

37 Bow Street, 04032
(207) 865-0512

Our cozy 1870 home is located off Main Street and only two blocks from L. L. Bean. Park your car and walk to the restaurants and many outlet stores. Stay in one of three country-decorated rooms: the Shaker room, quilt room, or the teddy bear room. Our rooms have hand-stenciled borders, handmade crafts, and either antique or reproduction furnishings. There is also a gift shop for guests.

Hosts: Roger and Kim Dubay
Rooms: 3 (1 PB; 2 SB) $55-75
Full Breakfast
Credit Cards: None
Notes: 2, 5, 7, 9, 10, 11, 12

GREAT CRANBERRY ISLAND

The Red House

Great Cranberry Island, 04625
(207) 244-5297

This is a place for total relaxation in a charming shorefront, former saltwater farm on a small island overlooking Mt. Cadillac and Acadia National Park. After a short, scenic passenger ferry ride from Northeast Harbor, you will be met at the dock and transported to an antique Cape with traditionally decorated rooms. There are many opportunities for walks on the shore and bicycle rides. A full home-cooked breakfast is served.

Hosts: Dorothy and John Towns
Rooms: 6 (3 PB; 3 SB) $60-75; $50-60 off-season
Full Breakfast
Credit Cards: A, B
Notes: 2, 4, 9, 10, 11, 13

KENNEBUNKPORT

The Captain Lord Mansion

P. O. Box 800, 04046
(207) 967-3141; (800) 522-3141

The Captain Lord Manion is an intimate and stylish Maine coast inn. Built during the War of 1812 as an elegant, private residence, it is now listed on the National Register of Historic Places. The large, luxurious guest rooms are furnished with rich antiques, yet have modern creature comforts. The gracious hosts and innkeepers and their friendly staff are eager to make your visit enjoyable. Family-style breakfasts are served in an atmospheric country kitchen.

Hosts: Bev Davis and Rick Litchfield
Rooms: 16 (PB) $75-175 January-April; $129-199 May to December
Full Breakfast
Credit Cards: A, B, D
Notes: 2, 5, 8, 9, 10

---

year; 6 Pets welcome; 7 Children welcome; 8 Tennis nearby; 9 Swimming nearby; 10 Golf nearby; 11 Skiing nearby; 12 May be booked through travel agent

English Meadows Inn
Route 35, 04043
(207) 967-5766

The English Meadows Inn is a 130-year-old Victorian farmhouse with attached carriage house nestled on a knoll within a ten-minute stroll of the village of Kennebunkport and a five-minute drive to the beach. There are 13 guest rooms, and rates include a full country breakfast. We promote a loving, family atmosphere in a warm and comfortable place to unwind. No smoking.

Hosts: Charlie and Bernice Doane
Rooms: 12 plus cottage (9 PB; 4 SB) $75-90
Full Breakfast
Credit Cards: A, B
Notes: 2, 5, 7 (over 10), 8, 9, 10

The Green Heron Inn
Ocean Avenue, P.O. Box 2578, 04046
(207) 967-3315

Comfortable, clean, and cozy ten-room bed and breakfast. Each guest room has private bath, air conditioning, and color TV. A full breakfast from a menu is served. "Best breakfast in town."

Hosts: Charles and Elizabeth Reid
Rooms: 10 (PB) $65-105
Full Breakfast
Credit Cards: None
Notes: 2, 5, 6 (in advance), 8, 9, 10

The Kennebunkport Inn
1 Dock Square, P.O. Box 111, 04046
(207) 927-2621

This classic country inn is in the heart of Kennebunkport near shops, historic district, beaches, boating, and golf. Originally a sea captain's home, the inn maintains its charm with antique furnishings, two elegant dining rooms, Victorian pub, and piano bar. Serving breakfast and dinner May through October, the inn is recognized for its fine food. Rooms are available year-round.

Hosts: Rick and Martha Griffin
Rooms: 34 (B) $69-155
Full Breakfast May-October
Continental Breakfast November-April
Credit Cards: A, B, C
Notes: 4, 5, 10

LAKE WELD

Kawanhee Inn Lakeside Lodge
Summer: Route 142, Webb Lake, 04285
Winter: 7 High Street, Farmington, 04938
(207) 585-2242 (summer); (207) 778-4306 (winter)

Kawanhee Inn is located on a high knoll and commands a beautiful view of the lake and mountains. A huge stone fireplace and forced hot air heat keep the building warm and cheerful. You will find a climate famous for its bracing mountain air. Blankets are a comfort nearly every night of the season, and the temperature ranges between 45 and 75 degrees.

Host: Marti Strunk
Rooms: 9 (4 PB; 5 SB) $45-125
Continental Breakfast

NOTES: Credit cards accepted: A Master Card; B Visa; C American Express; D Discover Card; E Diners Club; F Other; 2 Personal checks accepted; 3 Lunch available; 4 Dinner available; 5 Open all

Credit Cards: A, B
Closed October 15-April 30
Notes: 2, 3, 4, 8, 9, 10

LUBEC

Breakers by the Bay
37 Washington Street, 04652
(207) 733-2487

Enjoy the breathtaking views of the sea from your own private deck in this blue and white New England home located close to the international bridge leading to Campobello and Roosevelt's house. Start your day with a full breakfast in the dining room. Then choose from the beautiful vistas of Quoddy Head State Park and Campobello, or just sit back and enjoy relaxing.

Hosts: E. M. Elg
Rooms: 4 (2 PB; 3 SB) $40-60
Suite: 1
Full Breakfast
Credit Cards: None
Closed November-April
Notes: 2, 10

MILLINOCKET

Katahdin Area Bed and Breakfast
94-96 Oxford Street, 04462
(207) 723-5220

We are located 17 miles south of the entrance to Baxter State Park, the gateway to Katahdin, Maine's highest peak. With a population fewer than 8,000, Millinocket has small-town charm. The spectacular "Grand Canyon of the East" on Gulf Hagas is a short distance from here off Route 11 South. Appalachian trail access; 156 miles of groomed trails; walking distance to Main Street, restaurants, shops, houses of worship.

Hosts: Rodney and Mary Lou Corriveau
Rooms: 5 (1 PB; 4 S2B) $40-50
Full Breakfast
Credit Cards: None
Notes: 2, 5, 7, 8, 9, 10

NAPLES

The Augustus Bove House
Rural Route 1, Box 501, 04055
(207) 693-6365

Historic Hotel Naples, recently restored to show off its gracious charm, offers authentic, colonial accommodations in a relaxing atmosphere at affordable prices. Overlooking Long Lake and the causeway within easy walking distance of water, restaurants, recreation, and shops. Airconditioning, color TV, VCR and movies, and phone are provided. Antique and gift shop are on the premises. Off-season specials.

Hosts: David and Arlene Stetson
Rooms: 7 (3 PB; 4 SB) $45-79
Full Breakfast
Credit Cards: A, B, D
Notes: 2, 4 (off-season), 5, 6, 7, 8, 9, 10, 11

---

year; 6 Pets welcome; 7 Children welcome; 8 Tennis nearby; 9 Swimming nearby; 10 Golf nearby; 11 Skiing nearby; 12 May be booked through travel agent

SEARSPORT

Thurston House Bed and Breakfast Inn
8 Elm Street, P. O. Box 686, 04974
(207) 548-2213

This beautiful Colonial home, circa 1830, with ell and carriage house was built as a parsonage for Stephen Thurston, uncle of Winslow Homer, who visited often. Now you can visit in a casual environment. The quiet village setting is steps away from Penobscot Marine Museum, beach park on Penobscot Bay, restaurants, churches, galleries, antiques, and more. Relax in one of four guest rooms, two with bay views, and enjoy the "forget about lunch" breakfasts.

Hosts: Carl and Beverly Eppig
Rooms: 4 (2 PB; 2 SB) $45-60
Full Breakfast
Credit Cards: None
Notes: 2, 5, 7, 8, 9, 10, 11, 12

SOUTH FREEPORT

Harborside Bed and Breakfast
14 Main Street, 04078
(207) 865-3281

Harborside Bed and Breakfast is an 1830s Greek Revival house situated on the street that leads to the harbor. Long gone is the Soule shipyard where ships were once launched that sailed to the West Indies and beyond. In its place are two bustling marinas, a "lobster in the rough" restaurant, and the harbor itself, to which local fishermen still bring their daily catch—lobster, claims, fish and mussels.

Hosts: Caroline and Jim Hendry
Rooms: 3 (PB) $65-80
Full or Continental Breakfast
Credit Cards: A, B
Notes: 2, 5, 6, 7, 8, 9, 10

SOUTHWEST HARBOR

Lindenwood Inn
P. O. Box 1328, 04679
(207) 244-5335

This lovely sea captain's home overlooks the harbor on the quiet side of the island, offering a warm, cozy atmosphere. Explore nearby Acadia National Park and come home to swing on the porch, relax in the parlor, or play our harpsicord. Send for free brochure.

Hosts: Marilyn and Gardiner Brower
Rooms: 7 (3 PB; 4 SB) $50-125
Cottage: 1 (PB) $105
Full Breakfast
Credit Cards: None
Notes: 2, 5, 6 (over 12), 8, 9, 10, 11, 12

The Island House
P. O. Box 1006, 04679
(207) 244-5180

Relax in a gracious, restful seacoast home on the quiet side of Mount Desert Island. We serve such island house favorites as blueberry coffee cake and

---

NOTES: Credit cards accepted: A Master Card; B Visa; C American Express; D Discover Card; E Diners Club; F Other; 2 Personal checks accepted; 3 Lunch available; 4 Dinner available; 5 Open all

sausage-cheese casserole. A charming, private loft apartment is available. Acadia National Park is only a five-minute drive away. Located across the street from the harbor, near swimming, sailing, biking, and hiking.

Host: Ann Gill
Rooms: 4 (SB) $50-95
Full Breakfast
Credit Cards: None
Closed January-March
Notes: 2, 7, (over 11), 9, 10

THOMASTON

Cap'n Frost Bed and Breakfast
241 West Main (U.S. Route 1), 04861
(207) 354-8217

Our 1840 Cape is furnished with country antiques, some of which are for sale. If you are visiting our mid-coastal area, we are a comfortable overnight stay, close to Monhegan Island and a two-hour drive to Acadia National Park. Reservations are helpful.

Hosts: Arlene and Harold Frost
Rooms: 3 (1 PB; 2 SB) $40-45
Full Breakfast
Credit Cards: A, B
Notes: 2, 5, 9, 11

WATERFORD

The Parsonage House Bed and Breakfast
Rice Road, P. O. Box 116, 04088
(207) 583-4115

Built in 1870 for the Waterford Church, this restored historic home overlooks Waterford Village, Keoka Lake, and Mt. Tirem. It is located in a four-season area providing a variety of opportunities for the outdoor enthusiast. The Parsonage is a haven of peace and quiet. Three double guest rooms are tastefully furnished. Weather permitting, we feature a full breakfast on the screened porch. Guests love our large, northeastern farm kitchen and its glowing, wood-burning stove.

Hosts: Joseph and Gail St-Hilaire
Rooms: 3 (1 PB; 2 SB) $40-50
Full Breakfast
Credit Cards: None
Notes: 2, 3, 5, 7, 9, 10, 11

Bell Buoy Bed and Breakfast

YORK HARBOR

Bell Buoy Bed and Breakfast
570 York Street, 03911
(207) 363-7264

At the Bell Buoy, there are no strangers, only friends who have never met. Lo-

---

year; 6 Pets welcome; 7 Children welcome; 8 Tennis nearby; 9 Swimming nearby; 10 Golf nearby; 11 Skiing nearby; 12 May be booked through travel agent

cated minutes from I-95 and U.S. 1, minutes from Kittery outlet malls, and a short walk to the beach. Enjoy afternoon tea served either on the large front porch or the living room fireplace and cable TV. Homemade breads or muffins are served with breakfast in the dining room each morning or on the porch.

Hosts: Wes and Kathie Cook
Rooms: 4 (1 PB; 3 SB) $55-80
Full Breakfast
Credit Cards: None
Notes: 2, 6, 7 (over 6), 9, 10

York Harbor Inn
Route 1A, P.O. Box 573, 03911
(207) 363-5119; (800) 343-3869

For more than 100 years, the historic charm and hospitality of York Harbor Inn have welcomed those seeking distinctive lodging and dining experiences. A short walk takes you to a peaceful, protected beach. A stroll along Marginal Way reveals hidden coastal scenes and classic estates. Golf, tennis, biking, deep-sea fishing, and outlet shopping are close by. Air conditioning, antiques, phones, private baths, ocean views, and fireplaces. Full dining room and tavern with entertainment.

Hosts: Joe and Garry Dominguez
Rooms: 32 (28 PB; 4 SB) $45-129
Continental Breakfast
Credit Cards: A, B, C, E, F
Notes: 2, 3, 4, 5, 7, 8, 9, 10, 11, 12

NOTES: Credit cards accepted: A Master Card; B Visa; C American Express; D Discover Card; E Diners Club; F Other; 2 Personal checks accepted; 3 Lunch available; 4 Dinner available; 5 Open all

Maryland

The Barn on Howard's Cove

ANNAPOLIS

The Barn on Howard's Cove
500 Wilson Road, 21401
(410) 266-6840

This is a restored 1850s barn on a secluded cove off the Severn River, three miles from historic Annapolis, state capital, and sailing center of the United States. Annapolis is the home of the U.S. Naval Academy and has easy access to Washington, D. C. and Baltimore. Enjoy beautiful gardens and rural setting, country decor with antique quilts and furniture. Guests may dock boats on a private dock.

Hosts: Dr. and Mrs. Graham Gutsche
Rooms: 2 (PB) $60
Full Breakfast
Credit Cards: None
Notes: 2, 5, 7, 8, 10, 12

Chez Amis Bed and Breakfast
85 East Street, 21401
(410) 263-6631

This renovated 70-year-old corner store combines yesteryear ambience with today's conveniences: central air conditioning, TVs, beverage centers. Nineteenth-century American antiques blend with European art and South American artifacts in an airy setting of west coast pastels. Centrally located in the historic district, it is one block from city dock, state capital, and U. S. Naval Academy. Enjoy romance and warm hospitality in America's sailing capital at "the place of friends."

Hosts: Tom and Valerie Smith
Rooms: 3 (PB) $75-90
Expanded Continental Breakfast
Credit Cards: None
Notes: 2, 5, 7, 9, 12

---

year; 6 Pets welcome; 7 Children welcome; 8 Tennis nearby; 9 Swimming nearby; 10 Golf nearby; 11 Skiing nearby; 12 May be booked through travel agent

Jonah Williams House, 1830

101 Severn Avenue, 21403
(401) 269-6020

Peach siding and brown trim grace this historic home in a charmingly light and healthy environment featuring 19 windows and Laura Ashley decor. Close to historic town shopping center, Main Street, and city dock; one block from Spa Creek and Severn River; one block from taxi pick-up to any location in the area, including the U.S. Naval Academy, three minutes away.

Hosts: Dorothy and Hank Robbins
Rooms: 4 (1 PB; 3 SB) $65-75
Continental Breakfast
Credit Cards: None
Notes: 2, 5, 9, 12

Prince George Inn Bed and Breakfast

232 Prince George Street, 21401
(410) 263-6418

An 1884 Victorian brick townhouse, the inn has been lovingly restored and filled with antiques and collectibles. It is in the historic district near shops, restaurants, and the U.S. Naval Academy with its beautiful chapel. The inn features a guest parlor, breakfast sun porches, garden courtyard, and gazebo. Buffet breakfast. Two rooms with private baths; suite with private bath accommodates four. Restrictions on children, smoking, and pets.

Hosts: Bill and Norma Grovermann
Rooms: 3 (PB) $85-110
Full Breakfast
Credit Cards: A, B, C
Notes: 5, 8, 10

BALTIMORE

The Admiral Fell Inn

888 South Broadway, 21231
(410) 522-7377; (800) 292-INNS

The seven connected buildings of the historic inn were constructed between 1780 and 1910. Guest rooms are unique in size and shape, many offering a view of the harbor, and each is furnished with period antiques. A working fireplace graces the drawing room, and the interior is accented by a four-story atrium. Guests are welcome to relax in the atrium area, drawing room, library, or in the comfort of their own rooms. At the water's edge in historic Fells Point, the inn is just minutes from Baltimore's inner harbor attractions and museums.

Host: Dominik Eckenstein
Rooms: 37 (PB) $76-125
Continental Breakfast
Credit Cards: B, C
Notes: 2, 3, 4, 5, 7

Mulberry House

111 West Mulberry Street, 21201
(410) 576-0111

From this historic inn in the downtown area, walk to shopping, restaurants, and attractions. Four deluxe double guest

---

NOTES: Credit cards accepted: A Master Card; B Visa; C American Express; D Discover Card; E Diners Club; F Other; 2 Personal checks accepted; 3 Lunch available; 4 Dinner available; 5 Open all

rooms feature antique armoires, four-poster or brass beds, and brass chandeliers. Grand piano, fireplace, and courtyard. Free parking, but a car is not necessary.

Hosts: Charlotte and Curt Jeschke
Rooms: 4 (SB) $65
Full Breakfast
Credit Cards: None
Notes: 2, 5, 12

ELKTON

Garden Cottage at Sinking Springs Herb Farm
234 Blair Shore Road, 21921
(410) 398-5566

With an early plantation house, including a 400-year-old sycamore, the garden cottage nestles at the edge of a meadow flanked by herb gardens and a historic barn with a gift shop. It has a sitting room with fireplace, bedroom, bath, air conditioning, and electric heat. Freshly ground coffee and herbal teas are offered with the country breakfast. Longwood Gardens and Winterthur Museum are 50 minutes away. Historic Chesapeake City is nearby with excellent restaurants.

Hosts: Bill and Ann Stubbs
Room: 1 (PB) $75
Full Breakfast
Credit Cards: A, B
Notes: 2, 5, 7, 8, 9, 10, 12

FREDERICK

Middle Plantation Inn
9549 Liberty Road, 21701-3246
(301) 898-7128

From this rustic inn built of stone and log, drive through horse country to the village of Mount Pleasant. The inn is located several miles east of Frederick on 26 acres. Each room is furnished with antiques and has a private bath, air conditioning, and TV. The keeping room, a common room, has stained glass and a stone fireplace. Nearby are antique shops, museums, and many historic attractions. Located within 40 minutes of Gettysburg, Pennsylvania, Antietam Battlefield, and Harpers Ferry.

Hosts: Shirley and Dwight Mullican
Rooms: 4 (PB) 75-85
Continental Breakfast (optional)
Credit Cards: A, B
Notes: 2, 5, 8, 9, 10, 12

Middle Plantation Inn

---

year; 6 Pets welcome; 7 Children welcome; 8 Tennis nearby; 9 Swimming nearby; 10 Golf nearby; 11 Skiing nearby; 12 May be booked through travel agent

GAITHERSBURG

Gaithersburg Hospitality Bed and Breakfast
18908 Chimney Place, 20879
(301) 977-7377

This luxury host home with all amenities is located in the beautifully planned community of Montgomery Village, close to churches, shops, restaurants, and theaters, just off I-270 and minutes from Washington, D.C. It is ideally situated for convenient driving north to Gettysburg, Pennsylvania and Harpers Ferry. Hosts are empty-nesters who enjoy catering to your travel needs. Home cooking! Private parking, TV, refrigerator, and laundry facilities are offered.

Hosts: Suzanne and Joe Danilowiiz
Rooms: 3 (2 PB; 1 SB) $50-55
Full Breakfast
Credit Cards: F
Notes: 2, 5, 7, 8, 9, 10, 12

Staat's
9311 Brink Road, 20879
(301) 963-3155

This lovely country setting is 12 minutes by Metro to Washington, D.C. and sightseeing in the nation's capital. Refresh yourself after sightseeing with a swim in the backyard pool. Enjoy the lovely flower gardens, gazebo, back yard with herb garden, Christian atmosphere, and a sumptuous breakfast featuring muffins in the glassed sunroom.

Hosts: Wesley and Jean Staat
Rooms: 3 (PB) $30-40
Full Breakfast
Credit Cards: None
Notes: 2, 5, 7, 9

HAGERSTOWN

Lewrene Farm Bed and Breakfast
9738 Downsville Pike, 21740
(301) 582-1735

Enjoy our quiet, Colonial country home on 125 acres near I-70 and I-81, a home away from home for tourists, business people, and families. We have room for family celebrations or seminars for 12 to 16 people. Sit by the fireplace or enjoy the great outdoors. Antietam Battlefifeld and Harpers Ferry are nearby; Washington, D. C. and Baltimore are one and one-half hours away. Quilts for sale.

Hosts: Irene and Lewis Lehman
Rooms: 6 (3 PB; 3 SB) $45-70
Full Breakfast
Credit Cards: None
Notes: 2, 5, 7, 8, 9

ST. MICHAELS

Parsonage Inn
210 North Talbot Street, 21663
(410) 745-5519

This late Victorian, circa 1883, was lavishly restored in 1985 with seven guest rooms, private baths, and brass beds with Laura Ashley linens. Three

---

NOTES: Credit cards accepted: A Master Card; B Visa; C American Express; D Discover Card; E Diners Club; F Other; 2 Personal checks accepted; 3 Lunch available; 4 Dinner available; 5 Open all

rooms have working fireplaces. The parlor and dining room are in the European tradition. Striking architecture! Two blocks to the maritime museum, shops, and restaurants.

Host: Will Workman
Rooms: 7 (PB) $82-108
Continental Breakfast
Credit Cards: A, B
Notes: 2, 5, 7, 8

Wades Point Inn on the Bay

Wades Point Inn on the Bay

P. O. Box 7, 21663
(410) 745-2500

For those seeking the serenity of the country and the splendor of the bay, we invite you to charming Wades Point Inn, just a few miles from St. Michaels. Complemented by the ever-changing view of boats, birds, and water lapping the shoreline, our 120 acres of fields and woodlands, with one mile walking or jogging trail, provide a peaceful setting for relaxation and recreation on Maryland's eastern shore.

Hosts: Betsy and John Feiler
Rooms: 15 winter, 25 summer (15 PB; 10 SB) $59-169
Continental Breakfast
Credit Cards: A, B
Notes: 2, 5, 7, 8, 10

SILVER SPRING

Varborg

2620 Briggs Chaney Road, 20905
(301) 384-2842

This suburban Colonial home in the countryside is convenient to Washington, D.C. and Baltimore, just off Route 29 and close to Route 95. Three guest rooms with a shared bath are available. This home has been inspected and given a two-star rating by the American Bed and Breakfast Association. No smoking.

Hosts: Robert and Patricia Johnson
Rooms: 3 (SB) $50
Full Breakfast
Credit Cards: None
Notes: 5, 7, 8

---

year; 6 Pets welcome; 7 Children welcome; 8 Tennis nearby; 9 Swimming nearby; 10 Golf nearby; 11 Skiing nearby; 12 May be booked through travel agent

Massachusetts

AMHERST

Allen House Victorian Bed and Breakfast Inn
599 Main Street, 01002
(413) 253-5000

An authentic 1886 Victorian bed and breakfast inn located on three acres in the heart of Amherst and within walking distance of the area colleges and the Emily Dickenson House. We feature spacious bed chambers, period decor, and a full breakfast. Brochure available. Winner of the 1991 Amherst Historic Commission Preservation Award.

Host: Alan
Rooms: 5 (PB) $55-95
Full Breakfast
Credit Cards: None
Notes: 2, 5

Andover Inn

ANDOVER

Andover Inn
Chapel Avenue, 01810
(508) 475-5903

Located in the national district of Andover Hill, better known as Phillips Academy, the Andover Inn offers guests the charm and hospitality of New England in a cultural and elegant atmosphere. Guests rooms have color TV, air conditioning, phone, and freshly baked chocolate chip cookies upon arrival! The dining room features continental cuisine, including scampi and tournedoes flambes, dover sole, and caesar salad, all prepared table-side and finished with a selection of pastry creations made by our own pastry chef.

Host: Harry Broekhoff
Rooms: 33 (23 PB; 10 SB) $64.75-112.25
Full Breakfast
Credit Cards: A, B, C, D
Notes: 2, 3, 4, 6 (small), 7

BARNSTABLE VILLAGE

Beechwood Inn
2839 Main Street, Route 6A, 02630
(508) 362-6618

NOTES: Credit cards accepted: A Master Card; B Visa; C American Express; D Discover Card; E Diners Club; F Other; 2 Personal checks accepted; 3 Lunch available; 4 Dinner available; 5 Open all

A romantic Victorian inn located on Cape Cod in historic Barnstable Village is within walking distance of the beach, harbor, whale watching, and shopping. Each room has its own charm, furnished with period antiques. Our most popular, the rose room, has an antique queen four-poster canopy bed with a fainting couch in front of a working fireplace. We serve a full breakfast at individual tables with candles and classical music.

Hosts: Anne and Bob Livermore
Rooms: 6 (PB) $95-125
Full Breakfast
Credit Cards: A, B, C
Notes: 2, 5, 7 (over 11), 8, 9, 10, 11 (XC), 12

BOSTON

Greater Boston Hospitality
P. O. Box 1142, Brookline, 02146
(617) 277-5430

This bed and breakfast reservation service represents more than 100 homes, unhosted apartments, and inns throughout historic areas of Beacon Hill, Back Bay, and waterfront in Boston, as well as surrounding suburbs and the north and south shore areas of Massachusetts. All have been personally inspected for comfort, cleanliness, and congeniality of hosts. Many include parking and are close to public transportation. Write for free brochure. $70-120. Kelly Simpson, coordinator.

CHATHAM—CAPE COD

The Cranberry Inn at Chatham
359 Main Street, 02633
(508) 945-9232; (800) 332-4667 reservations

A historic landmark conveniently located in a quaint, seaside village, the Cranberry Inn is Chatham's oldest inn. It is completely restored. All guest rooms are individually appointed with antiques and four-poster and canopy beds. Suites and rooms with fireplaces are available. Some rooms have decks. Air conditioning, TV, phones. Walk to beaches, golf, tennis, shops, and restaurants.

Host: Peggy DeHan and Richard Morris
Rooms: 14 (PB) $90-160
Expanded Continental Breakfast
Credit Cards: A, B, C
Notes: 2, 7 (over 12), 9, 10

The Old Harbor Inn
22 Old Harbor Road, 02633
(508) 945-4434; (800) 942-4434

Experience enchantment in this English country-style inn. Guest rooms offer king, queen, or twin beds, decorator fabrics and linens. A home-baked buffet breakfast is served in the sunroom or on the outside deck. Enjoy the gathering room with fireplace. Beaches, art galleries, museums, golf, tennis, fishing, boating, quaint shops, wildlife pre-

---

year; 6 Pets welcome; 7 Children welcome; 8 Tennis nearby; 9 Swimming nearby; 10 Golf nearby; 11 Skiing nearby; 12 May be booked through travel agent

108 Massachusetts

The Old Harbor Inn

serve, theater, outdoor concerts, and fine restaurants are all within easy walking distance. A warm welcome and pleasurable memory-making await you. AAA-rated three diamonds.

Hosts: Tom and Sharon Ferguson
Rooms: 7 (PB) $95-140
Expanded Continental Breakfast
Credit Cards: A, B, C, D
Notes: 2, 5, 8, 9, 10

CHELMSFORD

Westsview Landing
P. O. Box 4141, 01824
(508) 256-0074

This large, contemporary home overlooking Hart's Pond is located three miles from Routes 495 and 3; 30 miles north of Boston, and 15 minutes south of Nashua, New Hampshire. It is close to historic Lexington, Concord, and Lowell. Many recreational activities including swimming, boating, fishing, and bicyling, are nearby; and there is a hot spa on the premises.

Hosts: Robert and Lorraine Pinette
Rooms: 3 (SB) $40-50
Full Breakfast
Credit Cards: None
Notes: 2, 6, 7, 8, 9, 10, 11

DEEFIELD-SOUTH

Deerfield's Yellow Gabled House
307 North Main Street, 01373
(413) 665-4922

This country house is located in the heart of a historical and cultural area and is the site of the Bloody Brook Massacre of 1675. It is furnished with period antiques and promises a comfortable stay with the ambience of yesteryear. One mile from the crossroads of I-91, Route 116 and Routes 5 and 10, and close to historic Deerfield.

Host: Edna Julia Stahelek
Rooms: 3 (1 PB; 2 SB) $50-80
Full Breakfast
Credit Cards: None
Notes: 2, 5, 7 (over 10), 8, 9, 10, 11, 12

NOTES: Credit cards accepted: A Master Card; B Visa; C American Express; D Discover Card; E Diners Club; F Other; 2 Personal checks accepted; 3 Lunch available; 4 Dinner available; 5 Open all

Massachusetts 109

DUXBURY

Black Friar Brook Farm
636 Union Street, 02332
(617) 834-8528

Enjoy a restful stay in the historic home of Josia Soule who, 285 years ago, left the pilgrim shore of Duxbury. See the oak gunstock beams throughout, and enjoy the hearty breakfasts prepared by your host. Blueberry pancakes are a specialty. Make this stop to see historic Plymouth, Boston, and Cape Cod. Hosts offer referral service for Christian hospitality in many areas on the east coast.

Hosts: Anne and Walter Kopke
Rooms: 2 (1 PB; 1 SB) $45
Full Breakfast
Credit Cards: None
Notes: 2, 5, 7, 8, 9, 10

Deerfield's Yellow Gabled House

EAST FALMOUTH

Bayberry Inn
226 Trotting Park, 02536-5665
(508) 540-2962

Bayberry Inn is an informal, relaxed setting where guests shed their anxieties and enjoy the peace and hospitality they crave. We welcome families with children or pets to come join us under the pines. Our home is secluded but near restaurants, shopping, and beaches. Special rates for clergy.

Hosts: Joel and Anna Marie Peterson
Rooms: 2 (SB) $50-60; $100 suite
Full Breakfast
Credit Cards: None
Notes: 2, 5, 6, 7, 9, 10

EAST ORLEANS

Nauset House Inn
143 Beach Road, Box 774, 02643
(508) 255-2195

A real old-fashioned country inn farmhouse, circa 1810, is located on three acres with an apple orchard, one-half mile from the ocean. No TV, no phones in the rooms. Large commons room and dining room have large fireplaces. Cozy, antiques, eclectic—a true fantasy.

Hosts: Diane and Al Johnson; Cynthia and John Vessell
Rooms: 14 (8 PB; 6 SB) $45-95
Full or Continental Breakfast
Credit Cards: A, B
Notes: 2, 8, 9, 10

Ship's Knees Inn
186 Beach Road, P. O. Box 756, 02643
(508) 255-1312

---

year; 6 Pets welcome; 7 Children welcome; 8 Tennis nearby; 9 Swimming nearby; 10 Golf nearby; 11 Skiing nearby; 12 May be booked through travel agent

This 170-year-old restored sea captain's home is a three-minute walk to beautiful sand-duned Nauset Beach. Inside the warm, lantern-lit doorways are 19 rooms individually appointed with special Colonial color schemes and authentic antiques. Some rooms feature authentic ship's knees, handpainted trunks, old clipper ship models, braided rugs, and four-poster beds. Tennis and swimming are available on the premises. Three miles away overlooking Orleans Cove, the Cove House property offers three rooms, a one-bedroom efficiency apartment, and two cottages.

Hosts: Jean and Ken Pitchford
Rooms: 22, 1 apartment, 2 cottages (11 PB; 14 SB) $45-100
Continental Breakfast
Credit Cards: A, B
Notes: 2, 5, 7 (Cove House property), 10, 12

Ship's Knees Inn

EDGARTOWN, MARTHA'S VINEYARD

The Arbor
222 Upper Main Street, P.O. Box 1228, 02539
(508) 627-8137

This turn-of-the-century Victorian is delightfully and typically New England and filled with the fragrance of fresh flowers. Relax in the garden, have tea in the parlor, stroll to the enchanting village and bustling harbor of Edgartown. Come, be our guest at The Arbor.

Host: Peggy Hall
Rooms: 10 (8 PB; 2 SB) $50-85 off-season; $75-125 in-season
Continental Breakfast
Credit Cards: A, B
Notes: 2, 8, 9, 10

Colonial Inn of Martha's Vineyard
38 North Water Street, 02539
(508) 627-4711; (800) 627-4701
FAX (508) 627-5904

The charm of Martha's Vineyard is echoed by the history and style of the Colonial Inn, overlooking the harbor in the heart of historic Edgartown. Affordable luxury awaits you. All rooms have heat, air-conditioning, color cable TV. Continental breakfast is served in the sunroom with patio seating available.

Host: Linda Malcouronne
Rooms: 42 (PB) $60-172
Continental Breakfast
Credit Cards: A, B, C
Closed January-March
Notes: 2, 3, 4, 7, 8, 9, 10, 12

ESSEX

George Fuller House
148 Main Street, 01929
(508) 768-7766

NOTES: Credit cards accepted: A Master Card; B Visa; C American Express; D Discover Card; E Diners Club; F Other; 2 Personal checks accepted; 3 Lunch available; 4 Dinner available; 5 Open all

Built in 1830, this handsome Federalist-style home retains much of its 19th-century charm, including Indian shutters and a captain's staircase. Two of the guest rooms have working fireplaces. Decoration includes handmade quilts, braided rugs, and caned Boston rockers. A full breakfast may include such features as Cindy's French toast drizzled with brandy lemon butter. The inn's 30-foot sailboat is available for day sailing or lessons.

Hosts: Cindy and Bob Cameron
Rooms: 5 (PB) $70-100
Full Breakfast
Credit Cards: A, B, C, D
Notes: 2, 5, 7, 8, 9, 10, 12

FALMOUTH

Captain Tom Lawrence House Bed and Breakfast Inn
75 Locust Street, 02540
(508) 540-1445

This 1861 Victorian whaling captain's residence is in a historic village close to the beach, shining sea bikeway, ferries, bus station, shops, and restaurants. Explore the entire cape, Vineyard, and Plymouth by day trips. Six beautiful, corner guest rooms have firm beds, some with canopies. Antiques, a Steinway piano, and fireplace in the sitting room. German spoken here.

Host: Barbara Sabo-Feller
Rooms: 6 (PB) $70-95
Full Breakfast
Credit Cards: A, B
Closed November-January
Notes: 2, 7 (over 12), 8, 9

The Palmer House Inn
81 Palmer Avenue, 02540
(508) 548-1230; (800) 472-2632

Located in the historic district, this turn-of-the-century Victorian offers eight rooms, antique furnishings, and a gourmet breakfast. Enjoy *pain perdue* with orange cream or Finnish pancakes with strawberry soup. Walk to beaches, shops, restaurants. Bicycles are available. Reservations suggested.

Hosts: Ken and Joanne Baker
Rooms: 8 (PB) $60-115
Full Breakfast
Credit Cards: A, B, C, D, E, F
Notes: 2, 5, 8, 10

Peacock's Inn on the Sound
P. O. Box 201, 02541
(508) 457-9666

This oceanfront bed and breakfast offers ten spacious guest rooms, fireplaces, country charm, and comfort. Enjoy the breathtaking view, sample our deluxe full breakfast, then spend your day touring year-round attractions. We are within walking distance of the island ferry, shops, and restaurants. Reservations suggested. Two-night minimum stay.

---

year; 6 Pets welcome; 7 Children welcome; 8 Tennis nearby; 9 Swimming nearby; 10 Golf nearby; 11 Skiing nearby; 12 May be booked through travel agent

112 Massachusetts

Hosts: Bud and Phyllis Peacock
Rooms: 10 (PB) $65-115
Full Breakfast
Credit Cards: A, B, C
Notes: 2, 5, 8, 9, 10

FALMOUTH HEIGHTS

The Moorings Lodge
207 Grand Avenue South, 02540
(508) 540-2370

A Victorian sea captain's home is across from a sandy beach with lifeguard safety and within easy walking distance of restaurants and island ferry. The homemade breakfast buffet is served on the large, glassed-in porch overlooking Martha's Vineyard. Comfortable, airy rooms, most with private baths. Call us "home" while you tour Cape Cod.

Hosts: Ernie and Shirley Bernard
Rooms: 8 (6 PB; 2 SB) $50-70
Full Breakfast
Credit Cards: A, B
Notes: 2, 7 (over 6), 8, 9, 10

GLOUCESTER

Williams Guest House
136 Bass Avenue, 01930
(508) 283-4931

Gloucester is a beautiful fishing town located on Cape Ann. Betty's Colonial Revival house borders the finest beach, Good Harbor. Rooms are furnished with comfort in mind, and a light breakfast is served. Boat cruises, sport fishing, whale watching trips, Hammond Castle, shops, and art galleries in both Rockport and Rocky Neck are nearby.

Hosts: Betty and Ted Williams
Rooms: 7 (5 PB; 2 SB) $50-58 in-season;
  $40-50 off-season
Continental Breakfast
Credit Cards: None
Closed November-April
Notes: 2, 9, 10

Round Hill Farm Non-Smokers'
Bed and Breakfast

GREAT BARRINGTON

Round Hill Farm Non-Smokers' Bed and Breakfast
17 Round Hill Road, 01230
(413) 528-3366

A haven for non-smokers, this classic, 19th-century hilltop horse farm is celebrated and meticulously maintained for comfortable and intelligent hospitality. The 1820s dairy barn, recently renovated and nationally rated "outstanding," offers two luxurious suites,

---

NOTES: Credit cards accepted: A Master Card; B Visa; C American Express; D Discover Card; E Diners Club; F Other; 2 Personal checks accepted; 3 Lunch available; 4 Dinner available; 5 Open all

one with kitchen and deck. The 1907 farmhouse has sunny, immaculate guest rooms, antiques, and books. Generous breakfasts are served whenever you choose. Three hundred spectacular acres, porches, wildlife, trout stream, cross-country skiing.

Hosts: Thomas and Margaret Whitfield
Rooms: 7 (2 PB; 5 SB) $65-150
Full Breakfast
Credit Cards: A, B, C
Notes: 2, 5, 6 (horses), 7 (over 15), 8, 9, 10, 11, 12

HARWICHPORT

Harbor Walk Guest House
6 Freeman Street, 02646
(508) 432-1675

Harbor Walk is in the beautiful Wychmere Harbor area of Harwichport. A few steps from the house will bring you a view of the harbor, and further along is one of the finest beaches on Nantucket Sound. The village of Harwichport is only one-half mile away and contains interesting shops and fine restaurants. We offer queen canopy beds, a good breakfast, and a cool breeze on the porch.

Hosts: Marilyn and Preston Barry
Rooms: 6 (4 PB; 2 SB) $45-70
Expanded Continental Breakfast
Credit Cards: None
Notes: 2, 6, (by arrangement), 7 (by arrangement), 8, 9, 10, 12

HYANNIS

The Inn on Sea Street
358 Sea Street, 02601
(508) 775-8030

This elegant 1849 Victorian inn is just steps from the beach and features fireplace, romantic guest rooms, canopy beds, antiques, and Oriental carpets. A gourmet breakfast includes homemade delights, fruit, and cheese. Close to island ferries, entertainment, and Kennedy Compound. Travel writers' choice bed and breakfast. One-night stays welcome.

Hosts: Lois Nelson and J. B. Whitehead
Rooms: 6 (3 PB; 3 SB) $70-90
Full Breakfast
Credit Cards: A, B, C, D
Notes: 2, 3, 4, 8, 9, 10

Sea Breeze Inn
397 Sea Street, 02601
(508) 771-7213

Sea Breeze is a 14-room quaint bed and breakfast. It is just a three-minute walk to the beach and 20 minutes to the island ferries. Restaurants, night life, shopping, golf, tennis are within a ten-minute drive. Some rooms have ocean views. An expanded continental breakfast is served between 7:30 and 9:30 each morning.

Hosts: Patricia and Martin Battle
Rooms: 14 (PB) $45-85

---

year; 6 Pets welcome; 7 Children welcome; 8 Tennis nearby; 9 Swimming nearby; 10 Golf nearby; 11 Skiing nearby; 12 May be booked through travel agent

Expanded Continental Breakfast
Credit Cards: None

LOWELL

Sherman-Berry House
163 Dartmouth Street, 01851-2425
(508) 459-4760

This charming 1893 Queen Anne Victorian home has been operating as a bed and breakfast since 1985. Located in a national historic district, the house contains wonderful collections of Victoriana, antiques, stained glass, and comfortable beds. Friendly hosts and breakfasts in the Victorian style make your stay like a step into the 1890s. Near Boston. No smoking.

Hosts: Susan Scott and David Strohmeyer
Rooms: 3 (SB) $50-60
Full Breakfast
Credit Cards: None
Notes: 2, 5, 7, 8, 9, 10, 11, 12

MARBLEHEAD

Harborside House
23 Gregory Street, 01945
(617) 631-1032

An 1840 Colonial overlooks picturesque Marblehead Harbor, with water views from the paneled livingroom with a cozy fireplace, period dining room, sunny breakfast porch, and third-story deck. A generous breakfast includes juice, fresh fruit, homeibaked goods, and cereal. Antique shops, gourmet restaurants, historic sites, and the beach are a pleasant stroll away. The owner is a professional dressmaker. Friendly resident cat. No smoking.

Host: Susan Blake
Rooms: 2 (SB) $55-70
Expanded Continental Breakfast
Credit Cards: None
Notes: 2, 5, 7 (over 10), 9, 10

Lindsey's Garret
38 High Street, 01945
(617) 631-2433

From this pre-Revolutionary War (1720) home in a historic district, walk to nearby shops, art galleries, restaurants, and antique shops. The self-contained studio apartment has beamed cathedral ceiling, fireplace, deck, and water view. It is furnished with country antiques and prints of the great ships of the China trade. Hosts are interested in the writings of C. S. Lewis, Morton Kelsey, and Matthew Fox. Discount plans with local gourmet restaurants. Full breakfast supplies in refrigerator.

Hosts: Richard C. Harrison and Sarah Lincoln-Harrison
Room: 1 (PB) $70
Full Breakfast
Credit Cards: A, B
Notes: 2, 5, 7 (over 3)

Spray Cliff on the Ocean
25 Spray Avenue, 01945
(508) 744-8924; (800) 626-1530

NOTES: Credit cards accepted: A Master Card; B Visa; C American Express; D Discover Card; E Diners Club; F Other; 2 Personal checks accepted; 3 Lunch available; 4 Dinner available; 5 Open all

Panoramic views stretch out in grand proportions from this English Tudor mansion, circa 1910, set high above the Atlantic. The inn provides a spacious and elegant atmosphere inside. The grounds include a brick terrace surrounded by lush flower gardens where eider ducks, black cormorants, and seagulls abound. Fifteen miles from Boston.

Hosts: Richard and Diane Pabich
Rooms: 7 (PB) $95-200
Continental Breakfast
Credit Cards: A, B, C, D

NANTUCKET

Bed 'n Breakfast on Nantucket Island
22 Lovers Lane, 02554
(508) 228-9040

Our accommodations are unique because we offer a suite that sleeps four, has a small kitchen, livingroom, bath, deck, and private entrance, all for the price of a single room. Located two miles from busy Main Street, a beautiful pine forest surrounds our home. Less than one mile down the quiet road brings our guests to a surf beach. Come to the island and let us spoil you! No smoking.

Hosts: Louise and Jim Ozias
Suite: 1 (PB) $70-90
Continental Breakfast
Credit Cards: None
Notes: 2, 7, 9

Hussey House—1795
15 North Water Street, Box 552, 02554
(508) 228-0747

The guest house offers large, comfortable, airy rooms with twin, double, king, and triple beds. Each room has a private bath. This carefully restored home has antiques, original floor boards, and a fireplace in every room. A main parlor, spacious grounds, gardens, bicycle racks, and off-street parking are also available.

Hosts: Mrs. H. Johnson
Rooms: 6 (PB) $85-125
Continental Breakfast
Credit Cards: None
Notes: 2, 7, 8, 9, 10

Martin's Guest House
61 Centre Street, P. O. Box 743, 02554
(508) 228-0678

In a stately 1803 mariner's home in Nantucket's historic district, a romantic sojourn awaits you—a glowing fire in a spacious, charming living/dining room; large, airy guest rooms with authentic period pieces and four-poster beds; a lovely yard and veranda for peaceful summer afternoons. Owners and resident innkeepers welcome you to their home for a memorable summer holiday or a romantic off-season getaway.

Hosts: Channing and Ceci Moore
Rooms: 13 (9 PB; 4 SB) $60-130
Continental Breakfast

Credit Cards: A, B, C
Notes: 2, 5, 7 (over 6), 8, 9, 10

The Woodbox Inn

29 Fair Street, 02554
(508) 228-0587

The Woodbox is Nantucket's oldest inn, built in 1709. It is one and one-half blocks from the center of town, serves the best breakfast on the island, and offers gourmet dinners by candlelight. There are rooms for two and one- and two-bedroom suites available.

Host: Dexter Tutein
Rooms: 9 (PB) $115-180
Full Breakfast
Credit Cards: None
Notes: 2, 4, 7, 8, 9, 10, 12

Morrill Place Inn

NEWBURYPORT

Morrill Place Inn

209 High Street, 01950
(508) 462-2808

Gracious bed and breakfast in an early-19th-century sea captain's mansion. We are within walking distance of Newburyport's restored Federal period downtown. Nearby, Plum Island's dunes and beaches are visited by more than 300 species of birds. Our Old South Church has had the Rev. Whitehead buried under its altar since the 18th century, and the First Religious Society's meeting house has possibly the finest steeple in New England!

Host: Rose Ann Hunter
Rooms: 9 (6 PB; 3 SB) $66-90
Continental Breakfast
Credit Cards: None
Notes: 2, 5, 6, 8, 9, 12

REHOBOTH

Gilbert's Bed and Breakfast

30 Spring Street, 02769
(508) 252-6416; (800) 828-6821

Our 150-year-old home is special in all seasons. The in-ground pool refreshes weary travelers, and the quiet walks through our 100 acres give food for the soul. Guests also enjoy the chickens and horses. We praise God for being allowed to enjoy the beauty of the earth and want to share this beauty with others.

Hosts: Jeanne and Peter Gilbert
Rooms: 3 (SB) $32-50
Full Breakfast
Credit Cards: None
Notes: 2, 5, 6, 7, 8, 9, 10

NOTES: Credit cards accepted: A Master Card; B Visa; C American Express; D Discover Card; E Diners Club; F Other; 2 Personal checks accepted; 3 Lunch available; 4 Dinner available; 5 Open all

ROCKPORT

Lantana House
22 Broadway, 01966
(508) 546-3535

An intimate guest house in the heart of historic Rockport, Lantana House is close to Main Street, the T-wharf, and the beaches. There is a large sun deck reserved for guests, as well as TV, games, magazines and books, a guest refrigerator, and ice service. Nearby you will find a golf course, tennis courts, picnic areas, rocky bays, and inlets. Boston is one hour away by car.

Host: Cynthia Sewell
Rooms: 7 (5 PB; 2 SB) $58-70
Continental Breakfast
Credit Cards: None
Notes: 2, 7, 8, 9

Linden Tree Inn
26 King Street, 01966
(508) 546-2494

This 1840 Victorian is located in picturesque Rockport. Charm and warm hospitality abound in our guest living and sitting rooms. It is a short walk to restaurants, gift and antique shops, art galleries, beaches, and the train to Boston. Enjoy Penny's famous breakfast, and lemonade and cookies in the afternoon.

Hosts: Larry and Penny Olson
Rooms: 18 (PB) $70-90
Continental Breakfast
Credit Cards: A, B
Notes: 2, 5 (some rooms), 8, 9, 10

Mooringstone for Non-smokers
12 Norwood Avenue, 01966-1715
(508) 546-2479

This is Rockport's only bed and breakfast exclusively for non-smokers. It has a central, quiet location and offers comfortable, ground-floor rooms with microwaves, air conditioning, cable TV, refrigerators, and parking. Rockport is an ideal base for day trips in New England. Ask about our "RSTnoB" special rates (Rooms, Sheets, Towels, and no Breakfast or housekeeping).

Hosts: David and Mary Knowlton
Rooms: 3 (PB) $70-79
Expanded Continental Breakfast
Credit Cards: A, B, C
Closed mid-October to mid-May
Notes: 2, 8, 9, 10, 12

SALEM

The Salem Inn
7 Summer Street, 01970
(508) 741-0680; (800) 446-2995

In the midst of the historical and beautifully restored city of Salem is The Salem Inn, originally three town houses built in 1834 by Captain Nathaniel West. The captain would have approved of the spacious, comfortably appointed guest rooms with a blend of period detail and antique furnishings. Some have working fireplaces. Ideal for families are two-room suites complete with equipped kitchen. All rooms have air conditioning, phones, TV. The Go Fish

---

year; 6 Pets welcome; 7 Children welcome; 8 Tennis nearby; 9 Swimming nearby; 10 Golf nearby; 11 Skiing nearby; 12 May be booked through travel agent

Seafood Emporium has two intimate dining rooms, rose garden, and brick terrace. Rail and bus transportation available to Boston, only 18 miles away.

Hosts: Richard and Diane Pabich
Rooms: 21 (PB) $80-125
Continental Breakfast
Credit Cards: A, B, C, D, E
Notes: 2, 3, 4, 5, 7, 8, 9, 10, 12

SANDWICH

Captain Ezra Nye House
152 Main Street, 02563
(508) 888-6142; (800) 388-2278

Whether you come to enjoy summer on Cape Cod, a fall foliage trip, or a quiet winter vacation, the Captain Ezra Nye House is the perfect place to start. Located 60 miles from Boston, 20 from Hyannis, and within walking distance of many noteworthy attractions, including Heritage Plantation, Sandwich Glass Museum, and the Cape Cod Canal.

Hosts: Elaine and Harry Dickson
Rooms: 6 (4 PB; 2 SB) $50-75
Expanded Continental Breakfast
Credit Cards: A, B, C, D
Notes: 2, 5, 7 (over six), 8, 10, 12

The Summer House
158 Main Street, 02563
(508) 888-4991

This exquisite 1835 Greek Revival home featured in *Country Living* magazine is located in the heart of historic Sandwich village and features antiques, hand-stitched quilts, flowers, large sunny rooms, and English-style gardens. We are within strolling distance of dining, museums, shops, pond, and the boardwalk to the beach. Bountiful breakfasts and elegant afternoon tea in the garden.

Hosts: David and Kay Merrell
Rooms: 5 (1 PB; 4 SB) $40-75
Full Breakfast
Credit Cards: A, B, C, D
Notes: 2, 5, 7 (over five), 8, 9, 10

STURBRIDGE

Bethlehem Inn
P. O. Box 451, 01566
(508) 347-3013

Located near Old Sturbridge Village in a quiet, wooded area by a babbling brook and less than one-quarter mile from Main Street, we feature home-baked blueberry muffins, orange juice, and coffee for breakfast. Kick off your shoes and join us in the livingroom for TV or conversation. The bed and breakfast is operated to defray expenses of Bethlehem in Sturbridge, a diorama on the life of Jesus.

Hosts: J. George and Agnes Duquette
Rooms: 2 (1 PB; 1 SB) $45-60
Continental Breakfast
Credit Cards: None
Notes: 2, 8, 9

Sturbridge Country Inn
530 Main Street, 01566
(508) 347-5503

NOTES: Credit cards accepted: A Master Card; B Visa; C American Express; D Discover Card; E Diners Club; F Other; 2 Personal checks accepted; 3 Lunch available; 4 Dinner available; 5 Open all

At this historic 1840s inn each room has a fireplace and private whirlpool tub. It is close to Old Sturbridge Village and within walking distance of restaurants, shops, antiques. Breakfast available in room.

Host: Mr. MacConnel
Rooms: 9 (PB) $69-149
Continental Breakfast
Credit Cards: A, B, C, D
Notes: 2, 5, 7, 8, 9, 10, 11, 12

VINEYARD HAVEN

Hanover House
10 Edgartown Road, P. O. Box 2107, 02568
(508) 693-1066

Hanover House is a large, old inn that has been brought into the 20th century while retaining the charm and personalized hospitality of the gracious, old inns of yesteryear. Decorated in a classic country style that typifies a New England inn, Hanover House offers a harmonious array of furnishings to assure your comfort.

Host: Barbara Hanover
Rooms: 16 (PB) $68-158
Continental Breakfat
Credit Cards: A, B, C
Notes: 2, 7, 8, 9, 10, 12

WARE

The 1880 Country Bed and Breakfast
14 Pleasant Street, 01082
(413) 967-7847; (413) 967-3773

Built in 1876, this Colonial has pumpkin and maple hardwood floors, beamed ceilings, six fireplaces, and antique furnishings. Afternoon tea is served by the fireplace; breakfast is served in the dining room or on the porch, weather permitting. It is a short, pretty country ride to historic Old Sturbridge Village and Old Deerfield Village; hiking and fishing are nearby. Midpoint between Boston and the Berkshires, this is a very comfortable bed and breakfast.

Host: Margaret Skutnik
Rooms: 5 (2 PB; 3 SB) $40-65
Full Breakfast
Credit Cards: None
Notes: 2, 5, 8, 9, 10, 11, 12

WAREHAM

Mulberry Bed and Breakfast
257 High Street, 02571
(508) 295-0684

Mulberry Bed and Breakfast is a cozy one and one-half-story home, probably originally occupied by a blacksmith in the 1840s. The seven-trunk mulberry tree lends its name to this homestay. The hostess and two cats welcome travelers and hope guests will consider Mulberry their home while visiting the area. Fresh fruit, homemade breads, jams and jellies, and beverages are served on the pleasant deck or in the bright kitchen. Mulberry is convenient to Plymouth, Cape Cod, Boston, Newport, and New Bedford.

Host: Frances A. Murphy
Rooms: 3 (SB) $42 October-May; $45 June-September
Continental Breakfast
Credit Cards: C
Notes: 2, 5, 7, 8, 9, 11

WELLFLEET

Inn at Duck Creeke

P. O. Box 364, 02667
(508) 349-9333

The Inn at Duck Creek on five acres is situated between a salt marsh and its own duck pond. The inn is a short walk to the village and close to bay and ocean beaches, national seashore park, Audubon sanctuary harbor, and marina. The inn is home to two fine restaurants located just across the drive. Enjoy pleasant accommodations in Cape Cod's most charming village.

Hosts: Robert Morrill and Judith Pihl
Rooms: 25 (17 PB: 8 SB) $48-80
Continental Breakfast
Credit Cards: A, B, C
Notes: 4, 7, 8, 9, 10

WEST BARNSTABLE

Honeysuckle Hill

591 Main Street, 02668
(508) 362-8418

Built in the early 1800s, Honeysuckle Hill is a comfortable, rambling place decorated in a Cape Cod version of English country, with chintz, feather-beds, down comforters, two shaggy dogs named Chloe and Annie, and a tin of homemade cookies at every bedside. Hearty, country breakfasts and afternoon tea are served. The inn is near West Parish Church, built in 1722, with a bell made and installed by Paul Revere.

Host: Barbara Rosenthal
Rooms: 3 (PB) $80-105
Full Breakfast
Credit Cards: A, B, C, D
Notes: 2, 5, 6 (small), 7 (over 5), 8, 9, 10, 12

WEST HARWICH BY THE SEA

Cape Cod Sunny Pines and Claddagh Tavern

P. O. Box 667, 02671
(508) 432-9628; (800) 356-9628

Enjoy Irish hospitality in a Victorian ambience reminiscent of a small Irish manor. A gourmet, family-style Irish breakfast is enjoyed by candlelight on bone china and crystal. All suites have private temperature controls. Relax on the Victorian veranda or in the spacious Jacuzzi overlooking the picnic grounds, pool, and garden. TV, air conditioning, and refrigerators. Quality AAA and ABBA approved.

Hosts: Jack and Eileen Connell
Rooms: 6 (PB) $75-100
Cottages: 2 (PB)
Full Breakfast
Credit Cards: A, B, C, D
Notes: 2, 3, 4, 8, 9, 10, 12

NOTES: Credit cards accepted: A Master Card; B Visa; C American Express; D Discover Card; E Diners Club; F Other; 2 Personal checks accepted; 3 Lunch available; 4 Dinner available; 5 Open all

Michigan

BATTLE CREEK

Greencrest Manor
6174 Halbert Road, 49017
(616) 962-8633

To experience Greencrest is to step back in time to a way of life that is rare today. From the moment you enter the iron gates, you will be mesmerized. This French Normandy mansion situated on the highest elevation of St. Mary's Lake is constructed of sandstone, slate, and copper. Three levels of formal gardens include fountains, stone walls, iron rails, and cut sandstone urns. Air conditioned.

Hosts: Tom and Kathy Van Daff
Rooms: 5 (3 PB; 2 SB) $75-150
Expanded Continental Breakfast
Credit Cards: A, B, C
Notes: 2, 5, 8, 10, 11

BAY CITY

Stonehedge Inn Bed and Breakfast
924 Center Avenue (M25), 48708
(517) 894-4342

With stained-glass windows and nine fireplaces, this 1889 English Tudor home is indeed an elegant journey into the past. The magnificent open foyer and staircase lead to large beautiful bedrooms on the upper floors. Original features include speaking tubes, a warming oven, chandeliers, and a fireplace picturing Bible stories and passages on blue Delft tiles. In the historic district, Frankenmuth is 20 miles away. Birth Run Manufacturer's Marketplace is 35 miles away.

Host: Ruth Koerber
Rooms: 7 (S3B) $65-85
Expanded Continental Breakfast
Credit Cards: A, B, c, D
Notes: 2, 5, 8, 9, 10, 11, 12

BIG RAPIDS

Taggart House
321 Maple, 49307
(616) 796-1713

Taggart House is a charming Victorian-style home in the heart of Big Rapids, home of Ferris State University. The warmth, friendliness, and elegant charm of this wonderful home creates an ambience that is sure to please you. Relax

---

year; 6 Pets welcome; 7 Children welcome; 8 Tennis nearby; 9 Swimming nearby; 10 Golf nearby; 11 Skiing nearby; 12 May be booked through travel agent

in the comfortable livingroom, or catch the news on television. Enjoy a continental breakfast in the formal dining room; or during the warmer months, on the beautiful, enclosed flagstone porch.

Host: Barbara Randle
Rooms: 5 (3 PB; 2 SB) $45-65
Continental Breakfast
Credit Cards: A, B
Notes: 2, 5, 7 (by arrangement), 8, 9, 10, 11

BLANEY PARK

Celibeth House

Route 1, Box 58A, Germfask, 49836
(906) 283-3409

This lovely house was built in 1895. It is situated on 85 acres overlooking Lake Anna Louise. Each room is tastefully furnished. Guests may also use the livingroom, reading room, and enclosed front porch, as well as a large outside deck and nature trails. Main House is open May 1 to November 1. Winter House is open November 1-May 1. Winter House is located one block from Main House.

Host: Elsa R. Strom
Rooms: 8 (PB) $35-50
Continental Breakfast
Credit Cards: A, B
Notes: 2, 5, 7, 9, 11, 12

CLIO

Chandelier Guest House

1567 Morgan Road, 48420
(313) 687-6061

Relax in our country home. Enjoy bed and breakfast comforts including choice of rooms with twin, full, or queen beds. You may wish to be served full breakfast in bed, or beneath the beautiful crystal chandelier, or on the sun porch with a view of surrounding woods. Located minutes from Clio Amphitheater, Flint Crossroad Village, Birch Run Manufacturer's Marketplace, Frankenmuth, and Chesaning. Senior citizen discount. Call for directions.

Hosts: Alfred and Clara Bielert
Rooms: 2 (1 PB; 1 SB) $45
Full Breakfast
Credit Cards: None
Notes: 2, 5, 7, 10

COLDWATER

Batavia Inn

1824 West Chicago Road, U.S. 12, 49036
(517) 278-5146

This 1872 Italianate country inn has original massive woodwork, high ceilings, and restful charm. Seasonal decorations are a specialty with Christmas an extra festival of trees. Located near recreation and discount shopping. In-ground pool available in season. Guest pampering is the innkeepers' goal with treats, turn down, homemade breakfasts. Perfect for small retreats.

Hosts: E. Fred and Alma Marquardt
Rooms: 6 (3 PB; 3 SB) $55-69
Full Breakfast
Credit Cards: None
Notes: 2, 5, 9, 10

NOTES: Credit cards accepted: A Master Card; B Visa; C American Express; D Discover Card; E Diners Club; F Other; 2 Personal checks accepted; 3 Lunch available; 4 Dinner available; 5 Open all

DAVISON

Oakbrook Inn
7256 East Court Street, 48423
(313) 658-1546

Oakbrook is located on 20 acres of rolling landscape with woods and creek less than five minutes from Flint. Guest rooms are furnished with antiques, handicrafts, and handmade quilts. The indoor pool and hot tub are open year-round. Enjoy the warm summer sun and cool, evening breezes on the deck.

Hosts: Jan and Bill Cooke
Rooms: 7 (PB) $49.05-98.10
Continental Breakfast
Credit Cards: A, B, C
Notes: 2, 5, 7, 8, 9, 10, 11

ELK RAPIDS

Cairn House Bed and Breakfast
8160 Cairn Highway, 49629
(616) 264-8994

Cairn House is a beautiful 1800 Colonial-style home located 15 miles north of Traverse City. Our area offers all types of vacation pleasures: tennis, golf, lakes, and gourmet restaurants. Our goal is to make your visit a happy one. We have three rooms. Smoking is restricted.

Hosts: Roger and Mary Vandervort
Rooms: 3 (PB) $60
Full Breakfast
Credit Cards: None
Notes: 2, 7, 8, 9, 10, 11, 12

FENNVILLE

The Kingsley House Bed and Breakfast
626 West Main Street, 49408
(616) 561-6425

This elegant Queen Anne Victorian was built by the prominent Kingsley family in 1886 and selected by *Inn Times* as one of 50 best bed and breakfasts in America. It was also featured in *Innsider* magazine. Near Holland, Saugatuck, Allegan State Forest, sandy beaches, cross-country skiing. Bicycles available, whirlpool bath, getaway honeymoon suite. Enjoy the beautiful surroundings, family antiques. Breakfast is served in the formal dining room.

Hosts: David and Shirley Witt
Rooms: 6 (PB) $65-125
Full Breakfast
Credit Cards: None

The Kingsley House Bed and Breakfast

year; 6 Pets welcome; 7 Children welcome; 8 Tennis nearby; 9 Swimming nearby; 10 Golf nearby; 11 Skiing nearby; 12 May be booked through travel agent

"The Porches" Bed and Breakfast
2297 70th Street (Lakeshore Drive), 49408
(616) 543-4162

Built in 1897, "The Porches" offers five guest rooms. Located three miles south of Saugatuck, we have a private beach and hiking trails. The large common room has a TV. We overlook Lake Michigan with beautiful sunsets from the front porch. Open May 1 to November 1.

Hosts: Bob and Ellen Johnson
Rooms: 5 (PB) $59-69
Full or Expanded Continental Breakfast
Credit Cards: A, B
Notes: 2, 8, 9, 12

FRANKENMUTH

Bed and Breakfast at the Pines
327 Ardussi Street, 48734
(517) 652-9019

"Come as a stranger; leave as a friend." Frankenmuth is one of Michigan's most popular family tourist attraction. Stay in our ranch-style home and walk to the many tourist areas. Enjoy a yard surrounded by evergreens and bedrooms tastefully decorated with heirloom quilts, ceiling fans, and antique accents. Sit down to a continental-plus breakfast of homemade breads and rolls, jams, fresh fruit, and beverage. Hosts enjoy traveling through the "eyes" of guests and have been hosting since 1986.

Hosts: Richard and Donna Hodge
Rooms: 3 (SB) $35-40
Expanded Continental Breakfast
Credit Cards: None
Notes: 2, 6, 7

GAYLORD

Heritage House Bed and Breakfast
521 East Main, 49735
(517) 732-1199

Our five bedroom, 1895-era, farm-style home features family-type hospitality and full, country breakfast. We are within walking distance of downtown Gaylord and within 45 minutes of numerous skiing and golfing resorts.

Hosts: Pat Teal and Phyllis Erb
Rooms: 5 (S2B) $45-75
Full Breakfast
Credit Cards: None

HOLLAND

Dutch Colonial Inn
560 Central Avenue, 49423
(616) 396-3664

Relax and enjoy a gracious 1928 Dutch Colonial. Your hosts have elegantly decorated their home with family heirloom antiques and furnishings from the 1930s. Guests enjoy the cheery sun porch, the "hideaway suite," or rooms with whirlpool tubs for two. Special, festive touches are everywhere during the Christmas holiday season. Nearby

---

NOTES: Credit cards accepted: A Master Card; B Visa; C American Express; D Discover Card; E Diners Club; F Other; 2 Personal checks accepted; 3 Lunch available; 4 Dinner available; 5 Open all

are Windmill Island, wooden shoe factory, Delftware factory, tulip festival, Hope College, Michigan's finest beaches, bike paths, and cross-country ski trails. Corporate rates are available for business travelers.

Hosts: Bob and Pat Elenbaas, Diana Klungel
Rooms: 5 (PB) $65-100
Full Breakfast
Credit Cards: A, B, C, D
Notes: 2, 5, 8, 9, 10, 11

MACKINAC ISLAND

Haan's 1830 Inn
Huron Street, P. O. Box 123, 49757
(906) 847-6244; winter (414) 248-9244

The earliest Greek Revival home in the Northwest Territory, this inn is on the Michigan Historic Registry and is completely restored. It is in a quiet neighborhood three blocks around Haldiman Bay from bustling 1800s downtown and Old Fort Mackinac. It is also adjacent to historic St. Anne's Church and gardens. Guest rooms are furnished with antiques. Enjoy the island's 19th-century ambience of horse-drawn buggies and wagons. Winter address: 1134 Geneva Street, Lake Geneva, Wisconsin 53147.

Hosts: Nicholas and Nancy Haan; Vernon and Joy Haan
Rooms: 7 (5 PB; 2 SB) $75-105
Expanded Continental Breakfast
Credit Cards: None
Closed late October to mid-May
Notes: 2, 7, 8, 9, 10

MCMILLAN

Helmer House Inn
Rural Route 3, County Road 413, 49853
(906) 586-6119

A designated historical landmark, Helmer House was built in the late 1800s. It has been restored to combine Old World charm with amenities of modern living. Original and authentic antique furnishings adorn its tastefully decorated guest rooms, common parlor, and dining room. Nestled between two lakes, it affords a variety of recreational activities. The inn has a ten-table restaurant serving lunch and dinner.

Hosts: Guy and Imogene Teed
Rooms: 5 (SB) $36-55
Full Breakfast
Credit Cards: A, B
Closed mid-October to mid-May
Notes: 2, 3, 4, 7, 9, 10, 11, 12

OMENA

Omena Shores Bed and Breakfast
13140 Isthmus Road, P. O. Box 15, 49674
(616) 386-7311

This gracious bed and breakfast is featured on the Leelanau home tour. You will love this special place and relax in its warm hospitality. The lovingly restored 1850s barn is sprinkled with antiques, wicker, and handmade quilts. It is 300 feet from Omena Bay with golf, swimming, tennis, biking, and cross-country skiing nearby.

Hosts: Charlie and Mary Helen Phillips
Rooms: 4 (2 PB; 2 SB) $65-85
Full Breakfast
Credit Cards: None
Notes: 2, 5, 8, 9, 10, 11, 12

Omena Shores Bed and Breakfast

ONEKAMA

Lake Breeze House
5089 Main Street, 49675-0301
(616) 889-4969

Our two-story frame house on Portage Lake is yours with a shared bath, livingroom, and breakfast room. Each room has its own special charm with family antiques. Come, relax and enjoy our back porch and the sounds of the babbling creek. By reservation only. Boating and charter service available.

Hosts: Bill and Donna Erickson
Rooms: 3 (SB) $55
Full Breakfast
Credit Cards: None
Notes: 2, 5, 8, 9, 10, 11

OWOSSO

Rossman's R&R Ranch
308 East Hibbard Road, 48867
(517) 723-2553 evening; (517) 723-3232 day

A newly remodeled farmhouse from the early 1900s, the ranch sits on 130 acres overlooking the Maple River valley. A large concrete circle drive with white-board fences leads to stables of horses and cattle. The area's wildlife includes deer, fox, rabbits, pheasant, quail, and song birds. Observe and explore from the farm lane, river walk, or outside deck. Countrylike accents adorn the interior of the farmhouse, and guests are welcome to use the family parlor, garden, game room, and fireplace. No smoking.

Hosts: Carl and Jeanne Rossman
Rooms: 2 (SB) $40-45
Continental Breakfast
Credit Cards: None
Notes: 2, 5, 6, 7, 9, 10

PETOSKEY

Stafford's Bay View Inn
613 Woodland, 49770
(616) 347-2771

Built in 1886 as part of Methodist chataqua, Bay View Association, the inn is now a nationally registered historic site and still a functioning chataqua

---

NOTES: Credit cards accepted: A Master Card; B Visa; C American Express; D Discover Card; E Diners Club; F Other; 2 Personal checks accepted; 3 Lunch available; 4 Dinner available; 5 Open all

open to the public. The inn keeps a retreat setting: no phones or TV in rooms, no alcohol for sale on premises. Decor is country Victorian, featuring Amish quilts and period furnishings. Fine dining available seasonally. Open May to October, plus winter weekends.

Hosts: Reg and Lori Smith
Rooms: 30 (PB) $84-128 per person
Full Breakfast
Credit Cards: A, B, C
Notes: 2, 3, 4, 7, 8, 9, 10, 11

The 1882 John Crispe House

Terrace Inn
P.O. Box 266, 49770
(616) 347-2856; (800) 530-9898

The Terrace Inn is set in the heart of the Christian summer community of Bay View. The chautauqua programs are still alive since being established in 1876. The ecumenical community offers religion, culture, and family activities. The inn was built in 1910 and has been recently restored. All guest rooms have private baths, and the dining room serves wonderful food, including planked whitefish. You have not seen Michigan until you have stayed at the Terrace Inn.

Hosts: Patrick and May Lou Barbour
Rooms: 44 (PB) $42-74
Continental Breakfast
Credit Cards: A, B
Notes: 2, 3, 4, 5, 7, 8, 9, 10, 11

PLAINWELL

The 1882 John Crispe House
404 East Bridge Street, 49080
(616) 685-1293

Enjoy museum-quality Victorian elegance on the Kalamazoo River. Situated between Grand Rapids and Kalamazoo just off U.S. 131 on Michigan 89, the John Crispe House is close to some of western Michigan's finest gourmet dining, golf, skiing, and antique shops. Air conditioned. No smoking or alcohol. Gift certifcates are available.

Hosts: Ormand J. and Nancy E. Lefever
Rooms: 5 (3 PB; 2 SB) $55-95
Full Breakfast
Credit Cards: A, B
Notes: 2, 7, 8, 10, 11

PORT HURON

The Victorian Inn
1229 Seventh Street, 48060
(313) 984-1437

The Victorian Inn features fine dining and guest rooms in authentically restored Victorian elegance. One hour north of metropolitan Detroit, it is located in the heart of the church district and one-half block from the museum. All food and beverages are prepared with the utmost attention to detail, which was the order of the day in a bygone era.

Host: Sheila Marinez
Rooms: 4 (2 PB; 2 SB) $55-65
Continental Breakfast
Credit Cards: A, B, C, D
Notes: 2, 3, 7, 8, 9, 10

TRAVERSE CITY

Cider House Bed and Breakfast
5515 Barney Road, 49684
(616) 947-2833

The emphasis here is on simple, warm, country life. Awake to the smell of apple blossoms in the spring and juicy, red apples in the fall. Relax and enjoy cider or homemade Scottish shortbread on the front porch of our contemporary "Bob Newhart Show" inn that overlooks the orchard. In winter, relax in front of our fireplace.

Hosts: Nan and Ron Tennant
Rooms: 4 (PB) $65-70
Full Breakfast
Credit Cards: None
Notes: 2, 5, 8, 9, 10, 11

WEST BRANCH

The Rose Brick Inn
124 East Houghton Avenue, 48661
(517) 345-3702

A 1906 Queen Anne-style home with a graceful veranda, white picket fence, and cranberry canopy, the Rose Brick Inn is tucked in the center two floors of the Frank Sebastian Smith house listed in Michigan's register of historic sites. It is located on downtown Main Street in Victorian West Branch. Golfing, hiking, biking, cross-country skiing, snowmobiling, hunting, shopping, and special holiday events await you year-round. Jacuzzi.

Host: Leon Swartz
Rooms: 4 (PB) $44-48
Continental Breakfast
Credit Cards: A, B
Notes: 2, 7, 8, 9, 10, 11

NOTES: Credit cards accepted: A Master Card; B Visa; C American Express; D Discover Card; E Diners Club; F Other; 2 Personal checks accepted; 3 Lunch available; 4 Dinner available; 5 Open all

Minnesota

CHATFIELD

Lunds' Guest House
218 Southeast Winona Street, 55923
(507) 867-4003

This charming 1920s home is decorated in the 1920s and 1930s style and located only 20 minutes from Rochester, at the gateway to beautiful Bluff country. Personalized service includes use of the kitchen, living and dining rooms, two screened porches, and washer and dryer.

Hosts: Shelby and Marion Lund
Rooms: 4 (2 PB; 2 S1.5B) $45-50
Continental Breakfast
Credit Cards: None
Notes: 2, 6, 7, 8, 9, 10, 11

Bakketopp Hus

FERGUS FALLS

Bakketopp Hus
Rural Route 2, Box 187 A, 56537
(218) 739-2915

Come to a spacious contemporary lake home with vaulted ceilings. Relax by the fireplace, in the hot spa, on the patio, with raised flower gardens, or decks on the wooded lakeside. Enjoy antique furnishings, regular and waterbeds, skylights, candlelight breakfast served on antique dishes by the patio windows that give a scenic lake view. At dusk you may hear the calling of the loons. Maplewood State Park is nearby.

Hosts: Dennis and Judy Nims
Rooms: 3 (1 PB; 2 SB) $60-85
Full Breakfast
Credit Cards: None
Notes: 2, 5, 7, 9, 10, 11

NORTH BRANCH

Red Pine Log Bed and Breakfast
15140 400th Street, 55056
(612) 583-3326

---

year; 6 Pets welcome; 7 Children welcome; 8 Tennis nearby; 9 Swimming nearby; 10 Golf nearby; 11 Skiing nearby; 12 May be booked through travel agent

Christian hosts invite you to our large, unique, hand-crafted log home on 30 acres near Taylors Falls. Two spacious bedrooms with queen beds, skylights, balcony, and a beautiful shared bath await you, with a table for two in each room for a private breakfast, if you wish. One hour from the twin cities, we are near parks and cross-country skiing. Warmth and hospitality are our calling card. Prepayment must accompany reservation.

Hosts: Lowell and Gloria Olson
Rooms: 2 (SB) $75-100
Full Breakfast
Credit Cards: None
Notes: 2, 4, 5, 10, 11

The Northrop-Oftedahl House

OWATONNA

The Northrop-Oftedahl House
358 East Main Street, 55060
(507) 451-4040

This 1898 Victorian with stained glass is three blocks from downtown. It has pleasant porches, grand piano, six-foot footed bathtub, souvenirs (antiques and collectibles from the estate). Northrop family-owned and operated, it is one of 12 historical homes in the area, rich in local history with an extensive reading library, backgammon, croquet, badminton, bocce, and more. Near hiking, biking trails, golf, tennis, parks, and 35 miles to Mayo Clinic.

Hosts: Jean and Darrell Stewart
Rooms: 5 (SB) $39-54
Continental Breakfast; Full breakfast on request
Credit Cards: None
Notes: 2, 3 (by arrangement), 4 (by arrangement), 5, 6 (by arrangement, 8, 9, 10, 11

ST. CHARLES

Thoreson's Carriage House Bed and Breakfast
606 Wabasha Avenue, 55972
(507) 932-3479

Located at the edge of beautiful Whitewater State Park with its swimming, trails, and demonstrations by the park naturalist, we are also in Amish territory and minutes from the world-famous Mayo Clinic. Piano and organ are available for added enjoyment. Please write for free brochure.

Host: Moneta Thoreson
Rooms: 2 (SB) $25-35
Full Breakfast
Credit Cards: None
Notes: 2, 5, 7, 8, 9, 10, 11

NOTES: Credit cards accepted: A Master Card; B Visa; C American Express; D Discover Card; E Diners Club; F Other; 2 Personal checks accepted; 3 Lunch available; 4 Dinner available; 5 Open all

This restored antebellum mansion of the Old South is in the town General U. S. Grant said was "too beautiful to burn." On the National Register of Historic Places, it has family heirloom antiques and canopied beds and is air conditioned. Your hosts' families have been in Mississippi for 200 years. Christ is the Lord of this house. "But as for me and my house, we will serve the Lord," Joshua 24:15. On U.S. Highway 61, adjacent to the Natchez Trace Parkway. Four-diamond rated by AAA.

Hosts: Mr. and Mrs. William Lum
Rooms: 10 (PB) $75-85; special family rates
Full Breakfast
Credit Cards: A, B, C, D
Notes: 2, 5, 7

VICKSBURG

The Vicksburg
801 Clay Street, 39180
(601) 636-4146; (800) 844-4146

Built in 1928 and completely renovated in 1983, the 200 rooms of the old Vicksburg Hotel were converted into 56 spacious, residential suites and rooms. Many of these are occupied by permanent residents. Your plantation breakfast is served in the nationally famous Old Southern Tea Room, also located in Vicksburg. The rooms and suites are beautifully furnished and have cable TV and private phones. Listed on the National Register of Historic Places.

Hosts: George and Carolyn Mayer
Rooms: 2 (PB) $65
Suites: 2
Full Breakfast
Credit Cards: A, B, C, D
Notes: 3, 4, 5, 7

---

year; 6 Pets welcome; 7 Children welcome; 8 Tennis nearby; 9 Swimming nearby; 10 Golf nearby; 11 Skiing nearby; 12 May be booked through travel agent

Missouri

BRANSON

Country Gardens Bed and Breakfast
HCR 4, Box 2202, Lakeshore Drive, 65616
(417) 334-8564

This bed and breakfast is located along Lake Taneycomo which provides excellent fishing and a parklike setting, only ten minutes from the majority of the music shows. We make reservations for shows on request. Honeymooners and special occasion guests welcomed. The rose suite has a private spa; the other two rooms share a spa on a deck overlooking the lake. All rooms have private entrances.

Hosts: Bob and Pat Cameron
Rooms: 3 (PB) $70-95
Full Breakfast
Credit Cards: A, B, D
Notes: 2, 9, 12

Ozark Mountain Country Bed and Breakfast
Box 295, 65616
(417) 334-4720; (800) 695-1546

Ozark Mountain Country reservation service has been arranging accommodations for guests in southwest Missouri and northwest Arkansas since 1982. In the current list of 80 homes and small inns, some locations offer private entrances and fantastic views, guest sitting areas, swimming pools, Jacuzzis, or fireplaces. Most locations are available all year. Personal checks accepted. Some homes welcome children; a few welcome pets (even horses). Coordinator: Kay Cameron. $35-95.

Brewer's Maple Lane Farm

NOTES: Credit cards accepted: A Master Card; B Visa; C American Express; D Discover Card; E Diners Club; F Other; 2 Personal checks accepted; 3 Lunch available; 4 Dinner available; 5 Open all

CARTHAGE

Brewer's Maple Lane Farm
Rural Route 1, Box 203, 64836
(417) 358-6312

Listed on the National Register of Historic Places, this Victorian home has 20 rooms furnished mostly with family heirlooms, four guest rooms, plus a two-bedroom cottage. Our 240-acre farm is ideal for family vacations and campers. We have a playground, picnic area, hunting, and fishing in our 22-acre lake. Nearby are artist Lowell Davis' farm and Sam Butcher's Precious Moments Chapel.

Hosts: Arch and Renee Brewer
Rooms: 4 (SB) $45
Expanded Continental Breakfast
Credit Cards: None
Notes: 2, 5, 7, 8, 10, 12

Hill House
1157 South Main, 64836
(417) 358-6145

Hill House is a brick Victorian mansion, circa 1887, with ten fireplaces, stained glass, and pocket doors. Unusual antiques are on display. Guest rooms have antique furniture and feather beds. We are approximately five miles from Precious Moments Chapel and Red Oak II. Breakfast features home-baked muffins, donuts, waffles, specialty jams, fruit, juice, bacon. The antique and gift shop is on the third floor.

Hosts: Dean and Ella Mae Scoville
Rooms: 4 (PB) $40-50
Full Breakfast
Credit Cards: None
Notes: 2, 5, 7, 8, 9, 10

Fifth Street Mansion

HANNIBAL

Fifth Street Mansion
213 South Fifth Street, 63401
(314) 221-0445

Built in 1858 in Italianate style by friends of Mark Twain, antique furnishings complement the stained glass, ceramic fireplaces, and original gaslight fixtures of the house. Two parlors, dining room, and library with hand-grained walnut paneling, plus wraparound porches provide space for conversation, reading, TV, games. Walk to Mark Twain historic district, shops, restaurants, riverfront. The mansion blends Victo-

---

year; 6 Pets welcome; 7 Children welcome; 8 Tennis nearby; 9 Swimming nearby; 10 Golf nearby; 11 Skiing nearby; 12 May be booked through travel agent

rian charm with plenty of old-fashioned hospitality. The whole house is available for reunions and weddings.

Hosts: Mike and Donalene Andreotti
Rooms: 7 (PB) $62-80
Full Breakfast
Credit Cards: A, B, C, D
Notes: 2, 5, 7, 8, 9, 10, 12

HERMANN

Die Gillig Heimat
HCR 62, Box 30, 65041
(314) 943-6942

Capture the beauty of country living on this farm located on beautiful rolling hills. The original Gillig home was built as a log cabin in 1842 and has been enlarged several times. Awake in the morning to beautiful views in every direction, and enjoy a hearty breakfast in the large, country kitchen. Stroll the pastures and hills of the working cattle farm while watching nature at its best. Historic Hermann is nearby.

Hosts: Ann and Armin Gillig
Rooms: 2 (PB) $50-55
Full Breakfast
Credit Cards: None
Notes: 2, 5, 7 (by arrangement)

PLATTE CITY

Basswood Country Inn Resort
15880 Interurban Road, 64079
(816) 431-5556

Come stay where the rich and famous relaxed and played in the 1940s and 1950s! These are the most beautiful, secluded, wooded, lakefront accommodations in the entire Kansas City area. Choose from two-bedroom, full kitchen suites, 1935 cottage, or single suites. Bring your pole—good fishing!

Hosts: Don and Betty Soper
Rooms: 7 (PB) $63-125
Cottage: 1 (PB) $93
Continental Breakfast
Credit Cards: A, B
Notes: 2, 5, 9, 10, 11

PT. LOOKOUT

Cameron's Crag
P. O. Box 526, 65726
(417) 335-8134; (800) 933-8529

Located high on a bluff overlooking Lake Taneycomo and the valley, three miles south of Branson, enjoy a spectacular view from a three-room private suite with king bed and Jacuzzi. A second room has a private entrance, queen bed, view of the lake, private spa on deck. The third room has twin or king beds.

Hosts: Glen and Kay Cameron
Rooms: 3 (PB) $50-85
Full Breakfast
Credit Cards: A, B, C
Notes: 2, 4

NOTES: Credit cards accepted: A Master Card; B Visa; C American Express; D Discover Card; E Diners Club; F Other; 2 Personal checks accepted; 3 Lunch available; 4 Dinner available; 5 Open all

ST. LOUIS

Lafayette House Bed and Breakfast

2156 Lafayette Avenue, 63104
(314) 772-4429

This 1876 Victorian mansion with modern amenities is in the center of things to do in St. Louis and on a direct bus line to downtown. It is air conditioned and furnished with antiques and traditional furniture. Many collectibles and large varied library to enjoy. Families welcome. Resident cats and dog.

Hosts: Sarah and Jack Milligan
Rooms: 5 (2 PB; 3 SB) $50-75
Full Breakfast
Credit Cards: None
Notes: 2, 5, 7, 8, 9, 10

Stelzer Bed and Breakfast

7106 General Sherman Lane, 63123
(314) 843-5757

Pat and Anita have a corner house with green siding and white awnings. Old family furniture is featured. The sleeping rooms are in the windowed "undercroft." One room has firm twin beds, the other has firm fold-out bed with waffle mattress. Each room has radio and clock with a color TV in the adjacent sitting room. A side driveway and entrance accommodate the guest area. We enjoy sharing the sunroom and livingroom with guests.

Hosts: Pat and Anita Stelzer
Rooms: 2 (SB) $20-30
Full Breakfast
Credit Cards: None
Notes: 2, 5, 7, 10

The Winter House

3522 Arsenal Street, 63118
(314) 664-4399

This gracious Victorian features a pressed tin ceiling in the lower bedroom and a suite on the second floor. Freshly squeezed orange juice is always served for breakfast in the dining room using crystal and antique china. Tea is served, and live piano music is available by reservation.

Hosts: Sarah and Kendall Winter
Rooms: 2 (PB) $52-65
Full Breakfast
Credit Cards: A, B, C, E, F
Notes: 2, 5, 7, 8, 9, 10, 12

SULLIVAN

Whip Haven Farm

Rural Route 1, Box 395, 63080
(314) 627-3717

A day in the country! The guest apartment chalet above the garage is full of country furnishings and has a fully equipped kitchen. A full country breakfast is served in the "big house," including fresh fruit and homemade bread, jams, and jellies. Enjoy a quiet walk to the Bourbeuse River, fish, listen to song birds, and look for wildlife. Meramec State Park and equestrian trail are nearby. Bed and bale available for horses. Complimentary beverage and snack upon arrival.

Hosts: Ginny and Rex Whipple
Apartment: 1 (PB) $70-80
Full Breakfast
Credit Cards: None
Notes: 2, 3, 4, 5, 7, 12

NOTES: Credit cards accepted: A Master Card; B Visa; C American Express; D Discover Card; E Diners Club; F Other; 2 Personal checks accepted; 3 Lunch available; 4 Dinner available; 5 Open all

Montana

BOZEMAN

Silver Forest Inn
15325 Bridger Canyon, 59715
(406) 586-1882

The Silver Forest Inn is a mountain hideaway built in the 1930s of huge logs. Surrounded by beautiful scenery, it is minutes from downhill and cross-country skiing, hiking, horseback riding, and mountain biking. It has an outdoor hot tub, private indoor Jacuzzi, excellent home cooking, and friendly hosts who offer you a unique experience in the Bridger Mountains. One and one-half hours from Yellowstone National Park.

Hosts: Kathryn and Richard Jensen
Rooms: 5 (3 PB; 2 SB) $50-70
Full Breakfast
Credit Cards: A, B
Notes: 2, 5, 6 (restricted), 7, 11, 12, 13

RED LODGE

Willows Inn
224 South Platt Avenue, P. O. Box 886, 59068
(406) 446-3913

Nestled beneath the majestic Beartooth Mountains in a quaint historic town, this delightful turn-of-the-century Victorian, complete with picket fence and porch swing, awaits you. A light and airy atmosphere with warm, cheerful decor greets the happy wanderer. Five charming guest rooms, each unique, are in the main inn. Two delightfully nostalgic cottages with kitchen and laundry are also available. Home-baked pastries are a specialty. Videos, books, games, afternoon refreshments, sun deck.

Hosts: Elven and Carolyn Boggio
Rooms: 5 (3 PB; 2 SB) $45-60
Cottages: 2 (no breakfast) $55
Continental Breakfast
Credit Cards: A, B, D
Notes: 2, 5, 7 (over 9 in main inn), 8, 9, 10, 11, 12

---

year; 6 Pets welcome; 7 Children welcome; 8 Tennis nearby; 9 Swimming nearby; 10 Golf nearby; 11 Skiing nearby; 12 May be booked through travel agent

Nebraska

OMAHA

The Jones'
1617 South 90th Street, 68124
(402) 397-0721

Large, private residence with large deck and gazebo in the back. Fresh cinnamon rolls are served for breakfast. Your hosts' interests include golf, travel, needlework, and meeting other people. Located five minutes from I-80.

Hosts: Theo and Don Jones
Rooms: 3 (1 PB: 2 SB) $25
Continental Breakfast
Credit Cards: None
Notes: 2, 5, 6, 7, 8, 10

Nevada

INCLINE VILLAGE

Haus Bavaria
593 North Dyer Circle, P. O. Box 3308, 89450
(702) 831-6122

This European-style residence in the heart of the Sierra Nevadas, is within walking distance of Lake Tahoe. Each of the five guest rooms opens onto a balcony, offering lovely views of the mountains. Breakfast, prepared by your host Bick Hewitt, includes a selection of home-baked goods, fresh fruit, juices, freshly ground coffee, and teas. A private beach and swimming pool are available to guests. Ski at Diamond Peak, Mt. Rose, Heavenly Valley, and other nearby areas.

Host: Bick Hewitt
Rooms: 5 (PB) $90
Full Breakfast
Credit Cards: A, B, C
Notes: 2, 5, 8, 9, 10, 11

New Hampshire

BETHLEHEM

The Old Homestead Bed and Breakfast
Route 302, 03574
(603) 639-9794

This late 18th-century carriage house and blacksmith shop has been totally renovated. Bedrooms have wood stoves, and a full breakfast of homemade breads and muffins is served. Close to ski areas and main area attractions.

Hosts: Jeanne Chenevert & Sons
Rooms: 8 (2 PB; 6 S3B) $30-35
Full Breakfast
Credit Cards: None
Notes: 2, 7, 8, 9, 10, 11

BRADFORD

The Bradford Inn
Rural Route 1, Main Street, Box 40, 03221
(603) 938-5309; (800) 669-5309

The Bradford Inn was built as a small hotel in the 1890s. It has two parlors for guest use, one with a fireplace, one with a TV. J. Albert's Restaurant features turn-of-the-century ragtime and rhapsodies, "grandma gourmet" cuisine, and was the 1991-92 winner Best Apple Pie in New Hampshire, *Yankee* magazine. The area abounds in outdoor activities in all seasons and offers craft and antique shops, auctions, summer theater, local fairs, and festivals. We can accommodate small groups (28-34) for retreats, family parties, or church outings.

Hosts: Tom and Connie Mazol
Rooms: 12 (PB) $59-79
Full Breakfast
Credit Cards: A, B, C, D, E
Notes: 2, 4, 5, 6, 7, 8, 9, 10, 11, 12

CLAREMONT

Goddard Mansion Bed and Breakfast
25 Hillstead Road, 03743
(603) 543-0603

Located on seven acres with panoramic mountain views, this delightful, restored early-1900s English Manor-style mansion has 18 rooms and expansive porches and tea house. Eight uniquely decorated guest rooms await, including

---

NOTES: Credit cards accepted: A Master Card; B Visa; C American Express; D Discover Card; E Diners Club; F Other; 2 Personal checks accepted; 3 Lunch available; 4 Dinner available; 5 Open all

an airy French-country room; step-back-in-time Victorian; whimsical cloud room; and romantic bridal suite. A full, natural breakfast starts each day. Four-season activities are nearby, national historic landmark, antique buffs' adventureland, smoke-free inside, clean air outside.

Hosts: Debbie and Frank Albee
Rooms: 8 (2 PB; 6 SB) $65-95
Expanded Continental Breakfast
Credit Cards: A, B, D, E, F
Notes: 2, 5, 7, 8, 9, 10, 11

COLEBROOK

Monadnock Bed and Breakfast

One Monadnock Street, 03576
(603) 237-8216

Located one block off Main Street, with easy access to shops and restaurants, in a quiet, picturesque, country community of 2,500 people, this 1916 house has a natural fieldstone porch, chimney, and foundation. Inside it has gorgeous, natural woodwork. Three guest bedrooms upstairs include two with double beds sharing facilities and one with a double and single bed with private half-bath. Common areas are available for relaxing or playing games and watching a large-screen TV. A roomy balcony is good for relaxing and soaking up the sun's rays.

Hosts: Barbara and Wendell Woodard
Rooms: 3 (SB) $43-54
Full Breakfast
Credit Cards: A, B
Notes: 2, 5, 7, 9, 10, 11

CONWAY

The Darby Field Inn

Bald Hill Road, Box D, 03818
(603) 447-2181

This renovated farmhouse, circa 1826, sits atop Bald Hill overlooking Mt. Washington Valley and the Presidential Range. It is a great place to relax and get away from it all. Candlelight dining with large fieldstone fireplace in the common rooms; lounge and outdoor pool on the premises. Cross-country skiing from back door. Hiking, downhill skiing, tennis, and golf nearby.

Hosts: Marc and Maria Donaldson
Rooms: 17 (15 PB; 2 SB) $70-140
Full Breakfast
Credit Cards: A, B
Notes: 2, 4, 5, 7, 8, 9, 10, 11

Kancamagus Swift River Inn

P.O. Box 1650, 03818
(603) 447-2332

This is a quality inn with that Old World flavor in a stress-free environment. Located in the White Mountains of New Hampshire in the Mt. Washington Valley on the most beautiful highway in the state, the Kancamagus Highway, one and one-half miles off Route 16. We are only minutes from all factory outlets, attractions, and fine restaurants.

---

year; 6 Pets welcome; 7 Children welcome; 8 Tennis nearby; 9 Swimming nearby; 10 Golf nearby; 11 Skiing nearby; 12 May be booked through travel agent

Hosts: Joseph and Jennie Beckenbach
Rooms: 10 (PB) $40-90
Continental Breakfast
Credit Cards: None
Notes: 2, 5, 7, 8, 9, 10, 11, 12

EATON CENTER

The Inn at Crystal Lake
Route 153, 03832
(603) 447-2120; (800) 343-7336

You deserve pampering! Unwind in our 1884 Victorian inn with balconies in a quiet picture-perfect village. Enjoy our antiques and extraordinary four-course, multi-entree, eye-appealing dinner presented on china, crystal, and lace in our metal-sculpture-enhanced dining room with fireplace. Begin the day with Irish soda bread and a full country breakfast. We have a Victorian parlor, a comfortable TV den/library, and a cozy lounge.

Hosts: Walter and Jacqueline Spink
Rooms: 11 (PB) $60-116 plus 15% service charge
Full Breakfast
Credit Cards: A, B, C
Notes: 2, 4, 5, 7, 8, 9, 10, 11

FREEDOM

Freedom House Bed and Breakfast
1 Maple Street, P.O. Box 478, 03836
(603) 539-4815

This Victorian home with six guest rooms is located 15 minutes from Conway. King Pine ski resort is five minutes away. Lake Ossipee and Loon Lake are great resort areas for enjoying an abundance of recreation. One church is located in the village; others are 15 minutes away. A smoke-free environment.

Hosts: Marjorie and Bob Daly
Rooms: 6 (SB) $60
Full Breakfast
Credit Cards: A, B
Notes: 2, 7, 8, 9, 10, 11

GREENLAND

Thomas Ayers Homestead Bed and Breakfast
47 Park Avenue, P.O. Box 15, 03840
(603) 436-5992

The Thomas Ayers House, begun in 1737 as a two-room post-and-beam structure, has been enlarged and remodeled many times in its 250-year history. Priscilla and Dave will tell you of the famous people, including Paul Revere, George Washington, and John Adams, who passed by its doors. Set on six acres on the historic village green, its nine rooms have wainscoting, exposed beams, and wide-board floors. Seven rooms have fireplaces. The bedrooms are made cozy with antiques, braided rugs, afghans, and rockers. Breakfast is served in the dining room on an antique table set in front of a brick fireplace with artfully displayed pewterware and ironware. The gourmet center of New England.

NOTES: Credit cards accepted: A Master Card; B Visa; C American Express; D Discover Card; E Diners Club; F Other; 2 Personal checks accepted; 3 Lunch available; 4 Dinner available; 5 Open all

New Hampshire 145

Hosts: David and Priscilla Engel
Rooms: 4 (2 PB; 2 SB) $50-55
Full Breakfast
Credit Cards: None
Notes: 2, 5, 7, 8, 9, 10, 11

Westwinds of Hancock

HAMPTON BEACH

The Oceanside
365 Ocean Boulevard, 03842
(603) 926-3542

This boutique hotel on the oceanfront has period furnishings, private baths, and is smoke free. Within easy walking distance of activities and shops. Intimate breakfast cafe, decks and sidewalk terrace, turn-down service. Beach towels and chairs are available.

Hosts: Skip and Debbie Windemiller
Rooms: 10 (PB) $77-105
Expanded Continental Breakfast except July and August
Credit Cards: A, B, C, D
Notes: 8, 10, 12

HANCOCK

Westwinds of Hancock
Route 1 (Old Bennington Road)
Box 635, 03449
(603) 525-6600

This turn-of-the-century Colonial sits on 19 acres with mountain view. All rooms have handmade quilts and antiques; morning sun porch; scrumptious, hot country breakfast (waffles or pancakes with fruit, sausage, bacon and eggs, muffins, juice, coffee), two guest sitting rooms with cable TV. Near state park with swimming and boating, near cross-country skiing, charming New England town.

Hosts: Christopher and Brenda Prahl
Rooms: 5 (3 PB; 2 SB) $ 50-65
Full Breakfast
Credit Cards: A, B, D
Notes: 2, 5, 8 (over eight), 8, 9, 10, 11

HOLDERNESS

The Inn on Golden Pond
Route 3, P. O. Box 680, 03245-0680
(603) 968-7269

An 1879 Colonial home is nestled on 50 wooded acres offering guests a traditional New England setting where you can escape and enjoy warm hospitality and personal service of the resident hosts. Rooms are individually decorated with braided rugs and country curtains and bedspreads. Hearty, home-cooked breakfast features farm fresh eggs, muffins, homemade bread,

year; 6 Pets welcome; 7 Children welcome; 8 Tennis nearby; 9 Swimming nearby; 10 Golf nearby; 11 Skiing nearby; 12 May be booked through travel agent

and Bonnie's most requested rhubarb jam.

Hosts: Bonnie and Bill Web
Rooms: 9 (PB) $85-135
Full Breakfast
Credit Cards: A, B
Notes: 2, 5, 8, 9, 10, 11, 12

JACKSON

Ellis River House
Route 16, P. O. Box 656, 03846
(603) 383-9339; (800) 233-8309

At this enchanting farmhouse inn, you can enjoy fine lodging and superb country dining, nestled in the heart of the White Mountains of New England overlooking the spectacular Ellis River. Enjoy homemade breads and pick your own farm-fresh eggs. Jackson's world-class cross-country ski trails are at our door. On-premises trout fishing, hiking in our magnificent White Mountains forest, and a Jacuzzi in our atrium. Warm and homey.

Hosts: Barry and Barbara Lubao
Rooms: 7 (2 PB; 5 SB) $40-120
Full Breakfast
Credit Cards: A, B, C
Notes: 2, 4, 6, 7, 8, 9, 10, 11

Inn at Thorn Hill
Thorn Hill Road, Box CBB, 03846
(603) 383-6448; (800) 289-8990

Enjoy spectacular mountain views and enticing cuisine at this 1895 Stanford White inn with antique-filled guest rooms in the main inn and a carriage house and three cottages furnished with a country touch—all smoke free. Activities available in every season at the inn and throughout the White Mountains. Air conditioned. Art workshops and special packages available. Ideal

Inn at Thorn Hill

NOTES: Credit cards accepted: A Master Card; B Visa; C American Express; D Discover Card; E Diners Club; F Other; 2 Personal checks accepted; 3 Lunch available; 4 Dinner available; 5 Open all

for small groups and special occasions. Recommended by *Bon Appetit, Yankee Guide, Travel and Leisure*, AAA.

Hosts: Peter and Linda La Rose
Rooms: 20 (18 PB; 2 SB) $80-182
Full Breakfast
Credit Cards: A, B, C
Closed April
Notes: 2, 4, 8, 9, 10, 11, 12

JEFFERSON

Applebrook
Route 115A, 03583
(603) 586-7713; (800) 545-6504

Taste our mid-summer raspberries while enjoying panoramic mountain views. Applebrook is a comfortable, casual bed and breakfast in a large Victorian farmhouse with a peaceful, rural setting. After a restful night's sleep, you will enjoy a hearty breakfast before venturing out for a day of hiking, fishing, antique hunting, golfing, swimming, or skiing. Near Santa's Village and Six-Gun City. Dormitory available for groups. Brochures available.

Host: Sandra J. Conley
Rooms: 8 plus dormitory (2 PB; 6 SB) $45-60
Full Breakfast
Credit Cards: A, B, D
Notes: 2, 4, 5, 6, 7, 8, 9, 10, 11

The Jefferson Inn
Route 2, 03583
(603) 586-7998; (800) 729-7908

This charming 1896 Victorian near Mt. Washington has a 360-degree mountain view. Summer activities include hiking from our door, a swimming pond, six golf courses nearby, summer theater, and excellent cycling. In the winter, enjoy Bretton Woods, cross-country skiing, and skating across the street. Afternoon tea is served daily. A family suite is available.

Hosts: Greg Brown and Bertie Koelewijn
Rooms: 10 (PB) $50-75
Full Breakfast
Credit Cards: A, B, C
Notes: 2, 7, 8, 9, 10, 11, 12

The Inn at New Ipswich

NEW IPSWICH

The Inn at New Ipswich
Porter Hill Road, P. O. Box 208, 03071
(603) 878-3711

The inn is situated at the heart of New England in New Hampshire's Monadnock region. The 1790 Colonial, with classic red barn, set amid stone walls and fruit trees, heartily welcomes guests.

Guest rooms feature firm beds and country antiques. Also featured are wide-pine floors and six original fireplaces. Downhill and cross-country skiing, hiking, antique shops, concerts, auctions are all nearby.

Hosts; Ginny and Steve Bankuti
Rooms: 6 (PB) $60
Full Breakfast
Credit Cards: A, B
Notes: 2, 5, 10, 11, 12

NEW LONDON

Pleasant Lake Inn

125 Pleasant Street, P. O. Box 1030, 03257
(603) 526-6271; (800) 626-4907

Our 1790 lakeside country inn is nestled on the shore of Pleasant Lake with Mt. Kearsarge as its backdrop. The panoramic location is only one of the many reasons to visit. All four seasons offer activities from our doorway: lake swimming, fishing, hiking, skiing, or just plain relaxing. Dinner is available. Call or write for a brochure.

Hosts: Margaret and Grant Rich
Rooms: 11 (PB) $75-90
Full Breakfast
Credit Cards: A, B
Notes: 2, 4, 5, 7 (over seven), 8, 9, 10, 11

NEWPORT

The Inn at Coit Mountain

HCR 63, Box 3, 03773
(603) 863-3583; (800) 367-2364

All four seasons provide nature's backdrop to this gracious, historic Georgian home. Whether you prefer the greening spring, languid summer afternoons, colorful autumn foiliage, or winter-white mornings, you will delight in a stay at the inn. Available for small retreats of ten to fifteen people.

Hosts: Dick and Judi Tatem
Rooms: 5 (2 PB; 3 SB) $85-125
Full Breakfast
Credit Cards: A, B, C
Notes: 2, 4 (by arrangement), 6, 7, 8, 9, 10, 11

NORTH CONWAY

The Buttonwood Inn

Mt. Surprise Road, P. O. Box 1817, 03860
(603) 356-2625; (800) 258-2625 outside New Hampshire

The Buttonwood is tucked away on Mt. Surprise in the heart of the White Mountains. It is secluded and quiet, yet only two miles from excellent town restaurants and factory outlet shopping. Built in 1820, this New England-style Cape Cod has antique-furnished guest rooms with wide-plank floors, a large outdoor pool, hiking, and cross-country skiing from the door. Alpine skiing is one mile away.

Hosts: Hugh, Ann, and Walter Begley
Rooms: 9 (3 PB; 6 S3B) $40-100
Full Breakfast
Credit Cards: A, B, C
Notes: 2, 5, 7, 8, 9, 10, 11, 12

NOTES: Credit cards accepted: A Master Card; B Visa; C American Express; D Discover Card; E Diners Club; F Other; 2 Personal checks accepted; 3 Lunch available; 4 Dinner available; 5 Open all

The Center Chimney— 1787

River Road, P. O. Box 1220, 03860
(603) 356-6788

Cozy, affordable Cape in a quiet location just off Saco River with swimming, canoeing, and fishing. Near Main Street and North Conway village with summer theater, free cross-country skiing, ice skating, shops and restaurants. Package plans available.

Host: Farley Whitley
Rooms: 4 (SB) $44-55
Continental Breakfast
Credit Cards: None
Notes: 2, 5, 7, 8, 9, 10, 11

Nereledge Inn

River Road, 03860
(603) 356-2831

Enjoy the charm, hospitality, and relaxation of a small 1787 bed and breakfast inn overlooking Cathedral Ledge. Walk to river or village. Close to all activities. Comfortable, casual atmosphere. Rates include delicious breakfast with warm apple pie.

Hosts: Valerie and Dave Halpin
Rooms: 9 (4 PB; 5 SB) $59-85
Full Breakfast
Credit Cards: A, B, C
Notes: 2, 5, 7, 8, 9, 10, 11

NORTH WOODSTOCK

Wilderness Inn Bed and Breakfast

Routes 3 and 112, 03262
(603) 745-3890

Located amid the White Mountains, the Wilderness Inn offers charming and intimate accommodations for couples and families. Skiing, hiking, canoeing, swimming, tennis, and golf are all close by. Gourmet breakfast includes fresh fruit, *cafe au lait,* cranberry-waltnut pancakes with pure maple syrup, and is served on our front porch in summer or fireside in winter.

Hosts: Rosanna and Michael Yarnell
Rooms: 7 (5 PB; 2 SB) $40-85
Full Breakfast
Credit Cards: A, B, C
Notes: 2, 5, 7, 8, 9, 10, 11, 12

OSSIPEE

Acorn Lodge

Box 144, 03864
(603) 539-2151

Acorn Lodge was named by former owner Grover Cleveland, who liked to fish on Duncan Lake, a very quiet and peaceful area. We offer a canoe, row boat, barbecue pit, badminton, horse-

---

year; 6 Pets welcome; 7 Children welcome; 8 Tennis nearby; 9 Swimming nearby; 10 Golf nearby; 11 Skiing nearby; 12 May be booked through travel agent

shoe court, and of course, swimming in crystal clear water. Two-night stay minimum.

Hosts: Julie and Ray Terry
Rooms: 6 (PB) $46
Continental Breakfast
Credit Cards: A, B
Notes: 2, 6, 7, 8, 9, 10

PLYMOUTH

Northway House
Rural Free Delivery 1, 03264
(603) 536-2838

Located in the heart of New Hampshire in the beautiful Pemiquewasset River Valley, the Northway House is near Newfound, Squam, and Winnepesaukee lakes, as well as the ski areas of Tenney, Waterville Valley, Loon, and Cannon. Hospitality-plus awaits the traveler in this charming Colonial house that is homey, comfortable, and reasonably priced.

Hosts: Micheline and Norman McWilliams
Rooms: 3 (SB) $25-40
Full Breakfast
Credit Cards: None
Notes: 2, 5, 6, 7, 9, 10, 11

RYE

Rock Ledge Manor Bed and Breakfast
1413 Ocean Boulevard, Route 1-A, 03870
(603) 431-1413

A gracious, traditional, seaside manor home with an excellent location offers an ocean view from all rooms. It is central to all New Hampshire and southern Maine seacoast activities; six minutes to historic Portsmouth and Hampton; 20 minutes to the University of New Hampshire; 15 minutes to Exeter Academy. Reservations are advised.

Hosts: Norman and Janice Marineau
Rooms: 4 (2 PB; 2 SB) $60-75
Full Breakfast
Credit Cards: None
Notes: 2, 5, 7 (over 10), 8, 9, 10, 11

STRAFFORD

Bed and Breakfast of New England
121 Barberry Lane, 03884
(603) 664-5492; (800) 285-5595

This reservation service represents small inns and bed and breakfasts in Maine, New Hampshire, Vermont, and Massachusetts. Choose accommodations near sea coves, ski areas, and mountain and lake regions. Near cultural centers and tourist attractions. $30-90 single; $40-120 double. Caren Raiche, coordinator.

SUTTON MILLS

The Village House at Sutton Mills
Box 151 Grist Mill Road, 03221
(603) 927-4765

This Village House is an 1857 country Victorian overlooking the quaint New

---

NOTES: Credit cards accepted: A Master Card; B Visa; C American Express; D Discover Card; E Diners Club; F Other; 2 Personal checks accepted; 3 Lunch available; 4 Dinner available; 5 Open all

England village of Sutton Mills. The location is quiet, yet convenient to New London, shopping, antiquing, and all summer and winter activities. The house is situated on four acres, and hikers, cross-country skiers, and snowmobilers enjoy starting out through our property. Guests enjoy the privacy of the guest house, tastefully decorated with antiques and old quilts. No smoking.

Hosts: Peggy and Norm Forand
Rooms: 3 (S2.5B) $45
Full Breakfast
Credit Cards: None
Notes: 2, 5, 8, 9, 10, 11

The Village House at Sutton Mills

WARNER

Jacob's Ladder Bed and Breakfast
Main Street, Rural Free Delivery 1
Box 11, 03278
(603) 456-3494

Situated in the quaint village of Warner, Jacob's Ladder is conveniently located between I-89, Exits 8 and 9. The early-1800s home is furnished predominantly with antiques, creating a tasteful country atmosphere. Cross-country ski and snowmobile trail on site with three ski areas within 20 miles. Lakes, mountains, covered bridges, arts and crafts, and more nearby. No smoking.

Hosts: Deb and Marlon Baese
Rooms: 4 (S2B) $40
Full Breakfast
Credit Cards: None
Notes: 2, 5, 7, 8, 10, 11

WILTON CENTER

Stepping Stones Bed and Breakfast
Bennington Battle Trail, 03086
(603) 654-9048

Stepping Stone is owned by a garden designer and weaver. Display gardens surround the 19th-century house set in the quiet, rural Monadnock region. A scrumptious breakfast is served on the porch or terrace in summer, and in the solar garden room year-round. Enjoy good reading, stereo, TV in the cozy livingroom, or watch active weaver and gardener at work in a serene and civilized atmosphere.

Host: Ann Carlsmith
Rooms: 3 (1 PB; 2 SB) $35-50
Full Breakfast
Credit Cards: None
Notes: 2, 5, 6, 7, 10, 11

New Jersey

AVON-BY-THE-SEA

Cashelmara Inn
22 Lakeside Avenue, 07717
(908) 776-8727; (800) 821-2976

A tastefully restored turn-of-the-century inn rests on the bank of a swan lake and the Atlantic Ocean. This desirable beachfront location offers a unique opportunity to smell the fresh salt air, to feel the ocean breeze, and to hear the sounds of the surf and sea gulls from the privacy of your seaside room. Hearty breakfasts are a tradition at Cashelmara Inn.

Host: Martin Mulligan
Rooms: 14 (PB) $60-150
Full Breakfast
Credit Cards: A, B, C
Notes: 2, 5, 7, 8, 9, 10

CAPE MAY

The Albert Stevens Inn
127 Myrtle Avenue, 08204
(609) 884-4717; (609) 884-2627

Built in 1890 by Dr. Albert G. Stevens as a wedding gift for his bride, Bessie, the inn is just a ten-minute walk to the beach and two blocks from Victorian shopping. The guest rooms are furnished with genuine antiques, and the two parlors have the original parlor furniture. A 102-degree, six-person Jacuzzi in the stress-reduction room is privately scheduled for guests' comfort. Dinner is included from November through March.

Hosts: Curt and Diane Rangen
Rooms: 7 (PB) $85-135
Full Breakfast
Credit Cards: A, B, C, D
Notes: 2, 4, 5, 8, 9, 10

Bedford Inn
805 Stockton Avenue, 08204
(609) 884-4158

The Bedford Inn is centrally located in Cape May, very near the ocean. Fully heated with a cozy fireplace in the parlor, the inn is completely Victorian and furnished with antiques. All rooms have air conditioning. On-site parking; mid-week discounts September to June. Many activitites nearby.

Hosts: Cindy and Al Schmucker
Rooms: 11 (PB) $85-145
Full Breakfast
Credit Cards: A, B, C
Notes: 2, 7, 8, 9, 10

NOTES: Credit cards accepted: A Master Card; B Visa; C American Express; D Discover Card; E Diners Club; F Other; 2 Personal checks accepted; 3 Lunch available; 4 Dinner available; 5 Open all

The Chalfonte Hotel
301 Howard Street, 08204
(609) 884-8409

The Chalfonte is situated in the historic district two blocks from the ocean. The gracious southern Victorian, built in 1876, is one of the last great, old hotels in Cape May. Guest rooms are quite simple, with original furnishings, ceiling fans, and claw foot tubs. The hotel is famous for southern cooking and hospitality. Breakfast and dinner are served in the long, airy dining room. Baby sitting and a variety of workshops are offered. The entire city of Cape May has been declared a national historic landmark for the more than 600 examples of 19th-century architecture in the district.

Hosts: Anne LeDuc and Judy Bartella
Rooms: 72 (11 PB; 61 SB) $74-145
Full Breakfast
Credit Cards: A, B
Notes: 2, 4, 7, 8, 9, 10, 11, 12

Bedford Inn

Duke of Windsor Inn
817 Washington Street, 08204
(609) 884-1355

This grande 1890 Victorian home offers gracious, relaxing accommodations furnished with period antiques, high-backed beds, and marble-topped tables and dressers. Two octagon rooms in our 40-foot turret are particularly fun and romantic. The dining room has five chandeliers and an elaborate plaster ceiling. We are within walking distance of the beach, historical attractions, tennis, and shopping. Open February to December.

Host: Bruce and Fran Prichard
Rooms: 9 (8 PB; 1 SB) $65-115
Full Breakfast
Credit Cards: A, B (for deposit only)
Notes: 2, 8, 9, 10

The Queen Victoria
102 Ocean Street, 08204
(609) 884-9349

The Queen Victoria includes three 1800s homes that have been restored and furnished with antiques. There are two parlors, one with fireplace and one with TV and games. Two dining rooms serve a hearty country breakfast and afternoon tea. Special services include free bicycles, beach showers and towels, and turned-down beds with a special chocolate on your pillow. All rooms are air conditioned.

Hosts: Dane and Joan Wells
Rooms: 22 (PB) $65-235

---

year; 6 Pets welcome; 7 Children welcome; 8 Tennis nearby; 9 Swimming nearby; 10 Golf nearby; 11 Skiing nearby; 12 May be booked through travel agent

Full Breakfast
Credit Cards: A, B
Notes: 2, 5, 7, 8, 9, 10

Windward House
24 Jackson Street, 08204
(609) 884-3368

An elegant, Edwardian seaside inn has an entry room and staircase that are perhaps the prettiest in town. Spacious, antique-filled guest rooms have queen beds and air conditioners. With three sun-and-shade porches, cozy parlor fireplace, and Christmas finery, the inn is located in the historic district, one-half block from the beach and shopping mall. Rates include homemade breakfast, beach passes, parking, and bicycles. Midweek discounts September to June; off-season weekend packages.

Hosts: Owen and Sandy Miller
Rooms: 8 (PB) $80-130
Full Breakfast
Credit Cards: A, B (deposit only)
Notes: 2, 5, 7 (over 12), 8, 9, 10

OCEAN CITY

BarnaGate Bed and Breakfast Inn
637 Wesley Avenue, 08226
(609) 291-9366

Enjoy the small, intimate accommodations of our 1895 seashore Victorian. The cozy rooms are decorated in country style with quilts on the antique beds and paddle fans to keep you cool. All rooms are named for flowers. Guests use our common area or front porch under burgundy awnings with white wicker rockers. Near Cape May, Atlantic City, county zoo, and antique shops. We've got everything—beach, boardwalk, and ocean. Hospitality is our specialty.

Hosts: Frank and Lois Barna
Rooms: 5 (1 PB; 4 SB) $50-70
Full Breakfast; Continental in sumnmer
Credit Cards: A, B
Notes: 2, 5, 7, 8, 9, 10

New Brighton Inn
519 Fifth Street, 08226
(609) 399-2829

This charming 1880 Queen Anne Victorian has been magnificently restored to its original beauty. All rooms and common areas (livingroom, library, sun porch) are elegantly and comfortably furnished with antiques. The front veranda is furnished with rockers and a large swing. Rates include beach tags and use of bicycles.

Hosts: Daniel and Donna Hand
Rooms: 4 (2 PB; 2 SB) $55-75
Full Breakfast
Credit Cards: A, B, C
Notes: 2, 5

Northwood Inn
401 Wesley Avenue, 08226
(609) 399-6071

Winner of the Cape May County beautification award, this elegantly restored

---

NOTES: Credit cards accepted: A Master Card; B Visa; C American Express; D Discover Card; E Diners Club; F Other; 2 Personal checks accepted; 3 Lunch available; 4 Dinner available; 5 Open all

1894 Queen Anne Victorian has 19th-century charm and 20th-century comfort. It features eight distinctive guest rooms, central air conditioning, fully stocked library/game room, two porches, and roof-top deck. It is three blocks from the beach, boardwalk, shops, and restaurants. Complimentary beach tags and off-street parking.

Hosts: Marj and John Loeper
Rooms: 8 (6 PB; 2 SB) $65-140
Full Breakfast; Continental weekdays
Credit Cards: A, B
Notes: 2, 5, 7 (over 9), 8, 10

Northwood Inn

OCEAN GROVE

The Cordova
26 Webb Avenue, 07756
(908) 774-3084 in season; (212) 751-9577 winter

Ocean Grove was founded as a religious retreat center at the turn of the century. This flavor has lasted in the quiet, peaceful atmosphere. Constant religious programs for the family are arranged in the 7,000-seat great auditorium. The Cordova rooms are uniquely charming and Victorian. Friendliness, hospitality, cleanliness, and quiet one block from the magnificent white sand beach and boardwalk. The porches have a splendid ocean view. Midweek specials; also, seven nights for the price of five.

Host: Doris Chernik
Rooms: 14 (1 PB; 13 SB) $30-62
Cottages: 2 (PB) $85-95
Continental Breakfast
Credit Cards: None
Notes: 2, 7, 8, 9, 12

Keswick Inn
32 Embury Avenue, 07756
(908) 775-7506

Built in 1875, the inn is near beach and shopping and is located in a Victorian village incorporated in 1969 as a camp meeting ground and seaside summer resort. The great auditorium seats 7,000, is a national historic monument, and houses a summer program of religious, cultural, and entertainment events.

Host: Robert Centorino
Rooms: 20 (18 PB; 2 SB) $24-70
Continental Breakfast
Credit Cards: A, B, C
Notes: 2, 8, 9, 10

SPRING LAKE

The Hewitt Wellington Hotel
200 Monmouth Avewnue, 07762
(908) 974-1212

156 New Jersey

Spring Lake's landmark in luxury. AAA four-diamond award winner. Twelve beautifully appointed single rooms and 17 two-room suites on the lake overlooking the ocean have private balconies, wraparound porches, air conditioning, ceiling fans, private marble baths, remote cable TVs, and phones. Heated pool and free beach passes. Refined dining in our intimate restaurant. Free brochure.

Rooms: 29 (PB) $70-210
Continental Breakfast
Credit Cards: A, B, C
Notes: 3, 4, 7, 8, 10

Sea Crest by the Sea
19 Tuttle Avenue, 07762
(201) 449-9031

Escape to the romantic refuge of a luxury bed and breakfast inn by the sea. For a week or a weekend, we will pamper you with warmth and hospitality that is friendly yet unobtrusive. The Sea Crest is our lovingly restored 1885 Victorian inn for ladies and gentleman on seaside holiday.

Hosts: John and Carol Kirby
Rooms: 12 (PB) $80-140
Expanded Continental Breakfast
Credit Cards: A, B
Notes: 2, 5, 8, 9, 10

Sea Crest by the Sea

NOTES: Credit cards accepted: A Master Card; B Visa; C American Express; D Discover Card; E Diners Club; F Other; 2 Personal checks accepted; 3 Lunch available; 4 Dinner available; 5 Open all

New Mexico

CEDAR CREST

The Apple Tree
12050 Highway 14 North, Box 287, 87008
(505) 281-3597; (800) 648-4262

Authentic adobe casita with rustic brick floors, log-beamed ceiling, and kiva fireplace; sleeps up to four. There is also a suite with separate bedroom/bath, queen bed, and sleeper sofa. Fireplace, kitchen, cable TV, air conditioning, phone. Breakfast includes blue-corn waffles, whole-wheat cinnamon rolls, southwestern quiche, and apple-raspberry tarts. Seven miles from Albuquerque on the scenic Turquoise Trail and less than two miles north of I-40.

Hosts: Garland and Norma Curry
Suites: 2 (PB) $55-105
Full Breakfast
Credit Cards: None
Notes: 2, 5, 6, 7, 8, 9, 10, 11

SANTA FE

Adobe Abode
202 Chapelle, 87501
(505) 983-3133

This charming bed and breakfast just three blocks from Santa Fe's plaza is a sophisticated mix of authentic Santa Fe style and European touches, featuring an eclectic art collection, fine antiques, and native New Mexican furniture. It offers two guest rooms in the main house and a guest house with twin beds and a walled patio.

Host: Pat Harbour
Rooms: 3 (PB) $85-110
Full Breakfast
Credit Cards: A, B
Notes: 2, 5, 7, 11, 12

Alexander's Inn
529 East Palace Avenue, 87501
(505) 986-1431

For a cozy stay in Santa Fe, nestle into a bed and breakfast featuring the best of American country charm, Alexander's Inn. Located in a lovely, residential neighborhood on the town's historic east side, Alexander's Inn is within walking distance of the downtown plaza, as well as Canyon Road, the art and soul of Santa Fe.

Hosts: Carolyn Delecluse and Mary Jo Schneider
Rooms: 5 (3 PB; 2 SB) $65-115
Continental Breakfast
Credit Cards: A, B
Notes: 2, 4, 7, (over 6), 8, 9, 10, 11

year; 6 Pets welcome; 7 Children welcome; 8 Tennis nearby; 9 Swimming nearby; 10 Golf nearby; 11 Skiing nearby; 12 May be booked through travel agent

Canyon Road Casitas

652 Canyon Road, 87501
(505) 988-5888; (800) 279-0755

Luxury accommodations are featured in this 100-year-old historic Territorial adobe within walking distance of distinctive art galleries, numerous museums, unique shops, and historic landmarks. Both guest rooms have kitchenettes, down quilts and pillows, feather beds, separate entrances, and private patios. This is a four-season retreat.

Host: Trisha Ambrose
Rooms: 2 (PB) $85-165
Continental Breakfast
Credit Cards: A, B, C, D
Notes: 2, 5, 7, 11, 12

El Paradero

220 West Manhattan, 87501
(505) 988-1177

El Paradero is located on a quiet, downtown side street, ideal for exploring the heart of historic Santa Fe. The owners have turned the old adobe Spanish farmhouse into a warm and relaxing experience of true southwestern comraderie and hospitality. The inn is furnished in the southwestern tradition with folk art and has an eccentric, rambling character typical of old adobes.

Hosts: Ouida MacGregor and Thom Allen
Rooms: 12 (8 PB; 4 SB) $50-130
Suites: 2
Full Breakfast
Credit Cards: None
Notes: 2, 3 (box), 5, 6, 7, 8, 9, 10, 11, 12

TAOS

Stewart House

P. O. Box 2326, 87571
(505) 776-2913

This Taos landmark was built over a 15-year period from what the artist/builder calls reclaimed parts of history. The inn is a mix of styles and textures, combining elements from Moorish to Mayan, Spanish to Scandinavian. The innkeepers have been in the fine art business for more than 20 years, so each room is filled with art and antiques. Enjoy mountain views, sunsets, outdoor hot tub, and hearty breakfasts only five minutes from Taos Plaza in a quiet, country setting.

Hosts: Mildred and Don Cheek
Rooms: 4 (PB) $70-120
Full Breakfast
Credit Cards: A, B
Notes: 2, 5, 7 (over 11), 8, 9, 10, 11, 12

El Paradero

NOTES: Credit cards accepted: A Master Card; B Visa; C American Express; D Discover Card; E Diners Club; F Other; 2 Personal checks accepted; 3 Lunch available; 4 Dinner available; 5 Open all

New York

ALBANY

Mansion Hil Inn
115 Philip Street at Park Avenue, 12202
(518) 465-2038

The urban inn is located around the corner from the New York state governor's executive mansion. The inn consists of 12 rooms and is in the mansion historic district in three separate buildings. It features an award-winning restaurant that serves regional American cuisine. Please write for a free brochure.

Hosts: Mary Ellen, Elizabeth, and Steve Stofelano
Rooms: 12 (PB) $105-145
Full Breakfast
Credit Cards: A, B, C, E
Notes: 2, 3, 4, 5, 6, 7, 8, 9, 10, 11, 12

Pine Haven Bed and Breakfast
531 Western Avenue, 12203
(518) 482-1574

A century-old Victorian home in Albany's finest neighborhood offers off-street parking and access to bus transportation to state capital offices, hospitals, colleges, and downtown. Restaurants, theater, and stores are within walking distance. Rooms are furnished with Victorian-era antiques, and beds have removable feather mattresses. Robes are provided for comfortable lounging, and there is a phone in each room. No smoking.

Host: Janice Tricarico
Rooms: 4 (S2B) $64
Continental Breakfast
Credit Cards: None
Notes: 2, 5, 7 (over 12), 12

Mansion Hill Inn

year; 6 Pets welcome; 7 Children welcome; 8 Tennis nearby; 9 Swimming nearby; 10 Golf nearby; 11 Skiing nearby; 12 May be booked through travel agent

ALBION

Friendship Manor
349 South Main Street, 14411
(716) 589-7973

This historic house, dating back to 1880, was built by the son of Joseph Hart, an original settler of Albion. It was purchased by Jack and Marilyn in 1986 and has been restored to capture its traditional turn-of-the-century beauty. The home is surrounded by one acre of land covered by lovely roses, herb garden, and comfortable sitting areas under shade trees. Located on the grounds is a swimming pool and tennis court. Central to Rochester, Buffalo, and Niagara Falls.

Hosts: Jack and Marylin Baker
Rooms: 4 (1 PB; 3 SB) $45
Continental Breakfast
Credit Cards: None
Notes: 2, 5, 8, 9, 10

AVERILL PARK

Ananas Hus Bed and Breakfast
Route 3, Box 301, 12018
(518) 766-5035

The Tomlinsons invite you to share the beauty, tranquility, and smoke- and pet-free environment of their hillside home on 30 acres with a panoramic view of the Hudson River valley. Ananas Hus lies just off Route 43 on South Road in West Stephentown, convenient to western Massachusetts and the state capital district of New York, which abounds with cultural, natural, historic, and sports attractions. Great ski country.

Hosts: Clyde and Thelma Olsen Tomlinson
Rooms: 3 (SB) $55
Full Breakfast
Credit Cards: C
Notes: 2, 5, 7 (over 12), 9, 10, 11

Gone with the Wind on Keuka Lake

BAINBRIDGE

Berry Hill Farm Bed and Breakfast
Rural Delivery 1, Box 128, 13733
(607) 967-8745

This restored 1820s farmhouse on a hilltop is surrounded by vegetable and flower gardens and 180 acres where you can hike, swim, bird-watch, pick berries, skate, cross-country ski, or sit on the wraparound porch and watch the natural parade. Our rooms are furnished with comfortable antiques. A ten-minute drive takes you to restaurants,

---

NOTES: Credit cards accepted: A Master Card; B Visa; C American Express; D Discover Card; E Diners Club; F Other; 2 Personal checks accepted; 3 Lunch available; 4 Dinner available; 5 Open all

golf, tennis, auctions, and antique centers. Cooperstown and most local colleges are only 45 minute away.

Hosts: Jean Fowler and Cecilio Rios
Rooms: 3 (SB) $55-65
Full Breakfast
Credit Cards: A, B
Notes: 2, 5, 7, 8, 9, 10, 11, 12

BOLTON LANDING

Hilltop Cottage Bed and Breakfast

Box 186, Lakeshore Drive, 12814
(518) 644-2492

A clean, comfortable, renovated farmhouse is near Lake George in the beautiful eastern Adirondack Mountains. Walk to beaches, restaurants, and marinas. Enjoy a quiet, home atmosphere with hearty breakfasts. In the summer, this is a busy resort area. Autumn offers fall foliage, hiking, skiing. There is a wood-burning stove for use in winter. A brochure is available.

Hosts: Anita and Charlie Richards
Rooms: 4 (1 PB; 3 SB) $45-55
Full Breakfast
Credit Cards: None
Notes: 2, 5

BRANCHPORT

Gone with the Wind on Keuka Lake

453 West Lake Road, 14418
(607) 868-4603

The name paints the picture of this 1887 stone Victorian on 14 acres on a slight rise overlooking a quiet lake cove that is adorned by an inviting gazebo. Feel the magic of total relaxation and peace of mind in the solarium hot tub, nature trails, three fireplaces, delectable breakfasts, private beach, and dock. One hour south of Rochester in the Finger Lakes of New York.

Hosts: Linda and Robert Lewis
Rooms: 6; $65-95
Full Breakfast
Credit Cards: None
Notes: 2, 5, 8, 9, 10, 11

BURDETT

The Red House Country Inn

4586 Picnic Area Road, 14818
(607) 546-8566

The inn is located in the beautiful 13,000-acre Finger Lakes National Forest with 28 miles of maintained hiking and cross-country ski trails. Six award-winning wineries are within ten minutes from the completely restored 1840s farmstead on five acres of groomed lawns and flower gardens. Enjoy beautifully appointed rooms, country breakfasts, in-ground pool, fully equipped kitchen. Twelve minutes north of Watkins Glen, 20 minutes from Ithaca, 30 minutes from Corning.

Hosts: Sandy Schmanke and Joan Martin
Rooms: 5 (S4B) $60-85
Full Breakfast

---

year; 6 Pets welcome; 7 Children welcome; 8 Tennis nearby; 9 Swimming nearby; 10 Golf nearby; 11 Skiing nearby; 12 May be booked through travel agent

Credit Cards: A, B, C, D
Notes: 2, 5, 9, 11, 12

CAMBRIDGE

Battenkill Bed and Breakfast
Route 313, Rural Delivery 1
Box 143, 12816-9717
(518) 677-8868

Relax in the beautiful Annaquassicoke Valley and enjoy our post-and-beam home. Veronica delights in creative cooking, and Walt is a jazz musician. In the winter, our bed and breakfast offers snow-shoeing on site and cross-country skiing nearby. Spring, summer, and fall offer you fishing, canoeing, tubing the beautiful Battenkill River, or biking through the valley. Equipment for all these activities is available at our rental office.

Hosts: Veronica and Walter Piekarz
Rooms: 2 (SB) $60
Full Breakfast
Credit Cards: A, B, C, D
Notes: 2, 3, 4, 5, 10, 11

CAZENOVIA

Brae Lock Inn
5 Albany Street (U.S. Route 20), 13035
(315) 655-3431; (800) 722-0674

This is as close to a Scottish inn as you will find this far west of Edinburgh. Built in 1805, the inn has been family-owned and operated since 1946 and features central New York's largest Scottish gift shop. Guest rooms carry the old-time charm of antiques and the classic luxury of Stickley furniture. Guests enjoy cross-country skiing, horseback riding, boating, and nearby golf privileges.

Host: Jim Barr
Rooms: 15 (14 PB; 1 SB) $75-125
Continental Breakfast
Credit Cards: A, B, C
Notes: 4, 5, 7, 8, 9, 10, 11, 12

Lincklaen House
79 Albany Street, Box 36, 13035
(315) 655-3461

To visit Lincklaen House is to return to an era of elegant hospitality. Lincklaen House is an extraordinary, four-season, country inn built in 1835 as a luxurious stopover for colonial travelers. Carefully renovated, the hotel provides the amenities that 20th-century travelers demand, while retaining a charm preserved since the 19th century. Afternoon tea is served.

Host: Howard M. Kaler
Rooms: 21 (PB) $70-130
Continental Breakfast
Credit Cards: A, B
Notes: 2, 3, 4, 5, 6, 7, 8, 9, 10, 11, 12

CLARENCE

Asa Ransom House
10529 Main Street, 14031
(716) 759-2315

NOTES: Credit cards accepted: A Master Card; B Visa; C American Express; D Discover Card; E Diners Club; F Other; 2 Personal checks accepted; 3 Lunch available; 4 Dinner available; 5 Open all

Warmth, comfort, and hospitality are our main attractions. Nine guest rooms have antique and period furnishings, seven of these have fireplaces. We also have a library, gift shop, and herb garden on a two-acre lot in the village. The original building housing the library, gift shop and tap room dates back to 1853. It was built by Asa Ransom who received the land from the Holland Lace Company in 1799.

Hosts: Bob and Judy Lenz
Rooms: 4 (PB) $85-135
Full Breakfast
Credit Cards: A, B, D
Closed Fridays and January
Notes: 2, 4, 7, 8, 9, 10

COOPERSTOWN

The Inn at Brook Willow
Rural Delivery 2, Box 514, 13326
(607) 547-9700

A pastoral retreat nestled in willows and pines, the Victorian house sits among meadows and hills and is furnished with antiques in the house and a "reborn" barn. A common room overlooks the gardens. Jack's famous muffins are served each morning. Chosen as one of the 100 best bed and breakfast homes in North America.

Hosts: Joan and Jack Grimes
Rooms: 4 (PB) $64-84
Full Breakfast
Credit Cards: None
Notes: 2, 5, 7, 8, 9, 10, 11

CORNING

1865 White Birch Bed and Breakfast
69 East First Street, 14830
(607) 962-6355

The White Birch, Victorian in structure but decorated in country, has been refurbished to show off its winding staircase, hardwood floors, and wall window in the dining room that overlooks the back yard. We are located in a residential area two blocks from restored historic Market Street and six blocks from the Corning Museum of Glass. A warm fire during the colder months welcomes guests in the common room where TV and great conversation are available. A full gourmet breakfast is served each morning.

Hosts: Kathy and Joe Donahue
Rooms: 4 (2 PB; 2 SB) $50-70
Full Breakfast
Credit Cards: A, B, C
Notes: 2, 5, 7, 8, 9, 10, 11

Delevan House
188 Delevan Avenue, 14830
(607) 962-2347

This southern Colonial house sits on a hill overlooking Corning. It is charming, graceful, and warm in quiet surroundings. Delicious breakfast.

Host: Mary De Pumpo
Rooms: 3 (1 PB; 2 SB) $55-75

---

year; 6 Pets welcome; 7 Children welcome; 8 Tennis nearby; 9 Swimming nearby; 10 Golf nearby; 11 Skiing nearby; 12 May be booked through travel agent

Full Breakfast
Credit Cards: None
Notes: 2, 5, 10, 11, 12

CUBA

Helen's Tourist Home
7 Maple Street, 14727
(716) 968-2200

Your hostess has been welcoming tourists in her turn-of-the-century home for 38 years. Guests have full use of the house, including the livingroom with TV. Coffee, a toaster, and a refrigerator are always available. Visit the Cuba Cheese Shop and historic Seneca Springs. Restaurants are nearby. Less than five minutes from Exit 28, Route 17. Reservations are appreciated.

Host: Dora Wittmann
Rooms: 5 (1 PB; 4 SB) $20-35
Credit Cards: None
Notes: 5, 7, 10, 11

DELMAR

American Country Collection of Bed and Breakfasts and Country Inns
4 Greenwood Lane, 12054-1606
(518) 439-7001 information; (800) 800-5908, ext. 21 reservations

This reservation service provides reservations for eastern New York, western Massachusetts, and all of Vermont. Just one call does it all. Relax and unwind at any of our 103 immaculate, personally inspected bed and breakfasts and country inns. Many include fireplace, Jacuzzi, and/or Modified American Plan. We cater to the budget-minded, yet also offer luxurious accommodations in older Colonial homes and inns. Urban, suburban, and rural locations available. $35-180. Arthur R. Copeland, coordinator.

DOWNSVILLE

Adams' Farmhouse Bed and Breakfast
Main Street, Route 206, P. O. Box 18, 13755
(607) 363-2757

Built in 1892, this is one of the oldest houses on the main street of this Catskills village. It is quiet, quaint, and beautiful, with a great front porch for relaxing, afternoon tea, and supper when requested. There is an antique store on the premises. Comfortable guest rooms are decorated in a country style. Three hours from New York City. Great antiquing, canoeing, horseback riding, swimming, tennis, walking, hunting, and fishing are nearby.

Hosts: Nancy and Harry Adams
Rooms: 3 (1 PB; 2 SB) $50
Full Breakfast
Credit Cards: None
Notes: 2, 3, 4, 8, 9, 10, 12

NOTES: Credit cards accepted: A Master Card; B Visa; C American Express; D Discover Card; E Diners Club; F Other; 2 Personal checks accepted; 3 Lunch available; 4 Dinner available; 5 Open all

DRYDEN

Margaret Thacher's Spruce Haven Bed and Breakfast
9 James Street, 13053
(607) 844-8052

This 1976 log home is warm and friendly and is surrounded by spruce trees that give the feeling of being in the woods, even though we are located in the village. Within 12 miles of Ithaca, Courtland, lakes, golf, skiing, colleges, museums, and restaurants.

Host: Margaret Thacher Brownell
Rooms: 2 (SB) Call for rates
Full Breakfast
Credit Cards: None
Notes: 2, 5, 6, 8, 9, 10, 11

EAST HAMPTON

Mill House
33 North Main Street, 11937
(516) 324-9766

This 1790 Colonial is located in "America's most beautiful village." Enjoy lemonade while overlooking the old Hook windmill, or take a restful nap in our back-yard hammock. In the off-season, enjoy hot cider by the fireplace or a brisk walk to the ocean beach. Antiquing, golf, tennis, Long Island wineries, and whale watching are nearby.

Hosts: Barbara and Kevin Flynn
Rooms: 8 (6 PB; 2 SB) $75-155
Full Breakfast
Credit Cards: A, B, C
Notes: 2, 5, 7 (over 11), 8

FAIR HAVEN

Frost Haven Resort, Inc.
West Bay Road, Box 241, 13064
(315) 947-5331

Located on Little Sodus Bay on the southern shores of Lake Ontario, the inn is surrounded with views of the waterfront and spacious, well-kept grounds. A full breakfast is served from 5:00 to 9:00 A.M. We make sure that fishermen are full as they try their luck with the famous trout and salmon fishing. All types of water sports are available with beaches and launch ramps nearby. July and August bring the Renaissance Faire. A full brochure is available upon request.

Hosts: Brad and Chris Frost
Rooms: 4 (SB) $66
Full Breakfast
Credit Cards: A, B
Notes: 2, 5, 7, 10, 11, 12

FORESTBURGH

The Inn at Lake Joseph
400 St. Joseph's Road, 12777
(914) 791-9506

The inn, previously owned by the Dominican sisters, was once the vacation estate used by Cardinals Hayes and Spellman of New York City. Its 125-year-old Queen Anne Victorian-style mansion is surrounded by 2,000 acres of wildlife preserve and hardwood forest on a 250-acre, unspoiled private lake. Rates include dinner.

Host: Ivan Weinger
Rooms: 9 (8 PB; 1 SB) $138-218
Full Braekfast
Credit Cards: A, B, C
Notes: 2, 4, 8, 9, 10, 11

FOSTERDALE

Fosterdale Heights House
205 Mueller Road, 12726
(914) 482-3369

This historic 1840 European-style country estate in the Catskill Mountains is less than two hours from New York City. It is gentle and quiet, with a bountiful breakfast. Enjoy the mountain view overlooking the pond, acres of Christmas trees (cut your own in season), natural forest, informal evenings of chamber music, and parlor games.

Host: Roy Singer
Rooms: 12 (3 PB; 9 SB) $52-105
Full Breakfast
Credit Cards: A, B
Notes: 4, 5, 8, 9, 10, 11

FULTON

Battle Island Inn
Rural Delivery 1, Box 176, 13069
(315) 593-3699

Battle Island Inn is a pre-Civil War farm estate that has been restored and furnished with period antiques. The inn is across the road from a golf course that also provides cross-country skiing. Guest rooms are elegantly furnished with imposing high-back beds, TVs, phones, and private baths. Breakfast is always special in the 1840s dining room.

Hosts: Joyce and Richard Rice
Rooms: 5 (PB) $60-85
Full Breakfast
Credit Cards: A, B, C, D
Notes: 2, 5, 7, 10, 11

Bellinger Woods Bed and Breakfast

HEMPSTEAD

Country Life Bed and Breakfast
237 Cathedral Avenue
On the Garden City Line, 11550
(516) 292-9219

This charming Dutch Colonial on the Garden City line is near airports, trains

---

NOTES: Credit cards accepted: A Master Card; B Visa; C American Express; D Discover Card; E Diners Club; F Other; 2 Personal checks accepted; 3 Lunch available; 4 Dinner available; 5 Open all

to New York City, beaches, universities, and Nassau coliseum. It is furnished with antique reproductions, and rooms have air conditioning and color TV. We offer on-site parking and are near many tourist attractions. No smoking.

Hosts: Richard and Wendy Duvall
Rooms: 5 (3 PB; 2 SB) $60-95
Full Breakfast
Credit Cards: A, B
Notes: 2 (deposit only), 4, 5, 7, 9, 10

HERKIMER

Bellinger Woods Bed and Breakfast
611 West German Street, 13350
(315) 866-2770

This Victorian bed and breakfast, circa 1860, is located one mile from I-90, New York State Thruway, Exit 30 in the village of Herkima. It offers comfortable elegance in the heart of central leatherstocking country, complete with marble fireplaces and crown plaster moldings. Area attractions include the Herkimer diamond mines, Remington Arms Museum, and antique shops. The Cooperstown area is just a 40-minute scenic ride away.

Hosts: Barbara and Paul Mielcarski
Rooms: 3 (2 PB; 1 SB) $35-55
Full Breakfast
Credit Cards: A, B
Notes: 2, 5, 8, 9, 10, 11, 12

HORSEHEADS

Burch Hill Bed and Breakfast
2196 Burch Hil Road, 14845
(607) 739-2504

This modern country home is minutes from Elmira, Corning, Watkins Glen, Ithaca, Finger Lakes, wineries, six colleges, international auto race track, museums, Mark Twain's grave site. Each room has its own water closet plus use of the large bathrooms. Rooms can accommodate four people by use of a sofa bed. Make our home yours when in the southern Finger Lakes area. No smoking.

Hosts: Bob and Doris Roller
Rooms: 2 (SB) $50
Full Breakfast
Credit Cards: None
Notes: 2, 3, 4, 5, 9, 10, 12

JAMESVILLE

High Meadows Bed-N-Breakfast
3740 Eager Road, 13078
(315) 492-3517

You are invited to enjoy country hospitality nestled in the tranquil hills just 12 miles south of Syracuse. High Meadows offers two guest rooms, a shared bath, air conditioning, fireplace, plant-filled solarium, and a wraparound

year; 6 Pets welcome; 7 Children welcome; 8 Tennis nearby; 9 Swimming nearby; 10 Golf nearby; 11 Skiing nearby; 12 May be booked through travel agent

deck with magnificent 40-mile view. The one queen and one double room are available. Syracuse area offers restaurants, museums, theaters, concerts, and collegiate and professional sporting events. Corporate and weekly rates and seniors' discounts available.

Hosts: Alexander and Nancy Mentz
Rooms: 2 (SB) $35-55
Continental Breakfast
Credit Cards: NOne
Notes: 2, 5, 7, 10, 11

LAKE LUZERNE

The Lamplight Inn Bed and Breakfast

2129 Lake Avenue, P. O. Box 70, 12846
(518) 696-5294

This romantic 1890 Victorian has individually decorated bedrooms with fireplaces and features antiques, wicker, fluffy comforters, and air conditioning. A memorable breakfast is served on the spacious sun porch with a mountain view. The southern Adirondack Mountains are one block from Lake Luzerne. Ten miles south of Lake George, 18 miles north of Saratoga Springs. Nearby endless activities include horseback riding, outlet shopping, white water rafting, antiquing.

Hosts: Eugene and Linda Merlino
Rooms: 10 (PB) $70-140
Full Breakfast
Credit Cards: A, B, C, D
Notes: 2, 5, 7 (over 12), 8, 9, 10, 11, 12

LAKE PLACID

Highland House Inn

3 Highland Place, 12946
(518) 523-2377

The Highland House Inn is centrally located in a lovely residential setting just above Main Street in the village of Lake Placid. Seven tastefully decorated rooms are available, along with a darling, fully efficient country cottage. A full breakfast is served, with blueberry pancakes a renowned specialty.

Hosts: Teddy and Cathy Blazer
Rooms: 7 plus cottage (PB) $47-85
Full Breakfast
Credit Cards: A, B
Notes: 2, 7, 8, 9, 10, 11

MOHAWK

Country Hills Bed and Breakfast

Rural Delivery 1, Box 80
(315) 866-1306

At this spacious 1860s farmhouse amid rolling lawns and private woods overlooking the Mohawk Valley, suites include kitchenette, a Murphy bed to comfortably accommodate up to four people, air conditioning, and TV. A separate entrance to suites insures privacy. It is a short scenic drive to famed Cooperstown, Remington Arms, Herkimer diamond digging, Jordanville Russian Orthodox Seminary, revolu-

---

NOTES: Credit cards accepted: A Master Card; B Visa; C American Express; D Discover Card; E Diners Club; F Other; 2 Personal checks accepted; 3 Lunch available; 4 Dinner available; 5 Open all

tionary period historic sites, and antique shops.

Hosts: Mary Ann and Jim Hill
Rooms: 2 (PB) $55-65
Full Breakfast
Credit Cards: A, B
Notes: 5, 7, 8, 9, 10, 11, 12

NEW YORK

Aaah! Bed and Breakfast
P. O. Box 200, 10108-0200
(212) 246-4000; FAX (212) 265-4346

This reservation service offers 170 hosted or unhosted (self-catered) accommodations throughout Manhattan. It offers a very personal approach to matching people to accommodations by travel dates, location, allergies, and smoking habits. No lists available; call to inquire. Studio and one- and two-bedroom apartments are also available. $60-80. William Salisbury, coordinator.

OXFORD

Whitegate Bed and Breafast in the Country
P.O. Box 917, 13830
(607) 843-6965

This charming 1820 Greek Revival farmhouse is located on 196 acres of serene meadows and lush woodlands midway between Cooperstown and the Finger Lakes. Stroll on the hiking paths, relax by one of the ponds, come inside and sit by the fire, or enjoy the view from the solarium. Traditional furniture and antiques combine to make Whitegate a most welcoming place.

Hosts: Wanda and Pual Mitten
Rooms: 4 (2 PB; 2 SB) $45-65
Full Breakfast
Credit Cards: A, B
Notes: 2, 3 & 4 (with reservations), 5, 8, 9, 10, 11, 12

PALMYRA

Canaltown Bed and Breakfast
119 Canandaigua Street, 14522
(315) 597-5553

This 1850s historic village home of Greek Revival architecture is located near antique stores, Erie Coverlet Museum, country store museum, Erie Canal hiking trail, canoe rental. Rooms are furnished with iron and brass beds and antiques. Enjoy the livingroom fireplace.

Hosts: Robert and Barbara Leisten
Rooms: 2 (SB) $50-60
Full Breakfast
Credit Cards: C
Notes: 2, 5, 6, 8, 10, 11, 12

PURLING

Shepherd's Croft
HCR 263 Mountain Avenue, 12470
(518) 622-9504

---

year; 6 Pets welcome; 7 Children welcome; 8 Tennis nearby; 9 Swimming nearby; 10 Golf nearby; 11 Skiing nearby; 12 May be booked through travel agent

Nestled in the northern Catskill Mountains approximately midway between the Hunter and Windham ski slopes, Shepherd's Croft has been an inn under various names and owners for more than 100 years. The entire property has undergone extensive renovations under the current owners during the last five years. Accommodations include six historic rooms in the main building, five motel rooms, and four suites with kitchen/living facilities. Children are welcome in the suites and motel rooms at no extra charge.

Hosts: Raimond and Linda Bang
Rooms: 15 (8 PB; 7 SB) $40-50
Full Breakfast; Continental weekdays
Credit Cards: A, B
Notes: 2, 5, 6, 7, 9, 10, 11, 12

Shepherd's Croft

QUEENSBURY

Crislip's Bed and Breakfast
Rural Delivery 1, Ridge Road, Box 57, 12804
(518) 793-6869

Located in the Adirondack area just minutes from Saratoga Springs and Lake George, this landmark Federal home provides spacious accommodations complete with period antiques, four-poster beds, and down comforters. The country breakfast menu features buttermilk pancakes, scrambled eggs, and sausages. Your hosts invite you to relax on the porches and enjoy the mountain view of Vermont.

Host: Ned and Joyce Crislip
Rooms: 3 (PB) $55-75
Full Breakfast
Credit Cards: A, B, C
Notes: 2, 5, 7

RICHFIELD SPRINGS

Country Spread Bed and Breakfast
23 Prospect Street, Route 28
P. O. Box 1863, 13439
(315) 858-1870

From our guest book.... "A refreshing night and fun conversation." Enjoy genuine hospitality in our 1893 country-decorated home. Located in the heart of central New York, we are close to the National Baseball Hall of Fame in Cooperstown, opera, antiquing, and four-season recreation. Delicious breakfasts (your choice) await. Member of local and national associations. Families welcome.

Hosts: Karen and Bruce Watson
Rooms: 2 (PB) $45-65

NOTES: Credit cards accepted: A Master Card; B Visa; C American Express; D Discover Card; E Diners Club; F Other; 2 Personal checks accepted; 3 Lunch available; 4 Dinner available; 5 Open all

Full Breakfast
Credit Cards: A, B
Notes: 2, 5, 7, 8, 9, 10, 11, 12

SENECA FALLS

Locustwood Inn
3563 Route 89, 13148
(315) 549-7132

Locustwood Inn is a charming, old country inn built in 1820. Located in the heart of the Finger Lakes, the inn is one of the oldest in Seneca County. Constructed of early brick, it still has the huge beams, wide-plank floors, and five fireplaces that were familiar to an era long past. Our guests are welcome to stroll the grounds, view the herbs and flowers, visit with our animal friends, or while away the hours in our hammock for two under the pines.

Hosts: Bob and Nancy Hill
Rooms: 3 (S2B) $60-80
Full Breakfast
Credit Cards: None
Note: 2

SOUTHOLD

Goose Creek Guesthouse
1475 Waterview Drive, 11971
(516) 765-3356

Goose Creek Guesthouse is a Civil War-era farmhouse secluded on a creek by the woods. We are in a resort area with many beaches, golf, charter boat fishing, antique shops, and museums. Near ferries to Connecticut or Montauk and the south shore via Shelter Island.

Host: Mary Mooney-Getoff
Rooms: 4 (SB) $45-70
Full Breakfast
Credit Cards: None
Notes: 2 (for deposit), 7, 8, 9, 10

TRUMANSBURG

Westwind Bed and Breakfast
1662 Taughannock Boulevard, 14886
(607) 387-3377

Westwind Bed and Breakfast

---

year; 6 Pets welcome; 7 Children welcome; 8 Tennis nearby; 9 Swimming nearby; 10 Golf nearby; 11 Skiing nearby; 12 May be booked through travel agent

Gracious hospitality and casual elegance await you in our 1870 Victorian farmhouse situated on the hillside above Cayuga Lake. Whether you are on vacation or a short getaway weekend, you will enjoy the country charm and convenience of Westwind. Located one-half mile south of Taughannock State Park and only 20 minutes from Cornell University and Ithaca College. Nearby is the Hangar Theatre, area golf courses, museums, antiques, and shopping.

Host: Sharon Scott
Rooms: 4 (S2B) $55-75
Full Breakfast
Credit Cards: A, B
Notes: 2, 5, 7 (over 10), 8, 9, 10, 11

UTICA

The Iris Stonehouse Bed and Breakfast
16 Derbyshire Place, 13501-4706
(315) 732-6720; (800) 446-1456

Enjoy city charm close to everything, three miles south of I-90, Exit 31. This stone Tudor house has leaded-glass windows that add charm to the eclectic decor of the three guest rooms. A guest sitting room offers a comfortable area for relaxing, reading, watching TV, or socializing in a smoke-free atmosphere. Air conditioned.

Hosts: Shirley and Roy Kilgore
Rooms: 3 (1 PB; 2 SB) $45-60
Full Breakfast
Credit Cards: A, B
Notes: 2, 5, 7 (over 7), 10, 11, 12

WARWICK

Willow Brook Inn
Warwick Turnpike, P. O. 375, 10990
(201) 853-7728

On the New York/New Jersey border, enjoy 120 acres of beauty with hiking trails, ponds with row boats, and outdoor party facilities. Inside we have clean and quiet sleeping rooms, TV lounge, pool table, and refrigerator and microwave for guest use. Indoor party facilities include a dining room that seats 60 people. We are less than one mile from the Appalachian Trail.

Host: Stan Streczyk
Rooms: 14 (4 PB; 10 SB) $44.50
Full Breakfast
Credit cards: None
Notes: 2, 3, 4, 5, 7, 8, 9, 10, 11

WESTHAMPTON BEACH

1880 Seafield House Bed and Breakfast
2 Seafield Lane, P. O. Box 648, 11978
(800) 346-3290

The Seafield House is a hidden, 100-year-old country retreat perfect for a romantic hideaway, a weekend of privacy, or just a change of pace from city life. Only 90 minutes from Manhattan, Seafield House is ideally situated on Westhampton Beach's exclusive Seafield Lane. The estate includes a swimming pool and tennis court and is a short, brisk walk to the ocean beach.

NOTES: Credit cards accepted: A Master Card; B Visa; C American Express; D Discover Card; E Diners Club; F Other; 2 Personal checks accepted; 3 Lunch available; 4 Dinner available; 5 Open all

The area offers outstanding restaurants, shops, and opportunities for antique hunting. Indoor tennis, Guerney's International Health Spa, and Montauk Point are nearby.

Host: Elsie Collins
Rooms: 3 (PB) $100-200
Full Breakfast
Credit Cards: C
Notes: 2, 5, 8, 9, 10

YOUNGSTOWN

The Cameo Manor North
3881 Lower River Road, 14174
(716) 745-3034

Located just seven miles north of Niagara Falls, our English manor house is the perfect spot for that quiet getaway you have been dreaming about. Situated on three secluded acres, the manor offers a great room with fireplaces, solarium, library, and an outdoor terrace for your enjoyment. Our beautifully appointed guest rooms include suites with private sunrooms, cable TV, and phones. A breakfast buffet is served daily.

Hosts: Greg and Carolyn Fisher
Rooms: 9 (5 PB; 4 SB) $60-125
Full Breakfast
Credit Cards: A, B
Notes: 2, 5, 7, 8, 9, 10, 11, 12

---

year; 6 Pets welcome; 7 Children welcome; 8 Tennis nearby; 9 Swimming nearby; 10 Golf nearby; 11 Skiing nearby; 12 May be booked through travel agent

North Carolina

ASHEVILLE

Aberdeen Inn
64 Linden Avenue, 28801
(704) 254-9336

We invite you to share our 1909 Colonial-style home six blocks from downtown and six minutes from Biltmore Estate. Lovely gardens and old shade trees provide privacy. Enjoy a buffet breakfast or a wicker rocker on our huge wraparound porch. The parlor and four of the nine bedrooms feature wood-burning fireplaces. Comfortable antiques, and collectibles. Friendly hosts, plus four cats, welcome you.

Hosts: Linda and Ross Willard
Rooms: 9 (PB) $55-75
Buffet Breakfast
Credit Cards: A, B
Notes: 2, 5, 8, 9, 10, 11

Cairn Brae
217 Patton Mountain Road, 28804
(704) 252-9219

A mountain retreat on three secluded acres above Asheville features beautiful views, walking trails, and a large terrace overlooking Beaver Dam Valley. Homemade full breakfast. Quiet, away from traffic, only minutes from downtown.

Hosts: Edward and Millicent Adams
Rooms: 3 (PB) $80-95
Full Breakfast
Credit Cards: A, B
Open April-November
Notes: 2, 3, 7 (over 5), 8, 9, 10

Cedar Crest Victorian Inn
674 Biltmore Avenue, 28803
(704) 252-1389; (800) 252-0310

This 1890 Queen Anne mansion is listed on the National Register of Historic Places. One of the largest and most opulent residences surviving Asheville's 1890s boom period. A captain's walk, projecting turrets, and expansive verandas welcome guests to lavish interior woodwork and stained glass. All rooms are furnished with antiques, with satin and lace trappings.

Hosts: Jack and Barbara McEwan
Rooms: 13 (9 PB; 4 SB) $70-120
Expanded Continental Breakfast
Credit Cards: A, B, C, D
Notes: 2, 5, 7 (over 12), 8, 9

NOTES: Credit cards accepted: A Master Card; B Visa; C American Express; D Discover Card; E Diners Club; F Other; 2 Personal checks accepted; 3 Lunch available; 4 Dinner available; 5 Open all

Dry Ridge Inn
26 Brown Street, Weaverville, 28787
(704) 658-3899

Part of this country-style inn was built in 1849 as a parsonage and was used as a hospital during the Civil War. The rest of the house was built in 1889. Large guest rooms have antiques and handmade quilts. In a small-town setting, it is ten minutes north of Ashville and all of its attractions.

Hosts: John and Karen VanderElzen
Rooms: 5 (PB) $50-60
Full Breakfast
Credit Cards: A, B, D
Notes: 2, 5, 7, 8, 9, 10

Dry Ridge Inn

Reed House
119 Dodge Street, 28803
(704) 274-1604

This comfortable Queen Anne Victorian with rocking chairs and swings on the porch has a rocking chair and fireplace in every room. Breakfast features homemade muffins, rolls, and jams and is served on the porch. Listed on the National Register of Historic Places; near Biltmore Estate.

Host: Marge Turcot
Rooms: 2 (SB) $50
Suite: 1 (PB) $75
Continental Breakfast
Credit Cards: A, B
Notes: 2, 7, 8, 9, 10, 11

BREVARD

The Red House Inn
412 West Probart Street, 28712
(704) 884-9349

The Red House was built in 1851 and has served as a trading post, a railroad station, the county's first courthouse, and the first post office. It has been lovingly restored and is now open to the public. Charmingly furnished with turn-of-the-century antiques. Convenient to the Blue Ridge Parkway, Brevard Music Center, and Asheville's Biltmore Estate.

Host: Mary Lynne MacGillycuddy
Rooms: 6 (1 PB; 5 S3B) $38-57
Full Breakfast
Credit Cards: A, B, C
Closed January-March
Notes: 2, 7, 8, 10

BRYSON CITY

Randolph House Inn
P.O. Box 816, 28713
(704) 488-3472

---

year; 6 Pets welcome; 7 Children welcome; 8 Tennis nearby; 9 Swimming nearby; 10 Golf nearby; 11 Skiing nearby; 12 May be booked through travel agent

The inn is located 60 miles southwest of Asheville in a quaint mountain town at the gateway to the Great Smoky Mountain National Park. It overlooks the town and is close to white-water activities, horseback riding, hiking, trout streams, Cherokee Indian Reservation, the Blue Ridge Parkway, Fontana Lake, and scenic trails and highways. Near depot and excursions on the Great Smoky Mountain railway. Listed on the National Register of Historic Places and recommended by the *New York Times*.

Hosts: Bill and Ruth Randolph Adams
Rooms: 6 (3 PB; 3 SB) $75
Full Breakfast
Credit Cards: A, B, C
Closed November-March
Notes: 2, 4, 8, 12

CHARLOTTE

The Morehead Inn
1122 East Morehead Street, 28204
(704) 376-3357; (800) 322-3965
FAX (704) 335-1110

A designated historic property, this inn is central to the downtown area and all other Charlotte-Mecklenburg suburbs. It is close to fine restaurants, shopping, buses, and airport. A southern estate, it is endowed with quiet elegance and spacious public areas. It is an excellent site for corporate and other executive conferences. Full catering service.

Room: 12 (PB) $79-115
Expanded Continental Breakfast

Credit Cards: A, B, C, E
Notes: 5, 7, 8, 10, 12

CLINTON

The Shield House
216 Sampson Street, 28328
(919) 592-2634

Reminiscent of "Gone with the Wind" and listed on the National Register of Historic Places, the Shield House has many dramatic features, including soaring Corinthian columns, wraparound porches, coffer ceilings with beading, and a large foyer with enclosed columns outlining a grand central-flight staircase. The red carpeted stairs twist up to a landing and then back to the front of the house. A large guest lounge is naturally lighted through glass doors that open only onto a balcony. Private phones, cable TV.

Hosts: Anita Green and Juanita G. McLamb
Rooms: 6 plus bungalow (PB) $45-75
Continental Breakfast
Credit Cards: A, B, D
Notes: 2, 4, 7, 8, 10

The Morehead Inn

NOTES: Credit cards accepted: A Master Card; B Visa; C American Express; D Discover Card; E Diners Club; F Other; 2 Personal checks accepted; 3 Lunch available; 4 Dinner available; 5 Open all

DURHAM

Arrowhead Inn
106 Mason Road, 27712
(919) 477-8430

The 1775 Colonial manor house is filled with antiques, quilts, samplers, and warmth. Located on four rural acres, Arrowhead features fireplaces, original architectural details, air conditioning, and homemade breakfasts. A two-room log cabin is also available. Easy access to restaurants, Duke University, University of North Carolina-Chapel Hill, Raleigh, and historic sites, including Duke Homestead Tobacco Museum and Bennett Place. Near I-85.

Hosts: Jerry, Barbara, and Cathy Ryan
Rooms: 8 (6 PB; 2 SB) $65-125
Full Breakfast
Credit Cards: A, B, C, E
Notes: 2, 5, 7, 8, 9, 10, 12

EAGLE SPRINGS

The Inn at Eagle Springs
Samarland Road, P. O. Box 56, 27242
(919) 673-2722

Previously a private girls' school, the inn is virtually unchanged but completely renovated. Located in the sandhills of North Carolina near Pinehurst, the golf capital of the world, it has access to more than 25 golf courses. One hour off Interstates 95, 85, 40, and 74. Can accommodate small conferences.

Hosts: Wes and Nora Smith
Rooms: 5 (PB) $50
Full Breakfast
Credit Cards: None
Notes: 2, 5, 7, 8, 9, 10, 12

FRANKLIN

Lullwater Retreat
950 Old Highlands Road, 28734
(704) 524-6532

The 120-year-old farmhouse and cabins are located on a river and creek in a peaceful mountain cove. Hiking trails, river swimming, tubing, and other outdoor activities are on the premises. It serves as a retreat center for church groups and family reunions. Guests cook their own meals or visit nearby restaurants. Chapel, rocking chairs, wonderful views, indoor and outdoor games. Christian videos, and reading materials are supplied.

Hosts: Robert and Virginia Smith
Rooms: 11 (5 PB; 6 SB) $30-45
Self-serve Breakfast
Credit Cards: None
Notes: 2, 5, 7, 8, 9, 10, 11

GLENDALE SPRINGS

Mountain View Lodge and Cabins
Blue Ridge Parkway Mile Post 256
P.O. Box 90, 28629
(919) 982-2233

---

year; 6 Pets welcome; 7 Children welcome; 8 Tennis nearby; 9 Swimming nearby; 10 Golf nearby; 11 Skiing nearby; 12 May be booked through travel agent

Secluded on the Blue Ridge Parkway, be pampered in our lodge with suites that offer fireplaces and beautiful views. Or enjoy a cabin with kitchenette. Families are welcome and play ground, picnic area, Jacuzzi, hiking, biking, skiing, canoeing are available. Breakfast and dinner are served in the lodge. Scenic and peaceful.

Hosts: George and Nellie Roth
Rooms: 12 (PB) $40-65
Expanded Continental Breakfast
Credit Cards: C
Notes: 2, 4 (limited weekends), 5, 7, 10, 11

GLENVILLE

Mountain High
Big Ridge Road, 28736
(704) 743-3094

Enjoy mountain views from an elevation of 4,200 feet in a quiet area with no houses nearby. Hike on trails around a private lake. Open July to November.

Host: George and Margaret Carter
Rooms: 3 (2 PB; 1 SB) $40
Full Breakfast
Credit Cards: None
Notes: 2, 8, 9, 10

Sunset Inn

HENDERSONVILLE

Claddagh Inn at Hendersonville
755 North Main Street, 28792
(704) 697-7778; (800) 225-4700 reservations

The Claddagh Inn at Hendersonville is a recently renovated, meticulously clean bed and breakfast that is eclectically furnished with antiques and a variety of collectibles. The inn is located two blocks from the main shopping promenade of beautiful, historic, downtown Hendersonville. The friendly, homelike atmosphere is complemented by a safe and secure feeling guests experience while at this lovely inn. The Claddaugh Inn is listed on the National Register of Historic Places.

Hosts: Vicki and Dennis Pacilio
Rooms: 15 (PB) $49-79
Full Breakfast
Credit Cards: A, B, C, D
Notes: 2, 5, 7, 8, 19, 10, 12

LAKE JUNALUSKA

Providence Lodge
207 Atkins Loop, 28745
(704) 456-6486

Providence Lodge is located on the assembly grounds of the United Methodist Church and near the Great Smoky Mountain National Park, Biltmore Estate, and the Cherokee Indian Reservation. The lodge is old, rustic, clean, and comfortable. Meals are especially

---

NOTES: Credit cards accepted: A Master Card; B Visa; C American Express; D Discover Card; E Diners Club; F Other; 2 Personal checks accepted; 3 Lunch available; 4 Dinner available; 5 Open all

good—bountiful, delicious food served family style in our large dining room.

Hosts: Ben and Wilma Cato
Rooms: 16 (10 PB; 6 SB) $45-80
Full Breakfast
Credit Cards: None
Closed September 15-June 1
Notes: 2, 4, 7, 8, 9, 10, 11, 12

Sunset Inn

300 North Lakeshore Drive, 28745
(704) 456-6114; (800) 733-6114

A beautiful mountain inn with large porches, comfortable rooms, and a location that lends itself to sight-seeing, area attractions, or rest. We take pride in maintaining our reputation for excellent food, and we try to make our guests feel pampered. Located on the assembly grounds of the United Methodist Church, which schedules daily programs in summer.

Hosts: Norma Wright and Wilma Cato
Rooms: 19 (15 PB; 4 SB) $60-80
Full Breakfast
Credit Cards: None
Notes: 2, 4, 8, 9, 10, 11, 12

NAGS HEAD

First Colony Inn

6720 South Virginia Dare Trail, 27959
(919) 441-2343; (800) 368-9390 reservations

Enjoy southern hospitality in our completely renovated historic inn with a boardwalk directly to our private ocean beach. We are the only historic bed and breakfast inn on North Carolina's outer banks. The Wright Brothers Memorial, lighthouses, Fort Raleigh (site of the first English colony in the New World) are nearby, or just rock on our two stories of wraparound verandas.

Hosts: The Lawrences
Rooms: 26 (PB) $50-100 winter; $60-110 spring/fall; $100-200 summer
Continental Breakfast
Credit Cards: A, B, D
Notes: 2, 4, 5, 7, 8, 9, 10, 12

NEW BERN

Harmony House Inn

215 Pollock Street, 28560
(919) 636-3810

Enjoy comfortable elegance in an unusually spacious Greek Revival inn built circa 1850 with final additions circa 1900. Guests enjoy a parlor, front porch with rocking chairs and swings, antiques and reproductions, plus a full breakfast in the dining room. Located in the historic district near Tryon Palace, shops, and restaurants.

Hosts: A. E. and Diane Hansen
Rooms: 9 (PB) $55-80
Full Breakfast
Credit Cards: A, B, C
Notes: 2, 5, 8, 10, 12

New Berne House Inn

709 Broad Street, 28560
(919) 636-2250; (800) 842-7688

---

year; 6 Pets welcome; 7 Children welcome; 8 Tennis nearby; 9 Swimming nearby; 10 Golf nearby; 11 Skiing nearby; 12 May be booked through travel agent

Just around the corner from Tryon Palace, New Berne House offers hospitality and comfortable English country decor in a lovingly restored brick Colonial. Seven guest rooms with private vintage baths, high antique beds piled with pillows and lace, air conditioning, phones, and optional TV are available. "Breakfasts that will be served in some small corner of heaven," the *Charlotte Observer*. Afternoon tea is served in the rose parlor or library.

Hosts: David and Gina Hawkins
Rooms: 7 (PB) $55-75
Full Breakfast
Credit Cards: A, B, C, D
Notes: 2, 5, 6 (by arrangement), 7, 8, 9, 10, 12

ORIENTAL

The Tar Heel Inn
205 Church Street, P. O. Box 176, 28571
(919) 249-1078

The Tar Heel Inn is more than 100 years old and has been restored to capture the atmosphere of an English country inn. Guest rooms have four-poster or canopy king and queen beds. Patios, gardens, and bicycles are for guest use. Six churches are within walking distance. Tennis, fishing, and golf are nearby. This quiet fishing village is known as the sailing capital of the Carolinas. Sailing cruises can be arranged.

Hosts: David and Patti Nelson
Rooms: 7 (PB) $65-75
Full Breakfast
Credit Cards: A, B
Notes: 2, 7, 8, 9, 10, 12

SALISBURY

The 1868 Stewart-Marsh House
220 South Ellis Street, 28144
(704) 633-6841

This Federal-style 1868 home is on a quiet, tree-lined street in the historic district. Spacious guest rooms have antiques, heart-of-pine floors, and air conditioning. Enjoy the cozy library and screened porch with wicker furniture. Homemade breads and muffins and the breakfast entree are served in the sunny dining room. Historic sites, churches, shopping, and restaurants are all within walking distance. One and one-half miles off I-85, Exit 76B.

Hosts: Gerry and Chuck Webster
Rooms: 2 (PB) $50-55
Expanded Continental Breakfast
Credit Cards: A, B
Notes: 2, 5, 7, 8, 10

The Tar Heel Inn

SPARTA

Turby-Villa
East Whitehead Street, Star Route 1
Box 48, 28675
(919) 372-8490

NOTES: Credit cards accepted: A Master Card; B Visa; C American Express; D Discover Card; E Diners Club; F Other; 2 Personal checks accepted; 3 Lunch available; 4 Dinner available; 5 Open all

At an altitude of 3,000 feet, this contemporary two-story home is the centerpiece of a 20-acre farm located two miles from town. The house is surrounded by an acre of trees and manicured lawn with a lovely view of the Blue Ridge Mountains. Breakfast is served either on the enclosed porch with white wicker furnishings or in the more formal dining room with Early American furnishings.

Hosts: Maybelline Turbiville
Rooms: 3 (PB) $35-50
Full Breakfast
Credit Cards: None
Notes: 2, 7, 8, 9

SPRUCE PINE

The Fairway Inn Bed and Breakfast
110 Henry Lane, 28777
(704) 765-4917

A lovely, inviting country home on an 18-hole golf course has a mountain view and five large bedrooms beautifully decorated with soft, appealing colors. Furnishings are eclectic. Your hosts offer tea and cheese in the afternoon. Morning coffee is provided for early risers, and a gourmet breakfast is served at your leisure. Open from April through December.

Hosts: Margaret and John Stevens
Rooms: 5 (PB) $50-70
Full Breakfast
Credit Cards: A, B
Notes: 2, 7, 8, 9, 10, 11

STATESVILLE

Aunt Mae's Bed and Breakfast
532 East Broad Street, 28677
(704) 873-9525

Once through the doors of our century-old home, you know you have stepped back in time. In her 90 years, Aunt Mae collected so many treasures that we cannot display them all at once. Hence, we have an ever-changing decor. Enjoy morning coffee left outside your door, a full breakfast, and homemade snacks. Convenient to I-40, I-77, historic downtown, and tennis courts. Golf and lake close by.

Hosts: Richard and Sue Rowland
Rooms: 2 (PB) $50
Full Breakfast
Credit Cards: A, B
Notes: 2, 5, 8, 9, 10, 12

TRYON

Fox Trot Inn
P. O. Box 1561, 28782
(704) 859-9706

This lovingly restored residence, circa 1915, is situated on six wooded acres within the city limits. It is convenient to everything, yet secluded with a quietly elegant atmosphere. Full gourmet breakfast, afternoon refreshments, heated swimming pool, fully furnished guest house with two bedrooms, kitchen, livingroom, deck with mountain views. Two guest rooms have sitting rooms.

Hosts: Betty Daugherty and Mimi Colby
Rooms: 4 (PB) $60-90
Guest House: $450 weekly
Full Breakfast
Credit Cards: None
Notes: 2, 8, 10

WAYNESVILLE

The Lodge at the Biodome
184 Shelton Cove Road, 28786
(704) 926-0273

The lodge is an eight-bedroom, four-bath bed and breakfast in the North Carolina biodome eco village. The village has eight homes, a Bunkminster Fuller geodesic dome as a greenhouse, organic gardens, solar and hydro systems, and many other aspects of a self-sufficient village. Rooms have twin, queen, or king beds.

Host: Hans Keller
Rooms: 8 (SB) $40
Contiental Breakfast
Credic Cards: A, B, C
Notes: 4, 5, 6, 7, 8, 9, 10, 11

Palmer House Bed and Breakfast
108 Pigeon Street, 28786
(704) 456-7521

Built in the 1880s, the Palmer House is the last of Waynesville's once numerous 19th-century hotels. Located less than one block from Main Street, the Palmer House is also near the Blue Ridge Parkway, the Great Smoky Mountains, Cherokee, and Biltmore Estate. Guests are entitled to a 10-percent discount off any purchase at the Palmer House Bookshop on Main Street.

Hosts: Jeff Minick and Kris Gillet
Rooms: 7 (PB) $50
Full Breakfast
Credit Cards: A, B, C
Notes: 2, 5, 7

WILSON

Miss Betty's Bed and Breakfast Inn
600 West Nash Street, 27893-3045
(919) 243-4447; (800) 258-2058 reservations

The inn is comprised of two historic structures. The Davis-Whitehead-Harriss house, circa 1858, which has been beautifully restored, has four bedrooms, two parlors, and a dining room. The adjacent Riley House, circa 1900, includes a large executive suite, three guest bedrooms, and a conference/workshop/meeting room, complete with all the necessary audio/visual aids. The theme of the inn is Victorian elegance with modern-day conveniences.

Host: Elizabeth A. Spitz
Rooms: 8 (PB) $60-80
Full Breakfast
Credit Cards: A, B, C, D
Notes: 2, 5, 8, 9, 10, 12

NOTES: Credit cards accepted: A Master Card; B Visa; C American Express; D Discover Card; E Diners Club; F Other; 2 Personal checks accepted; 3 Lunch available; 4 Dinner available; 5 Open all

North Dakota

DICKINSON

Joyce's Home Away from Home Bed and Breakfast
1561 First Avenue East, 58601
(701) 227-1524

All white brick, this large ranch-style home was built in 1983. It is located just off I-94 Exit 13, just minutes from shopping malls. The house features a large family room with fireplace and cable TV/VCR. An exercise room is also available. Jacuzzi; freshly baked goodies. Coffee is always on.

Host: Joyce Scott
Rooms: 4 (2 PB; 2 SB) $40-65
Continental Breakfast
Credit Cards: None
Notes: 2, 3, 4, 5, 8, 9, 10

LIDGERWOOD

Kaler's Bed and Breakfast
9650 Highway 18, 58053
(701) 538-4848

Enjoy country living on this 640-acre small grain farm situated in pheasant heartland. This older home has four beautiful bedrooms upstairs. A delicious full breakfast is served, and children are most welcome.

Host: Dorothy Kaler
Rooms: 4 (SB) $30
Full Breakfast
Credit Cards: None
Notes: 2, 5, 7, 8, 9, 10

---

year; 6 Pets welcome; 7 Children welcome; 8 Tennis nearby; 9 Swimming nearby; 10 Golf nearby; 11 Skiing nearby; 12 May be booked through travel agent

Ohio

Yesterday Bed and Breakfast

CENTERVILLE

Yesterday Bed and Breakfast
39 South Main Street, 45458
(513) 433-1660

Yesterday Bed and Breakfast is located ten miles south of downtown Dayton in the Centerville historic district, which features unique shops and museums. Lavender and Old Lace, featuring vintage linens and fine bath products, is on our premises. Yesterday is an easy drive from the Air Force Museum, Kings Island Amusement Park, historic towns, and antique centers. Your hosts, longtime area residents, will be happy to suggest other attractions in the area. Discount of $5 for stay of three nights or more.

Hosts: Tom and Barbara Monnig
Rooms: 3 (PB) $60-65
Expanded Continental Breakfast
Credit Cards: None
Notes: 2, 5, 7 (over 11), 8, 10, 11

DANVILLE

The White Oak Inn
29683 Walhonding Road, 43014
(614) 599-6107

This turn-of-the-century farmhouse on 14 acres in the rolling hills of northcentral Ohio features rooms with antiques and quilts or comforters. Three rooms have fireplaces; four have queen beds. With a large fireplace, the common room is comfortable for reading, playing board games, or socializing. The grounds and adjacent conservation land are ideal for hiking, canoeing, and other outdoor activities. Area attractions include the largest Amish population in the world, antiqueing, and a restored, historic canal town, Roscoe

---

NOTES: Credit cards accepted: A Master Card; B Visa; C American Express; D Discover Card; E Diners Club; F Other; 2 Personal checks accepted; 3 Lunch available; 4 Dinner available; 5 Open all

Village. Facilities are available for meetings, retreat, weddings, and receptions.

Hosts: Joyce and Jim Acton
Rooms: 10 (PB) $60-130
Full Breakfast
Credit Cards: A, B
Notes: 2, 4, 5, 8, 10, 12

EAST FULTONHAM

Hill View Acres Bed and Breakfast
7320 Old Town Road, 43735
(614) 849-2728

Old World hospitality and comfort await each of our guests. During your visit, wander over the 21 acres, relax on the deck or patio, use the pool or year-round spa, or cuddle up by the fireplace in the cooler months. A hearty, country breakfast with homemade breads, jams, and jellies is served. We are located ten miles southwest of Zanesville.

Hosts: Jim and Dawn Graham
Rooms: 2 (SB) $35-40; 5% discount for cash
Full Breakfast
Credit Cards: A, B
Notes: 2, 3, 4 (by arrangement), 5, 6 (by arrangement), 7, 9, 10

GENEVA-ON-THE-LAKE

Otto Court Bed and Breakfast
5653 Lake Road, 44041
(216) 466-8668

Otto Court Bed and Breakfast is a family-run business situated on two acres of lakefront property. There are eight cottages and a 19-room hotel overlooking Lake Erie. Besides a small game room, there is a horseshoe pit, a volleyball court, picnic tables, and plenty of beach with area for a bonfire. Within walking distance is the Geneva State Park and Marina. The Old Firehouse winery, Geneva-on-the-Lake Amusement Center, and the Jennie Munger Museum are nearyby.

Hosts: Joyce Otto and family
Rooms: 12 (8 PB; 4 SB) $45
Full Breakfast
Credit Cards: A, B, F
Notes: 2, 4, 5, 7, 9, 10, 12

LEXINGTON

The White Fence Inn
8842 Denman Road, 44904
(419) 884-2356; (800) 628-5793

The White Fence Inn is a beautiful country retreat situated among 73 acres. The 100-year-old farmhouse is decorated in a warm, country style. Common rooms include a large dining room with French doors, a parlor with fireplace and piano, a spacious sitting room with fireplace and TV. Breakfast is served indoors or outdoors. Guest rooms are decorated in individual themes—primitive, baskets and bottles, Victorian, Southwest, Amish, and country. One room has a fireplace and cathedral ceiling.

---

year; 6 Pets welcome; 7 Children welcome; 8 Tennis nearby; 9 Swimming nearby; 10 Golf nearby; 11 Skiing nearby; 12 May be booked through travel agent

Hosts: Bill and Ellen Hiser
Rooms: 6 (4 PB; 2 SB) $49-90
Full Breakfast
Credit Cards: None
Notes: 2, 5, 6, 7, 8, 10, 11

MILLERSBURG

Adams Street Bed and Breakfast

175 West Adams Street, 44654
(216) 674-0766

This homey bed and breakfast in a century-old home with white fence is in Holmes County, the center of Ohio's large Amish community. The cozy library has a cookbook collection and books on the Amish. Gourmet breakfast, porches, air conditioning. Abigail Adams, the resident cat, welcomes guests.

Host: Alma Kaufman
Rooms: 2 (SB) $45-55
Full Breakfast
Credit Cards: None
Note: 2

Kaufman's Bed and Breakfast

9905 State Route 39, 44654
(216) 674-4123

Welcome to an Amish-Mennonite home in scenic Holmes County with a quiet country setting and comfortable rooms. Relax in the large family room with fireplace, enjoy a book, or a play a game of Ping-Pong. There are two rooms with a shared bath and an apartment with private bath. Advance reservations advised; deposit required.

Hosts: Reuben and Elva Kaufman
Rooms: 2 plus apartment (1 PB; 2 SB) $45-60
Full Breakfast
Credit Cards: None
Notes: 2, 5, 7, 9, 10

NEWARK

Pitzer-Cooper House

6019 White Chapel Road, Southeast, 43056
(614) 323-2680

Step back into a quieter, simpler time at this recently restored 1858 country home listed on the National Register of Historic Places. Enjoy the large porch with swings, perennial and herb gardens, and pond. Inside, there are a common room and a music room with stereo and baby grand piano for the enjoyment and relaxation of guests. Delicious breakfasts feature fruit and homemade breads. A quiet, rural setting only five minutes from I-70.

Hosts: Joe and Teresa Cooper
Rooms: 2 (SB) $55
Full Breakfast
Credit Cards: None
Notes: 5, 7, 9, 10, 12

NEW RICHMOND

Hollyhock Bed and Breakfast

1610 Altman Road, 45157
(513) 553-6585

NOTES: Credit cards accepted: A Master Card; B Visa; C American Express; D Discover Card; E Diners Club; F Other; 2 Personal checks accepted; 3 Lunch available; 4 Dinner available; 5 Open all

An 1853 restored farmhouse on ten acres is nestled by hundreds of acres of woods, hills, and streams. The hostess tends a small flock of Dorset sheep, raising new lambs each spring. A small farm operates with many flower gardens, a pond to fish in, and wildlife aplenty. The queen suite is comprised of a bedroom and private parlor with fireplace. It is on the first floor with access to patio and deck for moonlit nights and beautiful sunsets and sunrises. A second room is available for couples traveling together.

Host: Evelyn Cutter
Room: 2 (PB) $55-75 rented together
Continental or Full Breakfast
Credit Cards: None
Notes: 2, 3, 4, 5, 6, 7, 8, 9, 10

PEEBLES

The Bayberry Inn Bed and Breakfast
25675 State Route 41, 45660
(513) 587-2221

You will find warm hospitality, cozy accommodations with comfortable appointments, and a front porch on which to relax after a hearty, old-fashioned breakfast. This Victorian farmhouse is located in Adams County, the hub for those with geological, historical, recreational, and agricultural interests. You are certain to enjoy visiting Serpent Mound, museums, natural wildlife areas, and herb gardens. Reservations are suggested.

Host: Marilyn F. Bagford
Rooms: 3 (SB) $45
Full Breakfast
Credit Cards: None
Closed November-April
Notes: 2, 7, 10

SANDUSKY

Bogarts Corner Bed and Breakfast
1403 East Bogart Road and U.S. 250, 44870
(419) 627-2707

We want you to feel at home, and people say that we have accomplished that. Our country-decor home is easily accessible to I-80 and I-90 for east-west travelers and only minutes from Lake Erie and all it has to offer. Near Cedar Point, a recreation park on more than 300 acres.

Hosts: Davilee and Zendon Willis
Rooms: 4 (2 PB; 2 SB) $35-45
Full Breakfast
Credit Cards: None
Closed October 1-April 30
Notes: 2, 7, 8, 9, 10

TIPP CITY

The Willow Tree Inn
1900 West State Route 571, 45371
(513) 667-2957

This restored pre-Civil War (1830) Federal manor home has a pond and combination springhouse and smokehouse. The original 1830 barn is also on the premises. Four working fireplaces,

---

year; 6 Pets welcome; 7 Children welcome; 8 Tennis nearby; 9 Swimming nearby; 10 Golf nearby; 11 Skiing nearby; 12 May be booked through travel agent

porches on which to swing and relax, and TV and air conditioning in all rooms; all but one room are suites. Easily located off Exit 68W from N75, just minutes north of Dayton.

Hosts: Tom and Peggy Nordquist
Rooms: 4 (1 PB; 3 SB) $45-65
Full Breakfast
Credit Cards: A, B
Notes: 2, 7 (over 8), 8, 9, 10

through present-day Zanesville, Lancaster, and Chillicothe, Ohio to Maysville, Kentucky. Guests enjoy breakfast in the dining room, which is part of the original house, or in the casual eating area of the newer addition.

Hosts: Anne and Paul Mechling
Rooms: 2 (SB) $35
Full Breakfast
Credit Cards: None
Notes: 2, 5, 7

Willow Tree Inn

Wal-Mec Farm Bed and Breakfast

THORNVILLE

Wal-Mec Farm Bed and Breakfast
5663 State Route 204 Northwest, 43076
(614) 246-5450

A stately Victorian house surrounded by lush trees and lawns, the Wal-Mec farm was built around 1860. It is located near the historic Zane's Trace, a highway built by Ebenezer Zane in 1797 that ran from Wheeling, West Virginia

WAVERLY

Governor's Lodge
171 Gregg Road, 45690
(614) 947-2266

Governor's Lodge is a place like no other. Imagine a beautiful, shimmering lake and an iridescent sunset. A quiet calm in the friendly atmosphere of an eight-room bed and breakfast open all

---

NOTES: Credit cards accepted: A Master Card; B Visa; C American Express; D Discover Card; E Diners Club; F Other; 2 Personal checks accepted; 3 Lunch available; 4 Dinner available; 5 Open all

year and situated on a peninsula in Lake White. Every room has a magnificent view. An affiliate of Bristol Village Retirement Community, we offer a meeting room and group rates for gatherings using the whole lodge.

Hosts: David and Jeannie James
Rooms: 8 (PB) $37-62
Expanded Continental Breakfast
Credit Cards: A, B
Notes: 2, 7, 9, 11

WEST MILTON

Locust Lane Farm Bed and Breakfast
5590 Kessler Cowlesville Road, 45383
(513) 698-4743

Delightful, old Cape Cod home in a rural setting 20 minutes north of Dayton and seven miles southwest of Troy. Browse through local antique shops, enjoy the nature center, golf course, and canoeing. Choose from queen or double guest rooms with private or shared bath. Relax in the library or in front of the fireplace. Full breakfast is served on the screened porch in the summer. I-75, Exit 69.

Hosts: Don and Ruth Shoup
Rooms: 3 (1 PB; 2 SB) $40-50
Full Breakfast
Credit Cards: None
Notes: 2, 5, 7, 10

Oklahoma

OKLAHOMA CITY

The Grandison
1841 Northwest 15th, 73106
(405) 521-0011

Built circa 1896 and updated in 1913, this brick and shingle three-story house is situated on lawns and gardens enhanced by fruit trees and a gazebo. Original stained glass and brass fixtures remain, and the decor is an airy, country Victorian. The bridal suite includes a working fireplace, white lace curtains, and a claw foot tub. Convenient to downtown Oklahoma City and the interstate system.

Hosts: Claudia and Bob Wright
Rooms: 5 (PB) $45-100
Full Breakfast
Credit Cards: A, B, C
Notes: 2, 4, 5, 12

NOTES: Credit cards accepted: A Master Card; B Visa; C American Express; D Discover Card; E Diners Club; F Other; 2 Personal checks accepted; 3 Lunch available; 4 Dinner available; 5 Open all

Oregon

ASHLAND

Mt. Ashland Inn
550 Mt. Ashland Road, 97520
(503) 482-8707

Enjoy mountain serenity and warm hospitality in this beautifully hand-crafted log inn 16 miles from Ashland. The craftsmanship and attention to detail is evident throughout in the hand carvings, Finelt-crafted furniture, stained glass, rock fireplace, and comfortable yet elegant decor. The inn's five guest rooms, including three romantic suites, all have spectacular views. Hike, bike, or cross-country ski from the inn's door, or downhill ski nearby.

Hosts: Jerry and Elaine Shanafelt
Rooms: 5 (PB) $75-125
Full Breakfast
Credit Cards: A, B
Notes: 2, 5, 10, 11, 12

BROOKINGS

Chetco River Inn
21202 High Prairie Road, 97415
(503) 469-8128

Old World hospitality with New World comfort is achieved while using alternative energy sources. The inn is small; guest numbers are limited to give you peaceful tranquility on the 35 wooded acres right along the river. Beds are comfortable, and the food is good. We are 17 miles from a small seacoast town with beautiful beaches.

Host: Sandra Brugger
Rooms: 4 (3 PB; 1 SB) $75-85
Full Breakfast
Credit Cards: A, B
Notes: 2, 3, 4, 9

Mt. Ashland Inn

---

year; 6 Pets welcome; 7 Children welcome; 8 Tennis nearby; 9 Swimming nearby; 10 Golf nearby; 11 Skiing nearby; 12 May be booked through travel agent

CANNON BEACH

Tern Inn
3663 South Hemlock, P. O. Box 952, 97110
(503) 436-1528

A personal touch in an impersonal world. Home-baked goods and homemade jams and jellies are part of the complete, hot breakfast or brunch cooked from scratch and served in your room anytime between 8:30 and 11:30 A.M. We are located on the north coast of Oregon in the arts resort of Cannon Beach. We offer light goose-down quilts for year-round comfort, private bath, and color TV. Choose between a fireplace or a sunroom to warm your heart.

Hosts: Gunter-Chris and Enken Friedrichsen
Rooms: 2 (PB) $75-95
Full Breakfast
Credit Cards: None
Closed January
Notes: 2, 8, 10

CLOVERDALE

Sandlake Country Inn
8505 Galloway Road, 97112
(503) 965-6745

This 1894 farmhouse on the Oregon historic register is the perfect hideaway for making marriage memories. The honeymoon suite offers a four-room sanctuary with private luxury bath, deck, view of Cape Lookout, parlor, and vintage movies. One mile from the beach; private garden spa; bikes and picnic lunches available; forest setting.

Hosts: Margo and Charles Underwood
Rooms: 4 (PB) $65-100
Full Breakfast
Credit Cards: A, B
Notes: 2, 3, 4, 5, 12

ELMIRA

McGillivray's Log Home Bed and Breakfast
88680 Evers Road, 97437
(503) 935-3564

Fourteen miles west of Eugene, on the way to the coast, you will find the best of yesterday and the comforts of today. King beds, air conditioning, and quiet. Old-fashioned breakfasts are usually prepared on an antique wood-burning cookstove. This built-from-scratch new log home is near Fern Ridge.

Host: Evelyn R. McGillivray
Rooms: 2 (PB) $50-70
Full Breakfast
Credit Cards: A, B
Notes: 2, 5, 7

EUGENE

Kjaer's House in the Woods
814 Lorane Highway, 97405
(503) 343-3234

The House in the Woods is a turn-of-the-century Craftsman-style home in a tranquil setting of fir, oak, azaleas, and rhododendrons. A respite from traffic and crowds, the house has a porch swing, quiet spots for reading

---

NOTES: Credit cards accepted: A Master Card; B Visa; C American Express; D Discover Card; E Diners Club; F Other; 2 Personal checks accepted; 3 Lunch available; 4 Dinner available; 5 Open all

and reflection, bird watching, walking, or listening to music.

Hosts: Eunice and George Kjaer
Rooms: 2 (1 PB; 1 SB) $40-65
Full Breakfast
Credit Cards: None
Closed December 20-January 3
Notes: 2, 7, 8, 9, 10

LA GRANDE

Pitcher Inn Bed and Breakfast
608 N Avenue, 97850
(503) 963-9152

The hosts have redecorated their 1925 home to maintain its original flavor. The homey dining room with oak floor and table welcomes you for a full breakfast. The unique, open staircase will lead you to your room. Each of four guest rooms has a touch of romance featuring a different color theme with accents of roses, bows, and pitchers. The honeymoon suite is a spacious room of lace and roses.

Hosts: Carl and Deanne Pitcher
Rooms: 4 (1 PB; 3 S2B) $55-80
Full Breakfast
Credit Cards: A, B
Closed January 2-15
Notes: 2, 8, 10, 11

LINCOLN CITY

The Rustic Inn
2313 Northeast Holmes Road, 97367
(503) 994-5111

This log cabin-style home has a comfortable, homey atmosphere in a garden setting within walking distance of the ocean. Rooms are decorated with antiques and have color TV. One room has a Jacuzzi for two, one room is handicapped accessible, and two rooms have a private entrance. We are near antique shops and a large outlet mall. We have a large front porch and rear deck for your relaxation.

Hosts: Evelyn and Lloyd Bloomberg
Rooms: 3 (PB) $40 Sunday through Thursday
Full Breakfast
Credit Cards: A, B
Notes: 2, 10, 12

Secluded Bed and Breakfast

NEWBERG

Secluded Bed and Breakfast
19719 Northeast Williamson Road, 97132
(503) 538-2635

This secluded, beautiful, country home on ten acres is an ideal retreat in a wooded setting for hiking, walking in the country, and observing wildlife. Located near Newberg behind the beautiful Red Hills of Dundee, it is convenient to George Fox College. McMinnville is a 20-minute drive, and the Oregon coast is one hour away. A delectable breakfast varies for your pleasure, tempting you with succulent French farm fruit from the famous Willamette Valley of Oregon. The home has many antiques and collectibles and stained glass in each room.

Hosts: Del and Durell Belanger
Rooms: 2 (1 PB; 1 SB) $40-50
Full Breakfast
Credit Cards: None
Notes: 2, 5, 7, 8, 9, 10

STAYTON

Horncroft
42156 Kingston-Lyons Drive, 97383
(503) 769-6287

This private home in a quiet, rural area southeast of Stayton is 12 miles east of Salem, the center of the Willamette Valley, a rich and scenic agricultural area. Mt. Jefferson Wilderness Area is one hour east; ocean beaches are one and one-half hours west.

Hosts: Dr. and Mrs. K. H. Horn
Rooms: 3 (1 PB; 2 SB) $35-45
Full Breakfast
Credit Cards: None
Closed Holidays
Notes: 2, 8, 9, 10, 11

WILSONVILLE

The Willows Bed and Breakfast
5025 Southwest Homesteader Road, 97070
(503) 638-3722

Surprisingly, this quiet, secluded spot is just two miles off I-5 and 20 minutes from downtown Portland. The home is furnished with many lovely antiques and surrounded by flowers, lawn, creek, and huge willow and fir trees. An elegant full breakfast includes a variety of fruits from the hosts' garden. Your private suite includes a phone, TV, and guest refrigerator. Travel information, with maps and brochures, is available to help you enjoy the many sights of the area.

Hosts: Dave and Shirlee Key
Rooms: 2 (PB) $45-55
Full Breakfast
Credit Cards: None
Notes: 2, 5, 7 (over 12), 8, 9, 10, 11

NOTES: Credit cards accepted: A Master Card; B Visa; C American Express; D Discover Card; E Diners Club; F Other; 2 Personal checks accepted; 3 Lunch available; 4 Dinner available; 5 Open all

Pennsylvania

ADAMSTOWN

Adamstown Inn
62 West Main Street, 19501-0938
(215) 484-0800; (800) 594-4808

Experience simple elegance in a Victorian home resplendent with leaded-glass windows and door, magnificent chestnut woodwork, and Oriental rugs. All four guest rooms are decorated with family heirlooms, handmade quilts, lace curtains, fresh flowers, and many distinctive touches. Accommodations range from antique to king beds. Two rooms have Jacuzzis for two. The inn is located in a small town brimming with antique dealers and only minutes from Reading and Lancaster.

Hosts: Tom and Wanda Berman
Rooms: 4 (PB) $65-95
Expanded Continental Breakfast
Credit Cards: A, B
Notes: 2, 5, 8, 9, 10, 12

AIRVILLE

Spring House
Muddy Creek Forks, 17302
(717) 927-6906

Built in 1798 of warm fieldstone, Spring House is a fine example of colonial architecture with original stenciling. Overlooking a river valley, the house has welcomed guests from around the world who seek a historic setting, tranquility, and access to Amish country and Gettysburg. Regional breakfast specialties and Amish cheeses welcome the traveler.

Host: Ray Constance Hearne
Rooms: 5 (3 PB; 2 SB) $60-85
Full Breakfast
Credit Cards: None
Notes: 2, 5, 7, 9, 10

Adamstown Inn

---

year; 6 Pets welcome; 7 Children welcome; 8 Tennis nearby; 9 Swimming nearby; 10 Golf nearby; 11 Skiing nearby; 12 May be booked through travel agent

ATGLEN

Glen Run Valley View Farm
Rural Delivery 1, Box 69, 19310
(215) 593-5656

In Chester County in southeastern Pennsylvania, this 50-acre farm is owned and operated by a Mennonite family. Guests can pick vegetables, blackberries, and wild strawberries in season and can help or watch the gathering of farm-fresh eggs and milking. Wholesome, country-style, home-cooked meals are eaten with the family. Nearby attractions include Gettysburg, Hershey chocolate plant, cloisters, Longwood Gardens, Wheatland, Lancaster County, Amish folk, Dutch Wonderland. Mrs. Stoltzfus also makes quilts for sale.

Hosts: Harold and Hanna Stoltzfus
Rooms: 3 (1 PB; 2 SB) $40-55
Full Breakfast
Credit Cards: None
Notes: 2, 4, 5, 6, 7, 10, 12

BEAUMONT

Ponda-Rowland Bed and Breakfast Inn and Farm Vacations
Rural Route 1, Box 349, 18612
(717) 639-3245; (800) 950-9130 noon to 4:00 P.M.

On this large, scenic farm in the endless mountain region of northeast Pennsylvania, guests enjoy 34 acres of a private wildlife refuge, including six ponds, walking and skiing trails, canoeing, swimming, ice skating, ice fishing, horseshoes, and badminton. Nearby are horseback riding, air tours, state parks, trout fishing, hunting, restaurants, county fairs, downhill skiing. The farmhouse, circa 1850, features a large stone fireplace, beamed ceilings, and museum-quality country antiques.

Hosts: Jeannette and Cliff Rowland
Rooms: 5 (4 PB; 1 SB) $50-70
Full Breakfast
Credit Cards: A, B
Notes: 2, 5, 7, 9, 10, 11, 12

BIRD-IN-HAND

Greystone Manor
P. O. Box 270, 17505
(717) 393-4233

Greystone Manor is a lovely, old, French Victorian mansion and carriage house with Victorian furnishings and decorative windows and doors. It sits on two acres of shaded lawn with flowering trees and plants. Surrounded by Amish farms, we are minutes from Lancaster, Lititz, Intercourse, and Strasburg. Near the farmers' market, outlet malls, and local craft shops.

Host: Sally Davis
Rooms: 13 (PB) $50-90
Continental Breakfast
Credit Cards: A, B
Notes: 2, 5, 7, 8, 9

NOTES: Credit cards accepted: A Master Card; B Visa; C American Express; D Discover Card; E Diners Club; F Other; 2 Personal checks accepted; 3 Lunch available; 4 Dinner available; 5 Open all

CAMBRIDGE SPRINGS

Bethany Guest House
325 South Main Street, 16403
(814) 398-2046; (800) 777-2046

Relax in the luxury of an 1876 Italianate home built in a Victorian resort community by one of the area's pionerring Christian families. This home on the National Register of Historic Places has been restored and is decorated with period furnishings. It has a parlor, drawing room, Greek Revival dining room, and library. The covenant room, with a double-wide whirlpool, is ideal for special occasions. Visit nearby Lake Erie, wildlife refuges, bicycle trails, and amusement parks. Christian missionaries stay at no charge Sunday through Thursday, and clergy discounts are available.

Hosts: David and Katie White
Rooms: 4 (PB) $35-55
Full Breakfast
Credit Cards: A, B, D
Notes: 2, 5, 7, 8, 9, 10, 11, 12

Line Limousin Farmhouse

CANADENSIS

Dreamy Acres
Route 447 and Seese Hill Road, 18325-0007
(717) 595-7115

Esther and Bill Pickett started Dreamy Acres as a bed and breakfast inn in 1959, doing bed and breakfast before it was in style. Situated on three acres with a stream and a pond, Dreamy Acres is in the heart of the Pocono Mountains vacationland, close to stores, churches, gift shops, and recreational facilities. Guest rooms have air conditioning, color cable TV, and some have VCRs. Continental breakfast served May 1 through October 31. Open year-round.

Hosts: Esther and Bill Pickett
Rooms: 6 (4 PB; 2 SB) $34-50
Expanded Continental Breakfast
Credit Cards: None
Notes: 2, 5, 8, 9, 10, 11

CARLISLE

Line Limousin Farmhouse
2070 Ritner Highway, 17013
(717) 243-1281

Relax and unwind in an 1864 brick and stone farmhouse on 100 acres, two miles off I-81, Exit 12. French Limousin cattle are raised here. Enjoy antiques, including a player piano, the use of a golf driving range. Join us for worship at our historic First Presbyterian Church. One suite and two rooms with king/twin extra-long beds. No smoking.

Hosts: Bob and Joan Line
Rooms: 3 (2 PB; 1 SB) $45-55
Full Breakfast
Credit Cards: None
Notes: 2, 5, 7, 10

CHAMBERSBURG

Falling Spring Inn
1838 Falling Spring Road, 17201
(717) 267-3654

Enjoy country living only two miles from I-81, Exit 6 and Route 30, on a working farm with animals and Falling Spring, a nationally renowned freshwater trout stream. A large pond, lawns, meadows, ducks, and birds all make a pleasant story. Historic Gettysburg is only 25 miles away. Relax in our air-conditioned rooms with queen beds.

Hosts: Adin and Janet Frey
Rooms: 5 (PB) $49-69
Full Breakfast
Credit Cards: A, B
Notes: 2, 7, 8, 9, 10

CHRISTIANA

Winding Glen Farm Guest Home
107 Noble Road, 17509
(215) 593-5535

Winding Glen is a dairy farm situated in a beautiful valley. Guests stay in the 250-year-old stone farmhouse with 16-inch walls. A full breakfast is served. You can watch the cows being milked and feed the calves. See "Our Way of Life" slide show set to music and narration. Handmade quilts are for sale. Many Amish shops and stores are nearby.

Host: Minnie B. Metzler
Rooms: 5 (SB) $35
Full Breakfast
Credit Cards: None
Notes: 2, 5, 7, 10

CLEARVILLE

Conifer Ridge Farm
Rural Delivery 2, Box 202A, 15535
(814) 784-3342

Conifer Ridge Farm has 126 acres of woodland, pasture, Christmas trees, and crops. There is a one-acre pond with a pier for swimming, fishing, and boating. The home's rustic exterior opens to a spacious contemporary design. You'll feel its country character in the old barn beams and brick walls that collect the sun's warmth for solar heat. Near Bedford Village and Raystown Dam.

Hosts: Dan and Myrtle Haldeman
Rooms: 2 plus cabin (1 PB; 1 SB) $30-50
Full Breakfast
Credit Cards: None
Notes: 2, 4, 5, 7, 9, 10, 11

CRESCO

LaAnna Guest House
Rural Route 2, Box 1051, 18326
(717) 676-4225

NOTES: Credit cards accepted: A Master Card; B Visa; C American Express; D Discover Card; E Diners Club; F Other; 2 Personal checks accepted; 3 Lunch available; 4 Dinner available; 5 Open all

The 111-year-old Victorian is furnished with Victorian and Empire antiques and has spacious rooms, quiet surroundings, and a trout pond. Walk to waterfalls, mountain views, and wildlife.

Hosts: Julie Wilson and Kay Swingle
Rooms: 3 (SB) $25-30
Continental Breakfast
Credit Cards: None
Notes: 2, 5, 7, 8, 9, 10, 11

Bechtel Mansion Inn

DONEGAL

Mountain View Bed and Breakfast and Antiques
Mountain View Road, 15628
(412) 593-6349

Enjoy lodging and breakfast in a quiet, pastoral setting in the heart of the Laurel Highlands in a restored 1850s farmhouse and barn furnished with 18th- and early 19th-century American furniture. See the magnificent views of the surrounding Laurel Mountains. Convenient to Fallingwater, ski resorts, rafting, hiking, and historic sites. Antiques available for sale. One mile east of Exit 9 on the Pennsylvania Turnpike. No smoking.

Host: Jerry and Lesley O'Leary
Rooms: 6 (3 PB; 3 SB) $75-125
Full Breakfast
Credit Cards: A, B, C, D, E
Notes: 2, 5, 9, 10, 11, 12

EAST BERLIN

Bechtel Mansion Inn
400 West King Street, 17316
(717) 259-7760

This charming Victorian mansion has been tastefully restored and furnished with antiques. Located on the western frontier of the Pennsylvania Dutch country, amid the East Berlin national historic district, the inn is a perfect location for a honeymoon, relaxing getaway, or visiting historic churches and sites in Gettysburg, York, or Lancaster. Gift certificates are available.

Hosts: Ruth Spangler; Charles and Mariam Bechtel
Rooms: 9 (7 PB; 2 SB) $72.50-130
Expanded Continental Breakfast
Credit Cards: A, B, C, D
Notes: 2, 7, 8, 9, 10

EAST MCKEESPORT

Gate House Bed and Breakfast
1035 Broadway, 15035
(412) 824-9399

Experience Victorian living in a quaint atmosphere. Most rooms have a working fireplace, soaking tub, and queen bed. The dining room is next door to the bed and breakfast. It is a five-minute walk to all churches; a 20-minute drive to downtown Pittsburgh. One block off U.S. 30 and 15 minutes from Pennsylvania Turnpike, Exit 6 or 7.

Host: Donna Taylor
Rooms: 6 (4 PB; 2 SB) $40-60
Full Breakfast
Credit Cards: A, B
Notes: 2, 5, 7, 8, 9

ELIZABETHTOWN

West Ridge Guest House
1285 West Ridge Road, 17022
(717) 367-7783

Tucked midway between Harrisburg and Lancaster, this European manor can be found four miles off Route 283 at Rheems-Elizabethtown Exit. Eight guest rooms are each decorated to reflect a different historical style. The exercise room with hot tub and large social room are in an adjacent guest house. Twenty to forty minutes to local attractions, including Hershey Park, Lancaster County Amish community, outlet shopping malls, masonic homes, Harrisburg state capital.

Host: Alice P. Heisey
Rooms: 8 (PB) $50-75
Full Breakfast
Credit Cards: A, B
Notes: 2, 7, 8, 10

EMLENTON

Whippletree Inn and Farm
Rural Delivery 3, Box 285, 16373
(412) 867-9543

The inn is a restored, turn-of-the-century home on a cattle farm. The house, barns, and 100 acres of pasture sit on a hill above the Allegheny River. A pleasant trail leads down to the river. Guests are welcome to use the one-half-mile race track for horses and carriages. Hiking, biking, cross-country skiing, canoeing, hunting, and fishing are nearby. Emlenton offers antique and craft shopping in the restored Old Mill.

Hosts: Warren and Joey Simmons
Rooms: 4 (2 PB; 2 SB) $47.20-53
Full Breakfast
Credit Cards: None
Notes: 2, 5, 7, 9, 10

EPHRATA

Clearview Farm Bed and Breakfast
355 Clearview Road, 17522
(717) 733-6333

This restored 1814 limestone farmhouse is surrounded by 200 acres of peaceful farmland that overlook a pond graced by a pair of swans. Although in the country, we are very easy to find and are just minutes from several major highways. Located in the heart of Penn-

---

NOTES: Credit cards accepted: A Master Card; B Visa; C American Express; D Discover Card; E Diners Club; F Other; 2 Personal checks accepted; 3 Lunch available; 4 Dinner available; 5 Open all

sylvania Dutch Lancaster County, excellent restaurants, antique malls, and outlet shopping are nearby. Featured in *Country Decorating Ideas*; AAA rated; a touch of elegance in a country setting.

Host: Mildred Wissler
Rooms: 5 (3 PB; 2 SB) $59-79
Full Breakfast
Credit Cards: A, B
Notes: 2, 5, 9, 10

The Guesthouse at Doneckers
318-324 North State and
301 West Main, 17522
(717) 733-8696

Indulge in country elegance in a turn-of-the-century guest house with suites, fireplaces, and Jacuzzis. Rooms are appointed with fine antiques and hand stenciling. There is exceptional shopping at our 18-department specialty store and fine dining at our renowned French restaurant. Artists and craftpersons are at work in 50 studios at the Artworks, all within walking distance of the Doneckers community. Nearby are major antique and collectibles markets. Call or write for prices.

Host: Jan Grobengieser
Rooms: 31 (29 PB; 2 SB)
Continental Breakfast
Credit Cards: A, B, C, D
Notes: 2, 3, 4, 5, 7, 8, 9, 10

Historic Smithton Inn
900 West Main Street, 17522
(717) 733-6094

Smithton is a classic Pennsylvania country inn, first opened in 1763, with a picturesque stone building and parlor, library, and dining room open to guests. All rooms offer working fireplaces, leather-upholstered furnishings, canopy or four-poster beds, candles, quilts, chamber music, feather beds, refrigerator, nightshirts, books, and fresh flowers. Located in the Pennsylvania Dutch farm country where Old Order Amish, Mennonite, and Brethren people live the "plain life" and farm with horses. Touring suggestions provided.

Host: Dorothy Graybill
Rooms: 7 (PB) $65-170
Full Breakfast
Credit Cards: A, B, C
Notes: 2, 5, 6 (by arrangement), 7, 8

GETTYSBURG—SEE ALSO HANOVER

The Brafferton Inn
44 York Street, 17325
(717) 337-3423

Stay in the first house built in Gettysburg's historic district. The inn offers 18th-century antiques and hospitality. One of Pennsylvania's finest restorations, it includes a wonderful mural of Gettysburg's historic buildings and

---

year; 6 Pets welcome; 7 Children welcome; 8 Tennis nearby; 9 Swimming nearby; 10 Golf nearby; 11 Skiing nearby; 12 May be booked through travel agent

is within walking distance of all the town's historic sites, the college, and entertainment.

Hosts: Mimi and Jim Agard
Rooms: 20 (6 PB; 4 SB) $65-95
Full Breakfast
Credit Cards: A, B
Notes: 2, 7 (over 7), 8, 9, 10, 11

Keystone Inn

231 Hanover Street, 17325
(717) 337-3888

The Keystone Inn is a large, brick Victorian home built in 1913. The high-ceilinged rooms are decorated with lace and flowers, and a handsome chestnut staircase rises to the third floor. The guest rooms are bright, cheerful, and air conditioned. Each has a reading nook and writing desk. Choose your own breakfast from our full breakfast menu. One suite available.

Hosts: Wilmer and Doris Martin
Rooms: 4 plus suite (3 PB; 2 SB) $59-100
Full Breakfast
Credit Cards: A, B
Notes: 2, 5, 7, 8, 9, 10, 11

HANOVER

Beechmont Inn

315 Broadway, 17331
(717) 632-3012; (800) 553-7009

Near Gettysburg, this elegant 1834 Federal inn is furnished with antiques and fireplaces and is air conditioned. Enjoy antiquing, outlet shopping, Codorus State Park's large lake, and nearby Amish countryside. Breakfast is a special event served outdoors, in your room, or in the dining room.

Hosts: Terry and Monna Hormel
Rooms: 7 (PB) $70-125
Full Breakfast
Credit Cards: A, B
Notes: 2, 5, 8, 9, 10

HESSTON

Aunt Susie's Country Vacations

Rural Delivery 1, Box 225, 16647
(814) 658-3638

Experience country living in a warm, friendly atmosphere with antiques and oil paintings. Nearby attractions include 28-mile-long Raystown Lake, historic houses, and a restored general store.

Hosts: John and Susan
Rooms: 8 (2 PB; 6 SB) $45-50
Expanded Continental Breakfast
Credit Cards: None
Notes: 2, 7, 9, 10

KINZERS

Sycamore Haven Farm

35 South Kinzer Road, 17535
(717) 442-4901

We have approximately 40 milking cows and many young cattle and cats for children to enjoy. Our farmhouse has three guest rooms, all with double beds and one single bed. We also have

---

NOTES: Credit cards accepted: A Master Card; B Visa; C American Express; D Discover Card; E Diners Club; F Other; 2 Personal checks accepted; 3 Lunch available; 4 Dinner available; 5 Open all

cots and a playpen. Located 15 miles east of Lancaster on Route 30.

Hosts: Charles and Janet Groff
Rooms: 3 (SB) $30-40
Continental Breakfast
Credit Cards: None
Notes: 2, 5, 6, 7, 8, 10

LAMPETER

Walkabout Inn
837 Village Road, 17537
(717) 464-0707

This 1925 brick Mennonite farmhouse features large wraparound porches, balconies, English gardens, and antique furnishings. The inn takes its name from the Australian word, which means to go out and discover new places. The Australian-born host will help you explore the Amish country surrounding the home. An elegant breakfast is served by candlelight. The honeymoon and anniversary suites are beautiful.

Hosts: Richard and Margaret Mason
Rooms: 4 (PB) $59-79
Suite: 1 (PB)
Full Breakfast
Credit Cards: A, B, C
Notes: 2, 3, 4, 5, 7, 8, 9, 10

LANCASTER—SEE ALSO LAMPETER

Buona Notte Bed and Breakfast
2020 Marietta Avenue, 17603
(717) 295-2597

This turn-of-the-century home has comfortable rooms, wraparound porch, and a large back yard. Hershey Park and Gettysburg are nearby. Pennsylvania Dutch country is only ten minutes away. Franklin and Marshall College is two miles away. Breakfast includes homemade breads, muffins, and jams. French and Italian are spoken here.

Hosts: Joe and Anna Kuhns Predoti
Rooms: 3 (1 PB; 2 SB) $40-50
Continental Breakfast
Credit Cards: None
Notes: 5, 7, 8

Lincoln Haus Inn Bed and Breakfast
1687 Lincoln Highway East, 17602
(717) 392-9412

Lincoln Haus Inn is the only inn in Lancaster County with a distinctive hip roof. It is furnished with antiques and rugs on gleaming, hardwood floors, and it has natural oak woodwork. The host is a member of the Old Order Amish Church, serving family-style breakfast with a homey atmosphere. Convenient location, close to Amish farmlands, malls, historic Lancaster; five minutes from Route 30 and Pennsylvania Dutch Visitors Bureau.

Host: Mary K. Zook
Rooms: 6 (PB) $45-65
Apartments: 2 (PB)
Full Breakfast
Credit Cards: None
Notes: 2, 5, 7, 8, 9, 10, 12

---

year; 6 Pets welcome; 7 Children welcome; 8 Tennis nearby; 9 Swimming nearby; 10 Golf nearby; 11 Skiing nearby; 12 May be booked through travel agent

New Life Homestead Bed and Breakfast
1400 East King Street (Route 462), 17602
(717) 396-8928

In the heart of the Amish area is a stately, brick Victorian close to all attractions, markets, farms, and outlets. Each room is decorated with family heirlooms and antiques. Full breakfast and evening refreshments are served. Tours and meals are arranged with local families. Worship with us in our Mennonite church.

Hosts: Carol and Bill Giersch
Rooms: (PB) $40-65
Full Breakfast
Credit Cards: None
Notes: 2, 5, 7, 8, 9, 10, 12

Witmer's Tavern—Historic 1725 Inn

Witmer's Tavern— Historic 1725 Inn
2014 Old Philadelphia Pike, 17602
(717) 299-5305

This three-story, all stone inn, originally built in 1725 and later added to, rests just off the nation's first turnpike. It is the sole survivor of some 62 pre-Revolutionary War inns and is listed on the local, state, and national registers of historic places and landmarks. Restored to the original, simple pioneer state, each romantic room has its own working fireplace, antique quilts, and fresh flowers. Pandora's antique and quilt shop is in the east end. Add your names to the guest list that includes John Adams, Marquis de Lafayette, and others. Villages of Bird-in-Hand and Intercourse are nearby.

Hosts: Brant Hartung and family
Rooms: 7 (2 PB; 5 SB) $60-100
Continental Breakfast
Credit Cards: None
Notes: 2, 5, 7, 8, 9, 10, 11

LIGONIER

Grant House Bed and Breakfast
244 West Church Street, 15658
(412) 238-5135

Grant House is an 1880 restored Victorian home in historic Ligonier, located 50 miles east of Pittsburgh and a three and one-half-hour drive west of the Washington, D. C./Baltimore, Maryland area. Walk three blocks to antique shops and restaurants. Visit Seven Springs, Hidden Valley skiing, and Frank Lloyd Wright's Fallingwater. Accommodations also available at our in-town Mellon Park Guest House, which has three bedrooms with queen beds and private baths.

NOTES: Credit cards accepted: A Master Card; B Visa; C American Express; D Discover Card; E Diners Club; F Other; 2 Personal checks accepted; 3 Lunch available; 4 Dinner available; 5 Open all

Hosts: Marilyn and Owen Grant
Rooms: 3 (1 PB; 2 SB) $65-75
Continental Breakfast
Credit Cards: None
Notes: 2, 5, 8, 9, 10, 11

Swiss Woods Bed and Breakfast

LIMA

Hamanassett

P.O. Box 129, 19037
(215) 459-3000

This 19th-century historic, country manor house is on 36 secluded acres of woodlands, gardens, and trails near Brandywine Valley. Near Winterthur, Hagley, Nemours Brandywine (Wyeth) museums, and Longwood Gardens. Well-appointed, large rooms have queen, double, twin, or canopied king beds, TVs, and amenities. Beautiful Federalist livingroom and extensive library; country breakfast of sophisticated cuisine. Near tennis, golf, and excellent dining opportunities. Two-night minimum stay.

Host: Evelene H. Dohan
Rooms: 6 (PB) $85-110
Full Breakfast

Credit Cards: None
Notes: 2, 5, 8, 10, 12

LITITZ

Swiss Woods Bed and Breakfast

500 Blantz Road, 17543
(717) 627-3358; (800) 594-8018

A visit to Swiss Woods is reminiscent of a trip to one of Switzerland's quaint, charming guest houses. Located in beautiful Lancaster County, this inn was designed with comfort in mind. Breakfast is a memorable experience of inn specialties. The gardens are a unique variety of flowering perennials and annuals. A massive sandstone fireplace dominates the sunny common room. Rooms feature natural woodwork and queen beds with down comforters, some with Jacuzzis, patios, and balconies. Enjoy our spectacular view and special touches. German spoken.

Hosts: Deborah and Werner Mosimann
Rooms: 7 (PB) $66-110
Full Breakfast
Credit Cards: A, B
Notes: 2, 7, 9, 12

MALVERN

The Great Valley House

110 Swedesford Road, Rural Delivery 3, 19355
(215) 644-6759

A pre-Revolutionary War stone farmhouse, circa 1690, is two miles from

---

year; 6 Pets welcome; 7 Children welcome; 8 Tennis nearby; 9 Swimming nearby; 10 Golf nearby; 11 Skiing nearby; 12 May be booked through travel agent

Valley Forge Park and convenient to Philadelphia, Lancaster, and Brandywine. Boxwoods line the walkway, and trees surround this 300-year-old house. Guest rooms include antiques, quilts, and hand stenciling. Guests enjoy full breakfast, swimming pool, refrigerator, microwave, and TV in their rooms. Featured in the *Washington Post* and the *Philadelphia Inquirer*, it is a wonderful blend of history with modern amenities.

Host: Pattye Benson
Rooms: 3 (2 PB; 1 SB) $65-80
Full Breakfast
Credit Cards: None
Notes: 2, 5, 7, 8, 9, 10, 12

MANHEIM

Wenger's Bed and Breakfast
571 Hossler Road, 17545
(717) 665-3862

Relax and enjoy your stay in the quiet countryside of Lancaster County. Our modern ranch-style house is within walking distance of our son's 100-acre dairy farm. The spacious rooms will accommodate families. You can get a guided tour through the Amish farmland. Hershey, the chocolate town, Pennsylvania's state capital at Harrisburg, and the Gettysburg battlefield are all within a one-hour drive.

Hosts: Arthur D. and Mary K. Wenger
Rooms: 2 (PB) $40-45

Full Breakfast
Credit Cards: None
Notes: 2, 5, 7, 10

The Great Valley House

MERCERSBURG

The Mercersberg Inn
405 South Main Street, 17236
(717) 328-5231

The Mercersberg Inn is a meticulously restored, 20,000-square-foot mansion with 15 guest rooms featuring working fireplaces, king beds, canopied beds, private balconies, and spectacular views of the Tuscarora Mountains. Just seven miles from Whitetail Ski Resort, the inn is also a short drive from Antietam, Harpers Ferry, and Gettysburg. Six-course, *prix fixe* meals are featured on weekends.

Host: Fran Wolfe
Rooms: 15 (PB) $105-175
Continental Breakfast
Credit Cards: A, B, D
Notes: 2, 4, 8, 10, 11, 12

NOTES: Credit cards accepted: A Master Card; B Visa; C American Express; D Discover Card; E Diners Club; F Other; 2 Personal checks accepted; 3 Lunch available; 4 Dinner available; 5 Open all

MONTOURSVILLE

The Carriage House at Stonegate
Road 1, Box 11A, 17754
(717) 433-4340

The Carriage House at Stonegate is the original carriage house for one of the oldest farms in the beautiful Loyalsock Valley. It offers 1,400 square feet of space on two levels and is totally self-contained and separate from the main house. It is located within easy access to I-80, I-180, and U.S. 15 and on the edge of extensive forests offering a wide range of outdoor activities in all seasons.

Hosts: Harold and Dena Mesaris
Rooms: 2 (SB) $50
Continental Breakfast
Credit Cards: None
Notes: 2, 5, 6, 7, 8, 9, 10, 11

MOUNT JOY

Cedar Hill Farm
305 Longenecker Road, 17552
(717) 653-4655

This 1817 stone farmhouse overlooks a peaceful stream. Each comfortable, charming guest room is centrally air conditioned. The honeymoon suite offers a private balcony. The host was born on this working farm located near Lancaster and Hershey. Farmers' markets, antique shops, and well-known restaurants abound. Gift certificates are available for anniversary or holiday giving.

Hosts: Russel and Gladys Swarr
Rooms: 4 (PB) $55-58
Expanded Continental Breakfast
Credit Cards: A, B, C
Notes: 2, 5, 7, 8, 10

Green Acres Farm Bed and Breakfast
1382 Pinkerton Road, 17552
(717) 653-4028

Our 1830 farmhouse is furnished with antiques and offers a peaceful haven for your getaway. The rooster, chickens, wild turkey, Pigmy goats, lots of kittens, pony, and 1,000 hogs give a real farm atmosphere on this 160-acre grain farm. Children love the pony cart rides, and everyone enjoys the trampoline and swings. We offer tour information in the Amish country.

Hosts: Wayne and Yvonne Miller
Rooms: 7 (5 PB; 2 SB) $45-50
Full Breakfast
Credit Cards: A, B
Notes: 2, 5, 6, 7, 8, 9, 10, 12

MT. POCONO

Farmhouse Bed and Breakfast
HCR 1, Box 6B, 18344
(717) 839-0796

---

year; 6 Pets welcome; 7 Children welcome; 8 Tennis nearby; 9 Swimming nearby; 10 Golf nearby; 11 Skiing nearby; 12 May be booked through travel agent

"Where the honor of our home is hospitality." An 1850 homestead on six manicured acres features two suites with fireplaces in the house and a separate cottage. The farm-style breakfast is complete with original, country recipes prepared by your host, a professional chef. Enjoy bedtime snacks baked fresh every day. Antiques adorn each room, with cleanliness being the order of the day. Accommodations have queen beds, TVs, and air conditioning. Totally non-smoking!

Hosts: Jack and Donna Asure
Rooms: 3 (PB) $75-95
Full Breakfast
Credit Cards: A, B, D
Notes: 2 (deposit), 5, 8, 9, 10, 11, 12

The Bodine House

MUNCY

The Bodine House
307 South Main Street, 17756
(717) 546-8949

The Bodine House, featured in the December 1991 issue of *Colonial Home* magazine, is located on tree-lined Main Street in the historic district. Built in 1805, the house has been authentically restored and is listed on the National Register of Historic Places. Most of the furnishings are antiques. The center of Muncy, with its shops, restaurants, library, and churches, is a short walk down the street. No smoking.

Hosts: David and Marie Louise Smith
Rooms: 4 (3 PB; 1 SB) $35-65
Full Breakfast
Credit Cards: A, B, C
Notes: 2, 7 (over six), 8, 9, 10, 11

OXFORD

Log House Bed and Breakfast
15225 Limestone Road, 19363
(215) 932-9257

This quiet, country farm in Chester County is in a wooded area away from city and traffic noises midway between Lancaster (Amish country), Philadelphia, and Wilmington. Historical events of Brandywine Valley and beautiful gardens, Herr's chip factory, picnic area, and hiking are nearby. No smoking.

Hosts: E. E. and Arlene E. Hershey
Rooms: 3 (2 PB; 1 SB) $45
Full Breakfast
Credit Cards: None
Notes: 2, 5, 7, 8, 9, 10, 11

NOTES: Credit cards accepted: A Master Card; B Visa; C American Express; D Discover Card; E Diners Club; F Other; 2 Personal checks accepted; 3 Lunch available; 4 Dinner available; 5 Open all

PARADISE

Maple Lane Farm Bed and Breakfast
505 Paradise Lane, 17562
(717) 687-7479

Clean, comfortable, air-conditioned rooms have antiques, quilts, poster and canopy beds. This working dairy farm has a winding stream, woodland, and a 40-mile view. Real Amish country, near museums, craft shops, antique shops, and farmers' markets.

Hosts: Edwin and Marion Rohrer
Rooms: 4 (2 PB; 2 SB) $45-55
Expanded Continental Breakfast
Credit Cards: None
Notes: 2, 5, 7, 8, 9, 10

PEACE BOTTOM

Pleasant Grove Farm
368 Pilottown Road, 17563
(717) 548-3100

Located in beautiful, historic Lancaster County, this 160-acre dairy farm has been a family-run operation for 110 years, earning the title of Century Farm by the Pennsylvania Department of Agriculture. As a working farm, it provides guests the opportunity to experience daily life in a rural setting. Built in 1814, 1818, and 1820, the house once served as a country store and post office.

Hosts: Charles and Labertha Tindall
Rooms: 4 (SB) $45-50
Full Breakfast
Credit Cards: None
Notes: 2, 5, 7, 9

Antique Row Bed and Breakfast

PHILADELPHIA

Antique Row Bed and Breakfast
341 South 12th Street, 19107
(215) 592-7802; (215) 592-9692

Comfortable, reasonably prices, home-style accommodations in a pleasantly furnished, 150-year-old town house lo-

---

year; 6 Pets welcome; 7 Children welcome; 8 Tennis nearby; 9 Swimming nearby; 10 Golf nearby; 11 Skiing nearby; 12 May be booked through travel agent

cated in Center City. Within walking distance of most cultural and historic attractions. Guest rooms have cable color TV and individually controlled air conditioning. Particularly attractive for longer stays is a separate suite with private entrance offering a bedroom with queen bed, sitting room with sofa bed, private bath, and fully equipped kitchen. Discounts available for extended stays.

Host: Barbara Pope
Rooms: 3 (1 PB; 2 SB) $55-65
Full Breakfast
Credit Cards: None
Notes: 2, 5, 7, 12

POINT PLEASANT

Tattersall Inn
Cafferty and River Road, Box 569, 18950
(215) 297-8233

This 18th-century plastered fieldstone home with its broad porches and manicured lawns resembles the unhurried atmosphere of a bygone era. Enjoy the richly wainscoted entry hall and formal dining room with marble fireplace and a collection of vintage photographs. Step back in time when you enter the colonial common room with beamed ceiling and walk-in fireplace. The spacious, antique-furnished guest rooms are a joy. Air conditioned.

Hosts: Gerry and Herb Moss
Rooms: 6 (PB) $75-95
Continental Breakfast
Credit Cards: A, B
Notes: 2, 5, 7, 8, 11

QUARRYVILLE

Runnymede Farm Guest House Bed and Breakfast
1030 Robert Fulton Highway, 17566
(717) 786-3625

Enjoy our comfortable farmhouse in south Lancaster County. The rooms are clean and air conditioned, and the lounge has a TV. Close to tourist attractions, but not in the main stream. Biking, hiking, picnicking. Country breakfast is optional.

Hosts: Herbert and Sara Hess
Rooms: 3 (SB) $35-40
Full Breakfast
Credit Cards: None
Notes: 2, 5, 7, 8, 9, 10

SCOTTDALE

Pine Wood Acres Bed and Breakfast
Rural Route 1, Box 634, 15683-9567
(412) 887-5404

A country home surounded by four acres of woods, wildflowers, and herb and flower gardens is ten miles from the Pennsylvania Turnpike and I-70, New Stanton exits; 25 miles from Frank Lloyd Wright's Fallingwater. Sumptuous breakfasts and warm hospitality are yours to enjoy at Pine Wood Acres, where your hosts are members of the Mennonite Church.

NOTES: Credit cards accepted: A Master Card; B Visa; C American Express; D Discover Card; E Diners Club; F Other; 2 Personal checks accepted; 3 Lunch available; 4 Dinner available; 5 Open all

Hosts: Ruth and James Horsch
Rooms: 3 (SB) $43-53
Expanded Continental Breakfast
Credit Cards: None
Notes: 2, 5, 6, 7, 8, 9, 10, 11, 12

SMOKETOWN

Homestead Lodging
184 East Brook Road, 17576
(717) 393-6927

Welcome to Homestead Lodging where quiet, country living and a homey atmosphere await you. After a leisurely morning coffee and danish, enjoy a walk down the lane to the scenic farmland around us. You can tour the countryside or go on a shopping spree in one of our many markets, quilt shops, antique shops, and craft shops. Restaurants are within walking distance.

Hosts: Robert and Lori Kepiro
Rooms: 4 (PB) $18-49
Continental Breakfast
Credit Cards: A, B
Notes: 2 (deposit only), 5, 7, 8, 9, 10, 11

STRASBURG

The Decoy Bed and Breakfast
958 Eisenberger Road, 17579
(717) 687-8585

This former Amish home is set in farmland with spectacular views and an informal atmosphere. Craft shops and attractions are nearby, and bicycle tours can be arranged. Two cats in residence.

Hosts: Debby and Hap Joy
Rooms: 4 (PB) $50-60; $40-50 December 1-April 30
Full Breakfast
Credit Cards: None
Notes: 2, 5, 7, 8, 10

THOMPSON

Jefferson Inn
Route 171, Rural Delivery 2, Box 36, 18465
(717) 727-2625

Built in 1871, the inn offers reasonably priced accommodations and a full-service restaurant. Situated in the rolling hills of northeast Pennsylvania, there are thousands of acres available nearby for fishing, boating, and some of the best deer and turkey hunting around. Other seasonal activities include skiing, snowmobiling, horseback riding, and golf. Good, Gospel-preaching churches are nearby.

Hosts: Douglas and Margie Stark
Rooms: 6 (3 PB; 3 SB) $25-50
Full Breakfast
Credit Cards: A, B
Notes: 2, 3, 4, 5, 6, 7, 8, 9, 10, 11 (XC), 12

TOWANDA

The Victorian Guest House
118 York Avenue, 18848
(717) 265-6972

Considered one of the grandest homes in Bradford County, this elegant 1897 structure is classic Victorian, with

---

year; 6 Pets welcome; 7 Children welcome; 8 Tennis nearby; 9 Swimming nearby; 10 Golf nearby; 11 Skiing nearby; 12 May be booked through travel agent

porches, arches, tower rooms, and a host of period architectural splendors. Bedrooms and open areas of the home are furnished with 19th-century antiques. Warm, cozy, Christian atmosphere.

Hosts: Tom and Nancy Taylor
Rooms: 11 (6 PB; 5 SB) $40-60
Continental Breakfast
Credit Cards: A, B, C, E
Notes: 2, 7, 8, 9, 10, 11 (XC)

VALLEY FORGE—SEE ALSO MALVERN

Valley Forge Mountain Bed and Breakfast
Box 562, 19481
(215) 783-7783; (800) 344-0123
FAX (215) 783-7783

George Washington headquartered here! Centrally located between Philadelphia, Lancaster County, Reading outlets, and the Brandywine Valley, this French Colonial is on three wooded acres adjacent to Valley Forge Park. Air conditioning, phones, TV/VCR, computer, printer, FAX, fireplaces, and bridle and hiking trail. Near fine shopping, antiquing, restaurants, cross-country skiing, horseback riding, golf. Two guest suites—one double Victorian, one California king.

Hosts: Dick and Carolyn Williams
Suites: 2 (PB) $50-65
Full or Continental Breakfast
Credit Cards: A, B, C, E
Notes: 2, 5, 7, 8, 9, 10, 11, 12

WELLSBORO

Kaltenbach's Bed and Breakfast
Stony Fork Road, Rural Delivery 6
Box 106A, 16901
(717) 724-4954; (800) 722-4954

This sprawling, country home with room for 32 guests offers visitors comfortable lodging, home-style breakfasts, and warm hospitality. Set on a 72-acre farm, Kaltenbach's provides ample opportunity for walks through meadows, pastures, and forests, picnicking, and watching the sheep, pigs, rabbits, and wildlife. All-you-can-eat country-style breakfasts are served. A honeymoon suite has a tub for two, and hunting and golf packages are available.

Host: Lee Kaltenbach
Rooms: 11 (9 PB; 2 SB) $60-125
Full Breakfast
Credit Cards: A, B
Notes: 2, 3, 4, 5, 7, 8, 9, 10, 11

WHITE OAK

The Easler's Bed and Breakfast
3401 Foster Road, 15131
(412) 673-1133

Encircled by silver maples on the highest hill in Allegheny County, this 1929 English Tudor mansion welcomes family travelers with three restful guest rooms. White Oak is located about 17 miles from the Pennsylvania Turnpike,

---

NOTES: Credit cards accepted: A Master Card; B Visa; C American Express; D Discover Card; E Diners Club; F Other; 2 Personal checks accepted; 3 Lunch available; 4 Dinner available; 5 Open all

Exits 6 and 7. Gourmet breakfasts are a specialty. Children under ten stay free in parents' room.

Host: Kathleen Easler
Rooms: 3 (1 PB; 2 SB) $50-75
Full Breakfast
Credit Cards: None
Notes: 2, 5, 6, 7, 8, 9, 10, 11

WRIGHTSVILLE

Roundtop Bed and Breakfast
Rural Delivery 2, P.O. Box 258, 17368
(717) 252-3169

Roundtop is situated high above the Susquehanna River on more than 100 acres of woodland. Built in 1880, this German stone house has been renovated to take full advantage of the spectacular views. Its many porches and fireplaces, as well as its spacious, attractive rooms, make it a romantic weekend getaway anytime of the year. It is halfway between York and Lancaster.

Hosts: Jodi and Tyler Sloen
Rooms: 6 (1 PB; 4 SB) $50-75
Full Breakfast
Credit Cards: A, B
Notes: 2, 7

Rhode Island

BLOCK ISLAND

The Barrington Inn
Beach Avenue, P. O. Box 397, 02807
(401) 466-5510

Known for its warmth and hospitality, The Barrington Inn is a century-old farmhouse situated on a knoll overlooking the New Harbor area of Block Island. There are six individually decorated guest rooms, five of which have spectacular water and sunset views. Block Island, approximately 12 miles off the coast, has recently been named as one of the 12 "last great places in the western hemisphere" by *Nature Conservancy*.

Hosts: Joan and Howard Ballard
Rooms: 6 (PB) $45-140
Expanded Continental Breakfast
Credit Cards: A, B
Notes: 2, 8, 9

Hotel Manisses
1 Spring Street, 02807
(401) 466-2421

The Hotel Manisses is an 1874 Victorian inn that was known as one of the best summer hotels in the East. Artistically renovated and restored, it is even more beautiful. Each charming room is decorated with authentic turn-of-the-century furniture. The decor throughout recaptures the gracious past and old-fashioned, hospitable atmosphere. Even the staff is dressed in fashions from that nostalgic era.

Hosts: Justin and Joan Abrams; Steve and Rita Draper
Rooms: 17 (PB) $55-225
Full Breakfast
Credit Cards: A, B, C
Notes: 2, 4, 7, 8, 9, 12

Hotel Manisses

The White House
Spring Street, 02807
(401) 466-2653

NOTES: Credit cards accepted: A Master Card; B Visa; C American Express; D Discover Card; E Diners Club; F Other; 2 Personal checks accepted; 3 Lunch available; 4 Dinner available; 5 Open all

This gracious, seaside mansion has ocean views from guest room balconies. The furnishings are French Provencial antiques, and the hosts have a presidential signature collection. Limousine service to and from ferries and the airport is available. Close to beaches, nature walks, gourmet restaurants, and churches. Although all rooms do not have private baths, the hosts prefer to make only two rooms available at one time, allowing each guest the use of a private bath.

Hosts: Joseph and Violette M. Connolly
Rooms: 5 (2 PB; 2 SB) $50-120
Full Breakfast
Credit Cards: A, B, C
Notes: 2, 5, 8, 9

CHARLESTOWN

General Stanton Inn
P. O. Box 222, 02813
(401) 364-8888

The inn stands on the old Boston Post Road (U.S. 1-A), about halfway between Narragansett and Watch Hill. It features old, original low ceilings, flaring fireplaces, brick ovens, and hand-hewn timbers. The inn serves breakfast, lunch, and dinner. On the premises is a large flea market open each Sunday from April to October.

Hosts: Angelo and Janice Falcone
Rooms: 15 (13 PB; 2 SB) $65-105
Full Breakfast
Credit Cards: A, B, C
Notes: 2, 4, 8, 9, 10

Inn the Meadow
1045 Shannock Road, 02813-3725
(401) 789-1473

A five-acre country setting where peace and quiet are plentiful is only minutes from the best in beaches, summer theater, seafood, shopping, and hiking. We offer queen or twin beds, a full breakfast from our menu, and a common room with fireplace, games, books, and piano. Make the inn your home away from home to explore all of Connecticut, Rhode Island, and Massachusetts. No smoking.

Host: Yolanda Day
Rooms: 4 (1 PB; 3 SB) $40-65
Full Breakfast
Credit Cards: A, B, D
Notes: 2, 5, 9, 12

GREEN HILL

Fairfield-By-The-Sea Bed and Breakfast
527 Green Hill Beach Road, 02879-5703
(401) 789-4717

An artist's contemporary home in an intimate, country setting offers beauty and seclusion. Stress reduction is the order of the day at this comfortable, airy house with an eclectic collection of art and an interesting library. Day trips are possible to Block Island, Martha's Vineyard, Cape Cod, Boston, Newport, Plymouth, and Mystic Seaport. Golf, bird watching, tennis, sailing, nature trails, fine shops, museums, historical sights, antiques, restaurants are all nearby.

---

year; 6 Pets welcome; 7 Children welcome; 8 Tennis nearby; 9 Swimming nearby; 10 Golf nearby; 11 Skiing nearby; 12 May be booked through travel agent

Host: Jeanne A. Lewis
Rooms: 2 (SB) $40-55
Expanded Continental Breakfast
Credit Cards: C
Notes: 2, 5, 7, 8, 9, 10, 11, 12

KINGSTON

Hedgerow Bed and Breakfast
1747 Mooresfield Road, P.O. Box 1586, 02881
(401) 783-2671

A lovely Colonial built in 1933 on two and one-quarter acres with tennis courts and formal gardens. Conveniently located 15 miles from Newport, 30 miles south of Providence, and next to the University of Rhode Island. The ferry to Block Island, beaches, and Mystic, Connecticut's seaport are within easy reach. Call for price information.

Hosts: Ann and Jim Ross
Rooms: 4 (S2B)
Full Breakfast
Credit Cards: None
Notes: 2, 5, 7, 8, 9, 10

MIDDLETOWN

Lindsey's Guest House
6 James Street, 02840
(401) 846-9386

We are located between two beaches off Routes 214 and 138 one mile from Newport's mansions, the Tennis Hall of Fame, and the art museum. The guest house is only two miles from the harbor, with its wharves, shops, and ocean drive. Close to the bird sanctuary and wildlife refuge. We pride ourselves on our clean, comfortable house with a large yard and deck.

Hosts: Dave and Anne
Rooms: 3 (1 PB; 2 SB) $40-80
Expanded Continental Breakfast
Credit Cards: None

NEWPORT

Admiral Farragut Inn
31 Clarke Street
Mailing address: 8 Fair Street, 02840
(401) 846-4256; (800) 343-2863

The Admiral Farragut Inn, circa 1702, is a most unique Colonial inn. Everywhere, in our guest rooms, great room, foyer, and halls, there are fresh interpretations of colonial themes, and even a bit of whimsy, to make anyone's stay a delight. Our personal favorites are the Shaker-style four-poster beds made by our in-house carpenter. There are painted armoires, gaily colored stencils, English antiques, faux-marble mantels with real Delft tiles. Located in one of Newport's historic areas and central to attractions. Afternoon tea is served.

Host: Evelyn Ramirez
Rooms: 10 (PB) $50-110
Expanded Continental Breakfast
Credit Cards: A, B, C, E
Closed January
Notes: 2, 7 (over 12), 8, 9, 10, 12

Admiral Fitzroy Inn
398 Thames Street
Mailing address: 8 Fair Street, 02840
(401) 846-4256; (800) 343-2863

NOTES: Credit cards accepted: A Master Card; B Visa; C American Express; D Discover Card; E Diners Club; F Other; 2 Personal checks accepted; 3 Lunch available; 4 Dinner available; 5 Open all

The Admiral Fitzroy Inn is a newly restored Victorian home designed by architect Dudly Newton and built in 1865. The inn has delightfully unique, hand-painted rooms decorated and furnished with a distinctive fashion to please the eye and lift the spirits. Quiet, restful, and relaxing, the inn is conveniently located in the heart of Newport's bustling waterfront district.

Host: Judy Rush
Rooms: 18 (PB) $65-150
Full Breakfast
Credit Cards: A, B, C, E
Notes: 2, 5, 7, 8, 10, 11, 12

Halidon Hill Guest House

Halidon Avenue, 02840
(401) 847-8318

Location is everything in Newport, and we are ten minutes from Hammersmith Farm, minutes from the beach, convenient to shopping areas, restaurants, and mansions. Our rooms are modern and spacious, and we have a deck and in-ground pool for your enjoyment.

Hosts: Helen and Ginger Burke
Rooms: 4 (2 PB; 2 SB) $55-125
Continental Breakfast
Credit Cards: C
Notes: 2, 5, 7, 8, 9, 10, 12

Spring Street Inn

353 Spring Street, 02840
(401) 847-4767

This charming, restored Empire Victorian home, circa 1858, has eight double guest rooms. The guest sitting rooms have cable TV, and a generous home-baked breakfast is served. The harborview suite has a balcony. Walk to all of Newport's highlights; one block from the harbor; on-site parking.

Host: Mrs. Parvin Latimore
Rooms: 8 (6 PB; 2 SB) $39-125
Full Breakfast
Credit Cards: A, B
Notes: 2, 5, 7 (over 12), 8, 9, 12

PROVIDENCE

State House Inn

43 Jewett Street, 02908
(401) 785-1235

A country inn usually means peace and quiet, friendly hosts, comfort and simplicity, with beautiful furnishings. The State House Inn has all of these qualifications, but just happens to be located in the city of Providence. Our inn has fireplaces, hardwood floors, Shaker or colonial furnishings, canopy beds, and modern conveniences such as FAX, TV, and phone. Located near downtown and local colleges and universities.

Hosts: Frank and Monica Hopton
Rooms: 10 (PB) $59-99
Full Breakfast
Credit Cards: A, B, C
Notes: 5, 7, 12

---

year; 6 Pets welcome; 7 Children welcome; 8 Tennis nearby; 9 Swimming nearby; 10 Golf nearby; 11 Skiing nearby; 12 May be booked through travel agent

SOUTH KINGSTOWN

Admiral Dewey Inn
668 Matunuck Beach Road, 02879
(401) 783-2090

This Victorian bed and breakfast first opened in 1898. Now on the National Register of Historic Places, the Admiral Dewey has been completely restored and is decorated and furnished entirely with a Victorian style. There is a large breakfast room with a tiled fireplace, a public parlor for lingering over coffee, and rockers on the wraparound porch for enjoying the off-shore breeze. The inn is near Theatre-by-the-Sea, the Trustom Pond Wildlife Refuge, and Matunuck and Moonstone beaches.

Host: Joan LeBel
Rooms: 10 (8 PB; 2 SB) $60-120
Continental Breakfast
Credit Cards: A, B
Notes: 7 (over 10)

WYOMING

The Cookie Jar Bed and Breakfast
64 Kingstown Road, 02898
(401) 539-2680

The heart of our home, the livingroom, was built in 1732 as a blacksmith's shop. Later, the forge was removed and a large granite fireplace was built by an American-Indian stonemason. The original wood ceiling, hand-hewn beams, and granite walls remain today. The property was called the Perry Plantation, and yes, they had two slaves who lived above the blacksmith's shop. We offer friendly, home-style living in a comfortable, country setting. On Route 138 just off I-95.

Hosts: Dick and Madelein Sohl
Rooms: 3 (1 PB; 2 SB) $55
Full Breakfast
Credit Cards: None
Notes: 2, 5, 7, 9, 10, 12

Admiral Dewey Inn

NOTES: Credit cards accepted: A Master Card; B Visa; C American Express; D Discover Card; E Diners Club; F Other; 2 Personal checks accepted; 3 Lunch available; 4 Dinner available; 5 Open all

South Carolina

The Breeden House Inn

BEAUFORT

TwoSuns Inn Bed and Breakfast
1750 Bay Street, 29902
(803) 522-1122; (800) 532-4244
FAX (803) 522-1122

Enjoy the southern charm of historic Beauford ("Prince of Tides" film site) and the informal ambience of a 1990-restored grand home, circa 1917, directly on the bay. Visit our quaint shops, galleries, and restaurants. Take a bicycle or carriage ride through our historic waterfront community and relax at TwoSuns Inn, which features Carrol's weavings, family collectibles, period decor, business amenities, handicap facilities, and warm hospitality. We are 45 miles north of Savannah, Georgia and 65 miles south of Charleston.

Hosts: Carrol and Ron Kay
Rooms: 5 (PB) $77-93
Full Breakfast
Credit Cards: A, B, C
Notes: 2, 3, 5, 8, 9, 10, 12

BENNETTSVILLE

The Breeden House Inn
404 East Main Street, 29512
(803) 479-3665

Built in 1886 as a wedding present for the builder's bride, the romantic Breeden House is a beautifully restored southern mansion on two acres. It is listed on the National Register of Historic Places and is located 20 minutes off I-95. The main house has a wraparound porch with 29 columns and rocking chairs. The carriage house has a porch with swings, rocking chairs, and ceiling fans. Beautiful decor, pool, cable TV in all rooms, phone in some rooms. One mile from a freshwater lake that has a mile-long jetty down the center; near muse-

---

year; 6 Pets welcome; 7 Children welcome; 8 Tennis nearby; 9 Swimming nearby; 10 Golf nearby; 11 Skiing nearby; 12 May be booked through travel agent

ums and antique shops. A haven for antique lovers and great for walkers and runners. Owned and operated by a Christian family. No smoking.

Hosts: Wesley and Bonnie Park
Rooms: 7 (PB) $50-55
Full Breakfast
Credit Cards: A, B, D
Notes: 2, 5, 9, 10, 12

CHARLESTON

The Belvedere
40 Rutledge Avenue, 19401
(803) 722-0973

A late 1800s Colonial mansion in the downtown historic district on Colonial Lake has an 1800 Georgian interior with mantels and woodwork. Three large bedrooms have antiques, Oriental rugs, and family collections. Easy acccess to everything in the area.

Hosts: David Spell and Rick Zender
Rooms: 3 (PB) $95
Continental Breakfast
Credit Cards: None
Closed December 1-February 15
Notes: 2, 7 (over 8), 8, 9, 10

Country Victorian Bed and Breakfast
105 Tradd Street, 29401-2422
(803) 577-0682

Come, relive the charm of the past. Relax in a rocker on the piazza of this historic home and watch the carriages go by. Walk to antique shops, churches, restaurants, art galleries, museums, and all historic points of interest. The house, built in 1820, is located in the historic district south of Broad. Rooms have private entrances and contain antique iron and brass beds, old quilts, antique oak and wicker furniture, and braided rugs over heart-of-pine floors. Homemade cookies will be waiting. Many extras!

Host: Diane Deardurff Weed
Rooms: 2 (PB) $65-90
Expanded Continental Breakfast
Credit Cards: None
Notes: 2, 5, 7, 8, 9, 10, 12

1837 Bed and Breakfast
126 Wentworth Street, 29401
(803) 723-7166

Enjoy accommodations in a wealthy cotton planter's home and brick carriage house centrally located in Charleston's historic district. Walk to boat tours, the old market, antique shops, restaurants, and main attractions. Near the Omni and College of Charleston. Full gourmet breakfast is served in the formal dining room and includes sausage pie, Eggs Benedict, ham omelets, and home-baked breads. The 1837 Tea Room serves afternoon tea to our guests and the public. Off-street parking.

Hosts: Sherri and Richard Dunn
Rooms: 8 (PB) $45-85
Full Breakfast
Credit Cards: A, B, C, D
Notes: 2, 8, 9, 10

NOTES: Credit cards accepted: A Master Card; B Visa; C American Express; D Discover Card; E Diners Club; F Other; 2 Personal checks accepted; 3 Lunch available; 4 Dinner available; 5 Open all

Historic Charleston Bed and Breakfast
43 Legare Street, 29401
(803) 722-6606

Through the auspices of this reservation service, you will enjoy your stay in a private home, carriage house, or mansion in a neighborhood of enchanting walled gardens, cobblestone streets, and moss-draped oaks. Each home is unique, with a warm and friendly atmosphere provided by a host who sincerely enjoys making guests welcome. All are historic properties dating from 1720 to 1920, yet all are up-to-date with private baths, air conditioning, phones, and TV. Sixty-five locations ranging from $50 to $135. Charlotte Fairey, coordinator.

The Kitchen House, Circa 1732

King George IV Inn and Guests
32 George Street, 29401
(803) 723-9339

This two-century-old, Federal-style historic house, circa 1790, in Charleston's downtown historic district was originally named the Freneau House after Peter Freneau. There are four stories in all, with three levels of lovely Charleston porches. All rooms have fireplaces, either Federal or plain Gothic Revival, ten-foot ceilings, six-foot ceilings, original wide-planked, hardwood floors, and six-foot oak doors. Walk to shopping, fine dining, antiques, and mansions.

Hosts: Jean, Bara, B. J., and Mike
Rooms: 8 (PB) $50-75
Continental Breakfast
Credit Cards: A, B
Notes: 2, 5, 6 (by arrangement), 7, 8, 9, 10, 12

The Kitchen House, Circa 1732
126 Tradd Street, 29401
(803) 577-6362

Nestled in the heart of the historic district, the Kitchen House is a completely restored 18th-century kitchen dwelling. Southern hospitality, absolute privacy, cozy fireplaces, antiques, patio, and colonial herb garden await you. The refrigerator and pantry are stocked for breakfast. The pre-Revolutionary War house was featured in *Colonial Homes* magazine and written up in the *New York Times*.

Host: Lois Evans
Rooms: 3 (PB) $75-150
Full Breakfast
Credit Cards: A, B
Notes: 2, 5, 7, 8, 9, 10, 12

---

year; 6 Pets welcome; 7 Children welcome; 8 Tennis nearby; 9 Swimming nearby; 10 Golf nearby; 11 Skiing nearby; 12 May be booked through travel agent

Rutledge Victorian Inn and Guest House

114 Rutledge Avenue, 29401
(803) 722-7551

Welcome to the past! This century-old Victorian house in Charleston's downtown historic district is quaint but elegant, with large, decorative porches, columns, and antique gingerbread. The authentic Old Charleston house has decorative fireplaces, hardwood floors, ten-foot doors and windows, old furnishings, and antiques. Modern amenities include air conditioning, TV, private or shared baths, ice machine, and refrigerator. Walking distance to all historic attractions.

Hosts: Jean, Sara, B. J., and Mike
Rooms: 11 (6 PB; 5 SB) $45-85
Continental Breakfast
Credit Cards: A, B
Notes: 2, 5, 6 (some), 7, 8, 9, 10, 12

Two Meeting Street Inn

2 Meeting Street, 29401
(803) 723-7322

Acclaimed as the belle of Charleston's bed and breakfasts, this 1890 Victorian mansion offers southern elegance. Located in the historic district at Battery Park, the inn is filled with antiques, Oriental rugs, and Tiffany windows. Your continental breakfast is served in the side garden or formal dining room, while the afternoons are enjoyed on the front porch rocking chairs. Within six blocks of most historic sites, restaurants, and shops.

Host: Karen M. Spell
Rooms: 9 (PB) $90-150
Continental Breakfast
Credit Cards: None
Notes: 2, 5, 7, (over 8), 9, 10

Two Meeting Street Inn

FORT MILL

Pleasant Valley Bed and Breakfast

1921 Blackwelder, 29715
(803) 547-7551

Nestled in the beautiful Olde English district, the inn is located in a wooded area in the peaceful countryside. Built in 1874, it has been restored and furnished with some antiques. Each bedroom has a TV, some have fireplaces. After breakfast in the spacious, country kitchen, take a stroll in the shade of 100-year-old oak trees. Equipped with facilities for the disabled, it is convenient to Carewinds Theme Park, Heritage USA, and Charlotte, North Carolina.

NOTES: Credit cards accepted: A Master Card; B Visa; C American Express; D Discover Card; E Diners Club; F Other; 2 Personal checks accepted; 3 Lunch available; 4 Dinner available; 5 Open all

Hosts: Bob and Gayla Lawrence
Rooms: 9 (PB) $39
Continental Breakfast
Credit Cards: None
Notes: 2, 7, 8, 9, 10, 12

GEORGETOWN

Ashfield Manor
3030 South Island Road, 29440
(803) 546-5111; (803) 546-0464

This Christian home offers southern hospitality in the style of a real southern plantation. Ashfield Manor offers an elegant country setting. All rooms are oversized and redecorated with period furnishings; private entrance and color TV. Continental breakfast is served in your room, the parlor, or on the 57-foot screened porch. Georgetown is quaint and historic with many attractions.

Hosts: David and Carol Ashenfelder
Rooms: 4 (SB) $40-55
Continental Breakfast
Credit Cards: A, B, C, D, E
Notes: 2, 5, 7, 8, 9, 10

The Shaw House
8 Cypress Court, 29440
(803) 546-9663

After eight years, we are still excited about everyone who visits. We have a wonderful location overlooking a beautiful marsh, seen from a spacious den with an all-glass view. Large bedrooms; many antiques; well-stocked with books and magazines; wonderful nooks to relax and read; piano. Only five blocks from downtown and great restaurants. Our guests always leave with a recipe or prayer tied with a ribbon.

Host: Mary Shaw
Rooms: 3 (PB) $50
Full Breakfast
Credit Cards: None
Notes: 2, 5, 7, 8, 9, 10

MCCLELLANVILLE

Laurel Hill Plantation
8913 North Highway 17, P. O. Box 190, 29458
(803) 887-3708

Laurel Hill faces the Atlantic Ocean and Intracoastal Waterway. Wraparound porches provide a spectacular view of creeks and marshes. The reconstructed house is furnished with country and primitive antiques that reflect the Low Country lifestyle. Boating on the waterway depends on the tide, weather, and availability of the captain. Thirty minutes north of Charleston.

Host: Jackie and Lee Morrison
Rooms: 4 (PB) $65-75
Full Breakfast
Credit Cards: None
Notes: 2, 5, 7 (over 6), 9, 10, 12

MYRTLE BEACH

Serendipity, an Inn
407 North 71st Avenue, 29577
(803) 449-5268

An award-winning, mission-style inn is just 300 yards from the ocean beach

---

year; 6 Pets welcome; 7 Children welcome; 8 Tennis nearby; 9 Swimming nearby; 10 Golf nearby; 11 Skiing nearby; 12 May be booked through travel agent

and has a heated pool and Jacuzzi. All rooms have air conditioning, color TV, and refrigerator. Secluded patio, Ping-Pong, and shuffleboard. Over 70 golf courses nearby, as well as fishing, tennis, restaurants, theaters, and shopping. Ninety miles to historic Charleston.

Hosts: Cos and Ellen Ficarra
Rooms: 12 (PB) $62
Expanded Continental Breakfast
Credit Cards: A, B, C, D
Notes: 7, 8, 9, 10, 12

SUMTER

Sumter Bed and Breakfast
6 Park Avenue, 29150
(803) 773-2903

This charming 1896 home has large, front porches and faces a lush green, quiet park in the historic district. The spacious guest rooms are upstairs and have fireplaces and private entrance. The livingroom also has a fireplace. Many antiques, HBO, library with numerous artifacts. The innkeepers offer a historic tour, spinning wheel demonstrations, and a golf package with 15 courses to choose from.

Hosts: Bob and Merilyn Carnes
Rooms: 4 (2 PB; 2 SB) $45-55
Continental Breakfast
Credit Cards: A, B
Notes: 2, 5, 8, 10

NOTES: Credit cards accepted: A Master Card; B Visa; C American Express; D Discover Card; E Diners Club; F Other; 2 Personal checks accepted; 3 Lunch available; 4 Dinner available; 5 Open all

South Dakota

CANOVA

Skoglund Farm
Route 1, Box 45, 57321
(605) 247-3445

Skoglund Farm brings back memories of Grandpa and Grandma's home. It is furnished with antiques and collectibles. A full, home-cooked evening meal and breakfast are served. You can sight-see in the surrounding area, visit Little House on the Prairie Village, hike, horseback ride, or just relax. Several country churches are located nearby.

Hosts: Alden and Delores
Rooms: 5 (SB) $30 each adult; $20 each teen; $15 each child; children 5 and under free
Full Breakfast
Credit Cards: None
Notes: 2, 4, 6, 7, 8, 9, 10

CUSTER

Custer Mansion Bed and Breakfast
35 Centennial Drive, 57730
(605) 673-3333

This historic 1891 Victorian Gothic mansion is on one acre and has a lovely patio and willow trees. Charmingly restored and beautifully decorated, it offers western hospitality and delicious home cooking in the unique setting of the beautiful Black Hills. Near Custer State Park, Mount Rushmore, and Crazy Horse Monument. Nearby restaurants. Recommended by *Bon Appetit* and *GMC Friends* magazines.

Hosts: Mill and Carole Seaman
Rooms: 6 (2 PB; 4 S2B) $45-65
Full Breakfast
Credit Cards: None
Notes: 2, 5, 7, 8, 9, 10, 11

RAPID CITY

Audrie's Cranbury Corner Bed and Breakfast
Rural Route 8, Box 2400, 57702
(605) 342-7788

The ultimate in charm and Old World hospitality, our country home and five-acre estate is surrounded by thousands of acres of national forest in a secluded Black Hills setting. Each comfortable room, suite, and cottage has private entrance, hot tub, patio, cable TV, and refrigerator. Free trout fishing, hiking, biking available on property.

---

year; 6 Pets welcome; 7 Children welcome; 8 Tennis nearby; 9 Swimming nearby; 10 Golf nearby; 11 Skiing nearby; 12 May be booked through travel agent

226 South Dakota

Hosts: Hank and Audry Kuhnhauser
Rooms: 6 (PB) $78-85
Full Breakfast
Credit Cards: None
Notes: 2, 5, 8, 9, 11

The Carriage House
721 West Boulevard, 57701
(605) 343-6415

The stately, three-story, pillared Colonial house is on a historic, tree-lined boulevard of Rapid City. The English country decor creates an ambience of elegance, refinement, and relaxing charm. Gourmet breakfasts are served in the formal dining room. The famous Black Hills and Badlands are minutes away, offering attractions like Mount Rushmore, Crazy Horse Monument, boating, and skiing.

Hosts: Betty and Joel King
Rooms: 5 (2 PB; 3 SB) $59-89
Full Breakfast
Credit Cards: A, B
Notes: 2, 5, 8, 9, 10, 11, 12

SENECA

Rainbow Lodge
HC 78, Box 81, 57473
(605) 436-6795

Spend a quiet, relaxing day or evening by the lake on the prairie. Beautiful landscaping and trees, meditation areas, and chapel. Homey atmosphere; handicapped accessible; full, country-style breakfast; four miles off Highway 212. Reservations required.

Hosts: Ralph and Ann Wheeler
Rooms: 3 (SB) $30-45
Full Breakfast
Credit Cards: None
Notes: 2, 4, 5, 7, 8, 9, 10

Mulberry Inn

YANKTON

Mulberry Inn
512 Mulberry Street, 57078
(605) 665-7116

The beautiful Mulberry Inn offers the ultimate in comfort and charm in a traditional setting. Built in 1873, the inn features parquet floors, six guest rooms furnished with antiques, two parlors with marble fireplaces, and a large porch. Minutes from the Lewis and Clark Lake and within walking distance of the Missouri River, fine restaurants, and downtown, the inn is listed on the National Register of Historic Places.

Host: Millie Cameron
Rooms: 6 (2 PB; 4 SB) $30-48 May-September; $25-43 October-April
Continental Breakfast; Full breakfast available with extra charge
Credit Cards: A, B, C
Notes: 2, 5, 7, 8, 9, 10

NOTES: Credit cards accepted: A Master Card; B Visa; C American Express; D Discover Card; E Diners Club; F Other; 2 Personal checks accepted; 3 Lunch available; 4 Dinner available; 5 Open all

Tennessee

HENDERSONVILLE

Monthaven Bed and Breakfast
1154 West Main Street, 37075
(615) 824-6319

Monthaven offers the serene tranquility of middle Tennessee and the convenience of being only 15 miles north of downtown Nashville. Built in the mid 1800s on the site of Indian camping grounds, Monthaven is an important example of Greek Revival architecture with Victorian decorative elements. Also located on the property is a 200-year-old log cabin rebuilt in 1938 with the original timbers and finished inside with white oak and cedar. All of Nashville's attractions are within 30 minutes.

Host: Hugh Waddell
Rooms: 3 (2 PB; 1 SB) $65-85
Cabin: 1 (PB)
Expanded Continental Breakfast
Credit Cards: A, B, C
Notes: 2, 3, 4, 5, 6, 7, 8, 9, 10, 12

KNOXVILLE

Langskomen Bed and Breakfast
1212 Nighthawk Lane, 37923
(615) 693-3797

You are invited to experience the Old World hospitality of Langskomen, a country bed and breakfast home located in a secluded, wooded area approximately three miles from I-75 and I-40, just west of Knoxville. Langskomen is convenient to many of the TVA lakes, the Great Smoky Mountains National Park, the University of Tennessee, cultural events, and art festivals. A wide selection of restaurants is nearby. Rooms are furnished with family antiques. Advance reservations required.

Hosts: Bill and Jan Groenier
Rooms: 2 (SB) $50
Full Breakfast
Credit Cards: None
Notes: 2, 5, 8, 10

---

year; 6 Pets welcome; 7 Children welcome; 8 Tennis nearby; 9 Swimming nearby; 10 Golf nearby; 11 Skiing nearby; 12 May be booked through travel agent

LIMESTONE

Snap Inn
Bed and Breakfast
Route 3, Box 102, 37681
(615) 257-2482

Your hosts will welcome you into this gracious 1815 Federal home furnished with antiques and set in farm country. Enjoy the peaceful mountain view from the full back porch, or play a game of pool. Located close to Davy Crockett State Park; 15 minutes to historic Jonesborough or Greenville.

Hosts: Dan and Ruth Dorgan
Rooms: 2 (PB) $50
Full Breakfast
Credit Cards: None
Notes: 2, 5, 6, 7 (1 only), 8, 9, 10, 12

MURFREESBORO

Clardy's Guest House
435 East Main Street, 37130
(615) 893-6030

This large Victorian home was built in 1898 and is located in Murfreesboro's historic district. You will marvel at the ornate woodwork, beautiful fireplaces, and magnificent stained glass overlooking the staircase. The house is filled with antiques, as are local shops and malls.

Hosts: Robert and Barbara Deaton
Rooms: 4 (2 PB; 2 SB) $30-40
Continental Breakfast
Credit Cards: None
Notes: 2, 5, 8, 9, 10

RUGBY

Grey Gables
Bed 'N Breakfast
Highway 52, P.O. Box 5252, 37733
(615) 628-5252; (800) 669-0052

Grey Gables, located one miles from the 1880s historic village of Rugby, offers visitors the best of its Victorian English heritage. The house is decorated with country and Victorian antiques and has porches with white wicker and rustic rockers. Enjoy an elegant evening meal and a hearty country breakfast. Access to golf, swimming, hiking, and bicycling; canoe rental and shuttle available. Private luncheons, teas, dinners, receptions, conferences, retreats, and group functions are accommodated by reservation. Horses boarded; no smoking.

Hosts: Bill and Linda Brooks Jones
Rooms: 8 (4 PB; 4 SB) $90
Full Breakfast
Credit Cards: A, B
Notes: 2, 3, 4, 5, 9, 10

SEVIERVILLE

Milk and Honey
Country Hideaway
2803 Old Country Way, 37864
(615) 428-4858

Just a few minutes from the Great Smoky Mountains National Park, Gatlinburg, and Pigeon Forge, this peaceful mountain hideaway awaits you with its big front porch, inviting interior furnished

---

NOTES: Credit cards accepted: A Master Card; B Visa; C American Express; D Discover Card; E Diners Club; F Other; 2 Personal checks accepted; 3 Lunch available; 4 Dinner available; 5 Open all

with antiques and quilts, and the aroma of a busy country kitchen. Enjoy a book or a game by the crackling fire in the parlor. Serving hearty Amish or country-style breakfast each morning.

Host: Fern Miller
Rooms: 6 (2 PB; 4 SB) $60-90 in-season; $49-79 off-season
Full Breakfast
Credit Cards: A, B
Notes: 2, 5, 8, 9, 10, 11, 12

Von-Bryan Inn

2402 Hatcher Mountain Road, 37862
(615) 453-9832

This mountaintop log home with panoramic view of the Great Smoky Mountains from the bedrooms has common areas and rockers on the porches. The inn offers Jacuzzis in some rooms, a swimming pool, and hot tub. Pick-up and delivery by helicopter. Near hiking, tubing, fishing, and picnicking in the mountains. Also near Dollywood, Pigeon Forge, and Gatlinburg. Afternoon refreshments. Separate three-bedroom, two-bath log chalet also available.

Hosts: D. J. and JoAnn Vaughn
Rooms: 5 plus log chalet (PB) $80-125
Full Breakfast
Credit Cards: A, B, C
Notes: 2, 4, 5, 9, 10, 11, 12

TOWNSEND

Smoky Bear Lodge

160 Bear Lodge Drive, 37882
(615) 448-6442; (800) 48-SMOKY

The Smoky Bear Lodge has a 1,500-square-foot conference room complementing the ideal Christian-oriented retreat site for youth, choirs, leadership, Sunday school classes, and pastors. The lodge is also perfect for that special family vacation. Situated in the foothills of the Great Smoky Mountains, the view from the rocker-lined front porch is incredible. Enjoy the activities, pool, hot tub, and beautiful sunrises and sunsets while you learn or relax. Call for brochure.

Hosts: Gary and Sandy Plummer
Rooms: 12 (10 PB; 2 SB) $55-85
Full Breakfast
Credit Cards: A, B, C
Notes: 2, 3, 4, 5, 7, 9, 10, 11

WAVERLY

The Nolan House Inn

Route 4, Highway 13 North, 37185
(615) 296-2511 day; (615) 535-2366 evening

The Nolan House is located seven miles from Loretta Lynn's dude ranch. It is ten miles from the Nathan Bedford Forest State Park, and 60 miles from Nashville and Opryland. This 1870 house is on the National Register of Historic Places and has the original cisterns, cellars, a shop with original artwork for sale, a dog trot, and original landscaping.

Hosts: Gordon and LaVerne Turner
Rooms: 4 (3 PB; 1 SB) $30-35
Continental Breakfast
Credit Cards: None
Notes: 2, 8, 9, 10

---

year; 6 Pets welcome; 7 Children welcome; 8 Tennis nearby; 9 Swimming nearby; 10 Golf nearby; 11 Skiing nearby; 12 May be booked through travel agent

Texas

ABILENE

Bolin's Prairie House Bed and Breakfast
508 Mulberry, 79601
(915) 675-5855

Nestled in the heart of Abilene is a 1902 home furnished with antiques and modern luxuries combined to create a homelike, warm atmosphere. Downstairs are high ceilings, hardwood floors, and a wood-burning stove. Upstairs are four unique bedrooms—Love, Joy, Peace, and Patience—each beautifully decorated. Breakfast is a special baked egg dish, fruit, and homemade bread served in the dining room on blue and white china.

Hosts: Sam and Ginny Bolin
Rooms: 4 (SB) $40-50
Full Breakfast
Credit Cards: A, B, C, D, E
Notes: 2, 5

FREDERICKSBURG

Baron's Creek Inn
110 East Creek Street, 78624
(512) 997-9398; (800) 800-4082

This turn-of-the-century home provides guests with unique accommodations: four complete suites, plus a Sunday house, each with private bath. A continental breakfast may be enjoyed on the front porch or veranda, or in the privacy of your suite. Located two blocks from the downtown area.

Hosts: Kenneth and Brooke Schweers
Rooms: 5 (PB) $85-95
Expanded Continental Breakfast
Credit Cards: A, B
Notes: 2, 5, 12

Baron's Creek Inn

Haus Wilhelmina
409 North Cora Street, 78624
(512) 997-3997; (512) 997-4712 reservations

NOTES: Credit cards accepted: A Master Card; B Visa; C American Express; D Discover Card; E Diners Club; F Other; 2 Personal checks accepted; 3 Lunch available; 4 Dinner available; 5 Open all

Located three blocks from historic downtown Marketplatz shopping district, museums, and German bakeries and cuisine, Haus Wilhemina is near beautiful churches of 25 denominations, including renowned Catholic and Lutheran edifices. Minna insists on serving hearty German breakfasts in the historic home that was once the city's kindergarten. English also spoken.

Host: Minna Knopp
Rooms: 2 (1 PB; 1 SB) $75
Full Breakfast
Credit Cards: A, B
Notes: 2, 5, 7, 8, 9, 10

J Bar K Ranch Bed and Breakfast

HC 10, Box 53 A, 78624
(512) 669-2471

A large German rock home with a historic marker on a Texas hill-country ranch is furnished with antiques. We offer a full country breakfast, Texas hospitality, and convenience to Fredericksburg, with its German heritage and architecture. Many quaint shops, antique stores, excellent restaurants, Nimitz Naval Museum, Enchanted Rock, and tours of Lyndon Johnson's ranch are nearby.

Hosts: Kermit and Naomi Kothe
Rooms: 4 (3 PB; 1 SB) $65
Full Breakfast
Credit Cards: None
Notes: 2, 7, 8, 9, 10

Magnolia House

101 East Hackberry, 78624
(512) 997-0306

Circa 1925; restored 1991. Enjoy southern hospitality in a grand and gracious manner. Outside, lovely magnolias and a bubbling fish pond and waterfall set a soothing mood. Inside, beautiful livingroom, game room, and formal dining room provide areas for guests to mingle. Four romantic rooms and two suites have been thoughtfully planned, appointed with antiques and original paintings by the owner. A southern-style, seven-course breakfast completes a memorable experience.

Host: Geri Lilley
Rooms: 4 (2 PB; 2 SB) $68-98
Suites: 2
Full Breakfast
Credit Cards: None
Notes: 2, 5, 8, 9, 10, 12

Schmidt Barn

Route 2, Box 112A3, 78624
(512) 997-5612

The Schmidt Barn is located one and one-half miles outside historic Fredericksburg. This 130-year-old limestone structure has been turned into a charming guest house with loft bedroom, livingroom, bath, and kitchen. The hosts live next door. German-style breakfast is left in the guest house for you. The house has been featured in national magazines and is decorated with antiques.

---

year; 6 Pets welcome; 7 Children welcome; 8 Tennis nearby; 9 Swimming nearby; 10 Golf nearby; 11 Skiing nearby; 12 May be booked through travel agent

Hosts: Dr. Charles and Loretta Schmidt
Guest House: 1 (PB) $70-100
Continental Breakfast
Credit Cards: A, B
Notes: 2, 6, 7, 8, 9, 10

GALVESTON

The Gilded Thistle

1805 Broadway, 77550
(409) 763-0894; (800) 654-9380

An oasis on Galveston Island. Enter a wonderland of Victorian collectibles, superb service, and bountiful amenities. Take tea with Blanche, Black Bart, and the other bears, and see their pretties. Be pampered by hosts who endeavor to share a feeling of history and that special sense of graciousness of times gone by. Featured in the *New York Times* and *Country Inns, Southern Living, House Beautiful* and other magazines. Call or write for brochure. Teddy bears are free.

Host: Helen Hanemann
Rooms: 3 (1 PB; 2 SB) $125-145
Full Breakfast
Credit Cards: A, B
Notes: 2, 3, 4, 5, 7, 8, 9, 10

The Victorian Bed and Breakast Inn

511 17th Street, 77550
(409) 762-3235

Galveston's first bed and breakfast, this 1899 home exudes Victorian romantic charm. A wraparound veranda, bird's eye maple floors, tiled fireplaces, and unique built-in benches welcome guests once they pass by 90-year-old palm and magnolia trees. Extremely large bedrooms offer guests king beds, porches, antiques, and warm, personal touches. Located in a historic district, the home is less than one mile from the gulf beach and an easy walk to museums, shopping, restaurants, and theaters.

Hosts: Janice and Bob Hellbusch
Rooms: 6 (2 PB; 4 SB) $55-125
Continental Breakfast
Credit Cards: A, B, C
Notes: 2, 5, 9, 10, 12

GRANBURY

Nutt House Hotel and Bed and Breakfast Inn

Town Square, 76048
(817) 573-5612

The Nutt House Hotel, located on the square, was built in 1893. Furnishings are from the 1880s with air conditioning and ceiling fans. The inn, a log cabin, is located one block from the square on a beautiful wooded lot on the water. The buffet-style restaurant specializes in country cooking, serving specialties of chicken and dumplings, bite-size cornbread, and homemade cobblers. After the ringing of the dinner bell, period-costumed young ladies are at your service.

Host: Sylvia (Sam) Overpeck
Rooms: 17 (8 PB; 9 SB) $39-75
Full or Continental Breakfast
Credit Cards: A, B, C
Notes: 3, 4, 5, 7, 9

NOTES: Credit cards accepted: A Master Card; B Visa; C American Express; D Discover Card; E Diners Club; F Other; 2 Personal checks accepted; 3 Lunch available; 4 Dinner available; 5 Open all

HOUSTON

The Highlander
607 Highland Street, 77009
(713) 861-6110

The Highlander is located in the re-emerging neighborhood of Woodland Heights at the northwest edge of downtown Houston. This 1922 four-square house has been transformed by the hosts. The beauty of The Highlander is well matched to the gracious hospitality you will receive. Enjoy tea in the parlor, a luxurious whirlpool bath, and lively conversation. Close to the theater district, city parks, jogging trail, and Houston's many attractions. The McIrvins will be happy to assist you in planning your stay in Houston.

Hosts: Arlen and Georgie McIrvin
Rooms: 4 (2 PB; 2 SB) $60-75
Full Breakfast
Credit Cards: A, B, C
Notes: 2, 5, 7, 8, 10

Robin's Nest
4104 Greeley, 77006
(713) 528-5821

This white two-story Victorian, circa 1894, started life as the main house for a dairy farm. The Holsteins and Jerseys are gone now, and somewhat astounding, it stands today in a vibrant, urban neighborhood nestled between downtown, universities, the theater district, and the Texas Medical Center. We have casual eateries as well as quality restaurants. Interesting attractions are too numerous to list. Advise us of your interests, and we can help plan your stay.

Host: Robin Smith
Rooms: 2 (1 PB; 1 SB) $45-75
Full Breakfast
Credit Cards: A, B
Notes: 2, 5, 8, 9, 10, 12

JEFFERSON

McKay House Bed and Breakfast Inn
306 East Delta, 75657
(903) 665-7322; (214) 348-1929

Jefferson is a town where one can relax, rather than get tired. The McKay House, an 1851 Greek Revival cottage, features a pillared front porch and many fireplaces, offering genuine hospitality in a Christian atmosphere. Heart-of-pine floors, 14-foot ceilings, and documented wallpapers complement antique furnishings. Guests enjoy a full "gentleman's" breakfast. Victorian nightshirts and gowns await pampered guests in each bed chamber.

Hosts: Tom and Peggy Taylor
Rooms: 4 plus 3 suites (PB) $70-125
Full Breakfast
Credit Cards: A, B
Notes: 2, 5, 10, 12

SAN ANTONIO

The Belle of Monte Vista
505 Belknap Place, 78212
(210) 732-4006

---

year; 6 Pets welcome; 7 Children welcome; 8 Tennis nearby; 9 Swimming nearby; 10 Golf nearby; 11 Skiing nearby; 12 May be booked through travel agent

J. Riely Gordon designed this 1890 Queen Anne Victorian home located conveniently in this famous Monte Vista historic district, one mile from downtown San Antonio. The house has eight fireplaces, stained-glass windows, hand-carved oak interior, and Victorian furnishings. Near zoo, churches, river walk, El Mercado, arts, and universities. Transportation to and from airport, bus, and train station upon request. Easy access from all major highways.

Hosts: Mary Lou and Jim Davis
Rooms: 8 (4 PB; 4 SB) $60
Full Breakfast
Credit Cards: None
Notes: 2, 5, 7, 8, 9, 10

The Belle of Monte Vista

UVALDE

Casa de Leona
1149 Pearsall, P. O. Box 1829, 78802
(512) 278-8550

The Spanish hacienda sits in the center of 17 acres along the Leona River on the old Fort Inge historic site. Enjoy flowing fountains, sun deck, gazebo on the river, hiking trails, bird watching, access to markets in Mexico, art and antique collections, and unique shopping boutiques. Four rooms plus guest cottage. Dinner by reservation.

Hosts: Carolyn and Ben Durr
Rooms: 4 plus cottage (3 PB; 1 SB) $55-76
Full or Continental Breakfast
Credit Cards: B, C, D
Notes: 2, 4

WINNSBORO

Thee Hubbell House
307 West Elm, 75494
(903) 342-5629

The spelling of "Thee" in our name denotes the Christian hospitality awaiting our visitors. Thee Hubbell House is hosted by the mayor and first lady of Winnsboro. You will be pampered with chocolate mints on your pillow, bubble baths, refreshments, and a full plantation breakfast. We offer honeymoon and anniversary packages and candlelight dinner by reservation. A 103-year-old, two-story Colonial home honored by a Texas historical marker and members of Texas Historical Hotel Association.

Hosts: Dan and Laurel Hubbell
Rooms: 5 (PB) $65-150
Full Breakfast
Credit Cards: A, B, C, D, E, F
Notes: 2, 3, 4, 7, 8, 9, 10, 12

NOTES: Credit cards accepted: A Master Card; B Visa; C American Express; D Discover Card; E Diners Club; F Other; 2 Personal checks accepted; 3 Lunch available; 4 Dinner available; 5 Open all

Utah

SAINT GEORGE

Seven Wives Inn
217 North 100 West, 84770
(801) 628-3737; (800) 484-1048 code 0165

The inn consists of two adjacent pioneer adobe homes with massive hand-grained moldings that frame windows and doors. Bedrooms are furnished with period antiques and handmade quilts. Some rooms have fireplaces; one has a whirlpool tub. Swimming pool on premises.

Hosts: Donna and Jay Curtis; Alison and Jon Bowcutt
Rooms: 13 (PB) $40-75
Full Breakfast
Credit Cards: A, B, C, E
Notes: 2, 5, 7, 8, 9, 10, 11

Vermont

ALBURG

Thomas Mott Homestead Bed and Breakfast
Blue Rock Road on Lake Champlain
Route 2, Box 149-B, 05440
(802) 796-3736; (800) 348-0843

Hosted by a criminology/American history major who enjoys gourmet cooking, this completely restored 1838 farmhouse has a guest livingroom with TV and fireplace overlooking the lake; game room with bumper pool and darts; quilt decor. Full view of Mt. Mansfield and Jay Peak. One hour to Montreal/Burlington; one and one-half hour to Lake Placid, New York and Stowe. Lake activities winter and summer. Amenities include Ben and Jerry's ice cream, lawn games, and horseshoes.

Host: Patrick J. Schallert, Sr.
Rooms: 4 (PB) $50-65
Full Breakfast
Credit Cards: None
Notes: 2, 4, 5, 7 (over 6), 9, 10, 11, 12

ANDOVER

The Inn at HighView
East Hill Road, 05143
(802) 875-2724

The Inn at HighView

NOTES: Credit cards accepted: A Master Card; B Visa; C American Express; D Discover Card; E Diners Club; F Other; 2 Personal checks accepted; 3 Lunch available; 4 Dinner available; 5 Open all

The Inn at HighView is located in wondrous seclusion high on East Hill in the tiny town of Andover and features panoramic views of the surrounding Green Mountains. The inn is a manificently restored farmhouse, circa 1800, with sauna, pool, and 52 acres of cross-country skiing and hiking trails. Excellent downhill skiing is located only 15 minutes away at Okemo Mountain. Located close to Weston, home of the famous Weston Priory and the Weston Playhouse. Dinner service on weekends.

Host: Greg Bohan
Rooms: 8 (PB) $80-125
Full Breakfast
Credit Cards: A, B
Notes: 2, 4, 5, 8, 9, 10, 11, 12

ARLINGTON

Hill Farm Inn
Rural Route 2, Box 2015, 05250
(802) 375-2269; (800) 882-2545

Hill Farm is one of Vermont's original farmsteads. The property was owned by the Hill family for more than 200 years after they received a land grant from King George III in 1775. It has been an inn since 1905 and retains much of the character of an old farm vacation inn with hearty home cooking, home-grown vegetables, and rooms decorated to capture the spirit and charm of New England farmhouses. Homemade jam is a complimentary take-home gift. Families welcome.

Hosts: George and Joanne Hardy
Rooms: 13 (8 PB; 5 SB) $60-95
Full Breakfast
Credit Cards: A, B, C, D
Notes: 2, 4, 5, 6 (limited), 7, 8, 9, 10, 11, 12

BELLOWS FALLS

Blue Haven Guest House
Bellows Falls, 05101
(802) 463-9008

This 1830 schoolhouse, lovingly restored by artist-hostess Helene, speaks of Old World roots. Homemade granola and prize-winning hot muffins prettily served with antique glassware are always a staple. Enjoy goose down-covered canopy beds set among hand-painted furniture in peaceful, cozy rooms. Claim one of the vintage rockers by the stone hearth and experience a singularly effective stress remedy. Midweek special rates; local train excursions; sleigh rides and hay rides.

Host: Helene Champagne
Rooms: 6 (3 PB; 3 SB) $58-78
Full Breakfast weekends; Continental breakfast weekdays
Credit Cards: A, B, C
Notes: 2, 5, 7, 8, 9, 10, 11, 12

BRATTLEBORO

The Green River Guest House
Rural Free Delivery 4, Box 789, 05301
(802) 254-4114

---

year; 6 Pets welcome; 7 Children welcome; 8 Tennis nearby; 9 Swimming nearby; 10 Golf nearby; 11 Skiing nearby; 12 May be booked through travel agent

Looking for an idyllic getaway? Nestled in a valley that time appears to have passed by, the Green River Guest House, situated on 13 acres of meadowland, is the perfect place to unwind. Relax and listen to the gentle rush of the Green River. Take a walk down a country road to the covered bridge, 200-year-old church, and old-fashioned swimming hole. Inside this charming and spacious home, comfort and warm hospitality await the guests. Romans 8:28.

Hosts: Patrick and Lorraine Ryan
Rooms: 2 (SB) $50
Full Breakfast
Credit Cards: A, B

BROOKFIELD

Birch Meadow Farm
East Street, Rural Route 1, Box 294A, 05036
(802) 276-3156

Capture the real Vermont on our 232-acre hilltop setting with panoramic views. Look down on a picturesque farm surrounded by pastures and mountains. Our elegant bed and breakfast suite has a wood-burning stove with fireplace screen, white and brass queen bed with down comforter, private bath, and private entrance. Also, fully equipped luxury log cabins, nestled in the woods have microwave ovens, gas grills, and picnic tables. Enjoy swimming, walking trails, and our pond stocked with trout. A country breakfast is served.

Hosts: Mary and Matthew Comerford
Rooms: 4 (PB) $80-90
Full or Continental Breakfast
Credit Cards: A, B
Notes: 2, 5, 7, 9, 10, 11, 12

Birch Meadow Farm

CHELSEA

Shire Inn
8 Main Street, P. O. Box 37, 05038
(802) 685-3031; (800) 441-6908

The Shire Inn was built in 1832, and the Federal brick facade is an architectural gem of the period. The inn still operates five of the original fireplaces, four of which are in guest bedrooms. At the inn, guests enjoy cycling, cross-country skiing, and hiking. Nearby they can swim, canoe, fish, hunt antiques, downhill ski, and go sleigh riding. Chelsea is within 30 to 34 miles of Woodstock/Quechee, Montpelier, or Hanover, New Hampshire, home of Dartmouth College.

Hosts: James and Mary Lee Papa
Rooms: 6 (PB) $80-165
Full Breakfast

NOTES: Credit cards accepted: A Master Card; B Visa; C American Express; D Discover Card; E Diners Club; F Other; 2 Personal checks accepted; 3 Lunch available; 4 Dinner available; 5 Open all

Credit Cards: A, B
Notes: 2, 4, 7 (over six), 8, 9, 10, 11

CHESTER

The Hugging Bear Inn and Shoppe
Main Street, 05143
(802) 875-2412

Teddy bears peek out the windows and are tucked in all the corners of this beautiful Victorian house built in 1850. If you love teddy bears, you'll love the Hugging Bear. There are six guest rooms with private shower baths and a teddy bear in every bed. Full breakfast and afternoon snack are served.

Hosts: Georgette, Paul, and Diane Thomas
Rooms: 6 (PB) $55-90
Full Breakfast
Credit Cards: A, B, C, D
Notes: 2, 5, 6 (limited, 7, 8, 9, 10, 11

The Stone Hearth Inn
Route 11 West, 05143
(802) 875-2525

Built in 1810, the Stone Hearth Inn is known for its informal hospitality. All of the guest rooms retain the romance of the period. Fully licensed pub, dining room, library, and large recreation room with whirlpool spa. Gift shop sells imported German nutcrackers. Near skiing and golf. Perfect for families.

Hosts: Janet and Don Strohmeyer
Rooms: 10 (PB) $60-100

Full Breakfast
Credit Cards: A, B, D
Notes: 2, 3, 4, 5, 7, 8, 9, 10, 11, 12

CUTTINGSVILLE

Buckmaster Inn
Lincoln Hill Road, Rural Route 1
Box 118, 05738
(802) 492-3485

The Buckmaster Inn (1801) was an early stagecoach stop in Shrewsbury. Standing on a knoll overlooking a picturesque barn scene and rolling hills, it is situated in the Green Mountains. A center hall, grand staircase, and wide-pine floors grace the home, which is decorated with family antiques and crewel handiwork done by your hostess. Extremely large, airy rooms, wood-burning stove, four fireplaces, two large porches.

Hosts: Sam and Grace Husselman
Rooms: 4 (2 PB; 2 SB) $45-60
Full Breakfast
Credit Cards: None
Notes: 5, 7, 8, 9, 10, 11

Maple Crest Farm
Lincoln Hill, Box 120, 05738
(802) 492-3367

This 27-room 1808 farmhouse has been preserved for five generations and is located in the heart of the Green Mountains in Shrewsbury. It has been a bed and breakfast for 21 years. Ten miles north of Ludlow and ten miles south of Rutland, an area that offers much to visitors. Pico, Killington, and Okemo are nearby for downhill skiing. Cross-country skiing and hiking are offered on the premises.

Hosts: William and Donna Smith
Rooms: 4 (SB) $20-25 per person
Full Breakfast
Credit Cards: None
Closed January
Notes: 2, 5, 7, 8, 11

Silas Griffith Inn

DANBY

Silas Griffith Inn
South Main Street, Rural Route 1
Box 66F, 05739
(802) 293-5567

Built by Vermont's first millionaire, this Victorian inn was built in 1891 in the heart of the Green Mountains, with spectacular mountain views. It features 17 delightful, antique-furnished rooms and a fireplace in the living and dining room. Hiking, skiing, antiquing nearby. Come and enjoy our elegant meals and New England hospitality.

Hosts: Paul and Lois Dansereau
Rooms: 17 (11 PB; 6 SB) $69-84
Full Breakfast
Credit Cards: A, B, C
Notes: 2, 4, 5, 7, 9, 10, 11, 12

FAIRLEE

Rutledge Inn and Cottages
Lake Morey Drive, 05045
(802) 333-9722

An outstanding lakeside resort offers genuine hospitality and excellent New England dining. It is located in the lovely Connecticut Valley on a spring-fed lake with a sandy beach and 1,000 feet of waterfront. No phones or TV! We have all kinds of activities for adults and young people that you can take part in, or just plain ignore. A place to step back in time to enjoy summer the way it was meant to be enjoyed.

Hosts: Bob and Nancy Stone
Rooms: 38 (33 PB; 5 SB) $75-108
Full Breakfast
Credit Cards: None
Open June to Labor Day
Notes: 2, 3, 4, 7, 8, 9, 10

Silver Maple Lodge and Cottages
Rural Route 1, Box 8, 05045
(802) 333-4326; (800) 666-1946

A historic bed and breakfast country inn is located in a four-season recreational area. Enjoy canoeing, fishing,

---

NOTES: Credit cards accepted: A Master Card; B Visa; C American Express; D Discover Card; E Diners Club; F Other; 2 Personal checks accepted; 3 Lunch available; 4 Dinner available; 5 Open all

golf, tennis, and skiing within a few miles of the lodge. Visit nearby flea markets and country auctions. Choose a newly renovated room in our old farmhouse or a handsome, pine-paneled cottage room. Many fine restaurants are nearby. Darmouth College is 17 miles away. Also offered are hot air balloon packages, inn-to-inn bicycling, canoeing, and walking tours. Brochure available.

Hosts: Scott and Sharon Wright
Rooms: 14 (12 PB; 2 SB) $42-62
Continental Breakfast
Credit Cards: A, B, C
Notes: 2, 5, 7, 8, 9, 10, 11, 12

Silver Maple Lodge and Cottages

JEFFERSON

Mannsview Inn
Rural Route 2, Box 4319, 05464
(802) 644-8321

Built in the mid 1800s, Mannsview Inn is a large, white Colonial with a Victorian flair, bay windows, French doors, and high ceilings. It is set on ten beautiful acres on a plateau near Smugglers' Notch, at the base of Mt. Mansfield, surrounded by beautiful mountain pastures, trout streams, maple and pine forests, and breathtaking mountain views. Enjoy skiing in the winter, maple syrup in the spring, outdoor sports in the summer, and gorgeous foliage in the fall.

Hosts: Bette and Kelley Mann
Rooms: 6 (4 PB; 2 SB) $40-70
Full Breakfast
Credit Cards: A, B, C
Notes: 2, 5, 7 (over 10), 8, 9, 10, 12

LOWER WATERFORD

Rabbit Hill Inn
Pucker Street and Route 18, 05848
(802) 748-5168; (800) 76-BUNNY

Full of whimsical and charming surprises, this Federal-period inn, established in 1795, has been lavished with love and attention. Many guest rooms have fireplaces and canopied beds. Chamber music, candlelit gourmet dining, and turn-down service make this an enchanting and romantic hideaway in a tiny, restored village overlooking the mountains. An award-winning, nationally acclaimed inn, our service is inspired by Philippians 2:7.

Hosts: John and Maureen Magee
Rooms: 18 (PB) $78-159
Full Breakfast
Credit Cards: A, B
Closed first two weeks of November and all of April
Notes: 2, 4, 9, 10, 11, 12

MIDDLEBURY

A Point of View
Rural Delivery 3, Box 2675, 05753
(802) 388-7205

Only three and one-half miles from the village, this country bed and breakfast has a view of the Green Mountains (hence its name) in a quiet setting in an exclusive neighborhood perfect for walking. Excellent beds in comfortable rooms with access to livingroom with large TV; game room with regulation pool table; bike. The atmosphere is warm and friendly; each guest is special.

Host: Marie Highter
Rooms: 2 (SB) $40-50
Full Breakfast
Credit Cards: None
Notes: 2, 5, 7 (by arrangement), 8, 10, 11

MOUNT HOLLY

The Hortonville Inn
Hortonville Road, Box 14, 05758
(802) 259-2587

The Hortonville Inn sits on a hilltop on 13 acres in an area known for its snow and reliable skiing. The inn was recently renovated and has a porch dining area with fireplace and wonderful mountain views. In-room movies are available, with more than 250 selections; complimentary wine and hors d'oeuvres are served by the fire at the end of the day. Herbal tea and homemade cookies are always available. Breakfast is country style, with four courses.

Hosts: Ray and Mary Maglione
Rooms: 5 (2 PB; 3 SB) $50-75
Full Breakfast
Credit Cards: A, B
Notes: 2, 4, 5, 7 (over 6), 8, 9, 10, 11, 12

NEWFANE

The Four Columns Inn
P. O. Box 278, 05345
(802) 365-7713

Built more than 150 years ago with hand-hewn beams and timbers, this stately house is located at the west end of the village green in the lovely town of Newfane. Explore the 150 acres of beautiful wooded land behind the inn with hiking trails. Enjoy the gardens around the inn or the back roads on your bicycles. Swim in the pool, or relax by the stream; in winter, alpine and cross-country skiing are close by. A healthful breakfast is served. No smoking. Pets accepted on approval with a $10 extra charge.

Hosts: Pam and Jacques Allembert
Rooms: 15 (PB) $100-170
Full Breakfast
Credit Cards: A, B, C
Notes: 2, 4, 5, 6, 7, 8, 9, 10, 11

STOWE

Inn at the Brass Lantern
717 Maple Street, 05672
(802) 253-2229; (800) 729-2980

NOTES: Credit cards accepted: A Master Card; B Visa; C American Express; D Discover Card; E Diners Club; F Other; 2 Personal checks accepted; 3 Lunch available; 4 Dinner available; 5 Open all

This traditional Vermont bed and breakfast country inn in the heart of Stowe is an award-winning restoration of an 1810 farmhouse and carriage barn overlooking Mt. Mansfield, Vermont's most prominent mountain. The inn features period antiques, quilts, and planked floors. The entire inn is air conditioned. Most rooms have views, and some have fireplaces. Special packages include honeymoon, skiing, golf, sleigh and surrey rides, and more. No smoking.

Hosts: Mindy and Andy Aldrich
Rooms: 9 (PB) $65-120
Full Breakfast
Credit Cards: A, B, C
Notes: 2, 5, 8, 9, 10, 11, 12

Ski Inn

Route 108, 05672
(802) 253-4050

Back in the 1940s, Larry and Harriet Heyer, the only original owners left in Stowe, designed their ski lodge along New England architectural lines. The result is a lovely, white Vermont country inn with fieldstone fireplace on a sloping hillside in a setting of green hemlocks and fir trees. In appearance, it is a traditional Old New England inn, but in comfort it is modern. Located back from the highway among the evergreens, this is a quiet, restful place to relax. Flat hiking, trout stream, cookouts, cross-country ski trails, close to downhill ski area.

Host: Harriet Heyer
Rooms: 10 (5 PB; 5 SB) $40-50

Continental Breakfast; Full breakfast in ski season
Credit Cards: None
Notes: 2, 4 (in winter), 5, 6 (by arrangement), 7, 8, 9, 10, 11

Stowe Bound Lodge

673 South Main Street, 05672
(800) 727-8693

Stowe Bound is located in the picturesque village of Stowe. A family-run lodge, the emphasis is on an enjoyable atmosphere and a memorable stay. Each morning a full breakfast is served. Evening meals are available in winter. Golf, mountain climbing, horseback riding, glider and airplane rides, skiing. Christian visitors are appreciated.

Hosts: Dick, Erika, and Sarah
Rooms: 12 (4 PB; 6 SB) $40-80
Full Breakfast
Credit Cards: None
Notes: 2, 4, 5, 6, 7, 8, 9, 10, 11

Timberhölm Inn

452 Cottage Club Road, 05672
(802) 253-7603; (800) 753-7603

This delightful country inn in a quiet, wooded setting serves afternoon tea and cookies in the summer and après ski soup in the winter. We have ten individually decorated rooms with quilts and antiques and a spacious, sunny great room with a large fieldstone fireplace. Game room with shuffleboard; deck overlooking the Worchester Mountains; outdoor hot tub; cable TV.

---

year; 6 Pets welcome; 7 Children welcome; 8 Tennis nearby; 9 Swimming nearby; 10 Golf nearby; 11 Skiing nearby; 12 May be booked through travel agent

Hosts: The Hildebrand family
Rooms: 10 (PB) $60-100
Full Breakfast
Credit Cards: A, B
Notes: 2, 5, 7, 8, 9, 10, 11, 12

WAITSFIELD

Mad River Barn
Route 17, 05673
(802) 496-3310

This classic Vermont lodge has spacious rooms, some with TVs and kitchenettes. There are three meeting rooms on the premises. Dinner is served by reservation. We are near skiing, hiking, and biking and have an outdoor pool, white perennial garden, and grand stone fireplace in the pub.

Host: Betsy Pratt
Rooms: 15 (PB) $24-48 per person
Full Breakfast
Credit Cards: A, B, C
Notes: 2, 4; 5, 7, 9, 10, 11, 12

Mountain View Inn
Rural Free Delivery Box 69, Route 17, 05673
(802) 496-2426

The Mountain View Inn is an old farmhouse, circa 1826, that was made into a lodge in 1948 to accommodate skiers at nearby Mad River Glen. Today it is a country inn with seven rooms. Meals are served family style around the antique harvest table where good fellowship prevails. Sip mulled cider around a crackling fire in our livingroom when the weather turns chilly.

Hosts: Fred and Suzy Spencer
Rooms: 7 (PB) $55-55 per person
Full Breakfast
Credit Cards: None
Notes: 2, 4, 5, 7, 8, 9, 10, 11, 12

Newtons' 1824 House Inn
Route 100, Box 159, 05673
(802) 496-7555

Enjoy relaxed elegance in one of six beautiful guest rooms at this quintessential farmhouse on 52 acres. The inn features antiques, chandeliers, fireplaces, and classical music. Breakfast by the fire includes such whimsical gourmet delights as soufflés, crepes, blueberry buttermilk pancakes, and freshly squeezed orange juice. Cross-country skiing and swimming hole are nearby.

Hosts: Nick and Joyce Newton
Rooms: 6 (PB) $75-105
Full Breakfast
Credit Cards: A, B, C
Notes: 2, 5, 7, 8, 9, 10, 11

WARREN

Beaver Pond Farm Inn
Golf Course Road
Rural Delivery Box 306, 05674
(802) 583-2861

Beaver Pond Farm Inn, a small, gracious country inn near the Sugarbush ski area, is located 100 yards from the first tee of the Sugarbush Golf Course, transformed into 40 kilometers of cross-country ski trails in the winter. *Bed &*

NOTES: Credit cards accepted: A Master Card; B Visa; C American Express; D Discover Card; E Diners Club; F Other; 2 Personal checks accepted; 3 Lunch available; 4 Dinner available; 5 Open all

Breakfast in New England calls it "The best of the best." Rooms have down comforters and beautiful views. Hearty breakfasts are served, and snacks are enjoyed by the fireplace. Continental dinners are offered three times a week. Hiking, biking, soaring, and fishing nearby. Ski and golf packages are available.

Hosts: Bob and Betty Hansen
Rooms: 6 (4 PB; 2 SB) $64-90
Full Breakfast
Credit Cards: A, B, C
Notes: 2, 4, 7 (over 5), 8, 9, 10, 11, 12

WATERBURY

Grünberg Haus Bed and Breakfast
Route 100 South, Rural Route 2,
Box 1595, 05676
(802) 244-7726; (800) 800-7760

Spontaneous, personal attention in a hand-built Austrian mountain chalet with a huge fieldstone fireplace, sauna, Jacuzzi, grand piano, trails, tennis court, and imaginative full breakfasts. Cozy Old World chalet guest rooms feature balconies and antiques. Innkeeper and professional musician Chris plays the piano regularly. Innkeeper Mark takes care of the chickens, cats, and guineas. "Like visiting a pal," *Hudson Dispatch*. "Quiet, romantic," *Vermont* magazine. Central to Stowe, Waitsfiefld, Sugarbush, Burlington, Montpelier. Home of Ben & Jerry's ice cream! Adventure packages.

Hosts: Christopher Sellers and Mark Frohman
Rooms: 10 (5 PB; 5 SB) $55-90
Full Breakfast
Credit Cards: A, B, C, D, F
Notes: 2, 4 (for 10 or more), 5, 7, 8, 9, 10, 11

Inn at Blush Hill
Blush Hill Road, Rural Route 1
Box 1266, 05676
(802) 244-7529; (800) 736-7522

This Cape Cod bed and breakfast, circa 1790, sits on five acres with spectacular mountain views. The inn has a large common room, library, antiques, and four fireplaces, one in a guest room. Enjoy a breakfast of Vermont products at a ten-foot farmhand's table in front of a bay window overlooking the Worcester Mountains. Afternoon refreshments are served. We are adjacent to Ben and Jerry's ice cream factory, and skiing at Stowe and Sugarbush are only minutes away.

Hosts: Gary and Pamela Gosselin
Rooms: 6 (4 PB; 2 SB) $55-110 seasonal
Full Breakfast
Credit Cards: A, B, C, D
Notes: 2, 5, 7, 8, 9, 10, 11, 12

WEST DOVER

Red Cricket Inn
Route 100, P. O. Box 396, 05356-0396
(800) 733-2742

This warm, comfortable inn offers old-fashioned hospitality in a relaxed and spacious atmosphere. All rooms have

---

year; 6 Pets welcome; 7 Children welcome; 8 Tennis nearby; 9 Swimming nearby; 10 Golf nearby; 11 Skiing nearby; 12 May be booked through travel agent

color cable TV and air conditioning. Fireside lounge, game room, sauna, fitness room. Small pets welcome; small and large groups welcome. Winter rates Modified American Plan; summer rates bed and breakfast. In the heart of the Mt. Snow Haystack, Stratton area.

Host: Barbara Hunter
Rooms: 24 (22 PB; 2 SB) $59-150
Full Breakfast
Credit Cards: A, B, D
Notes: 2, 4, 5, 6, 7, 8, 9, 10, 11, 12

The Wilder Homestead Inn

WESTON

The Wilder Homestead Inn
Lawrence Hill Road, Rural Route 1
Box 106D, 05161
(802) 824-8172

Built in 1827 with Rumford fireplaces and original Moses Eagon stenciling, the inn has been carefully restored by us and has quiet surroundings and antique furnishings. Walk to village shops, museums, summer theater. Nearby are Weston Priory, fine restaurants, skiing. Weston is a village that takes you back in time. No smoking.

Hosts: Peggy and Roy Varner
Rooms: 7 (5 PB; 2 SB) $60-95
Full Breakfast
Credit Cards: A, B (deposit only)
Notes: 2, 7 (over 6), 8, 9, 10, 11

WILMINGTON

Shearer Hill Farm Bed and Breakfast
P. O. Box 1453, 05363
(802) 464-3253; (800) 437-3104

This is country living at its finest. Located on a pristine gravel road five miles from Wilmington, large, charming guest rooms await. Awake to the aroma of freshly brewed coffee, homemade muffins, and bread. Cross-country skiing on the premises; downhill skiing, swimming, boating, horseback riding, and hiking nearby.

Hosts: Bill and Patti Pusey
Rooms: 4 (PB) $70-80
Continental Breakfast
Credit Cards: A, B
Notes: 2, 5, 7, 8, 9, 10, 11

Virginia

ALEXANDRIA—DISTRICT OF COLUMBIA

Morrison House
116 South Alfred Street, 22314
(703) 838-8000

Awarded 1990 "Best Inn of the Year," Morrison House is an 18th-century-style manor house in historic Old Town Alexandria, just minutes from Washington, D.C. Elegant Federal-period reproductions, including mahogany four-poster beds, marble baths, crystal chandeliers, and decorative fireplaces.

Hosts: Robert and Rosemary Morrison
Rooms: 45 (PB) $135-400
Full Breakfast Available
Credit Cards: A, B, C, D
Notes: 2, 3, 4, 5, 9, 10

ALTAVISTA

Castle To Country House
1010 Main Street, 24517
(804) 369-4911

Lodging in bed and breakfast establishments is a European tradition combining comfort, privacy, and the many advantages of being a guest in a private home. Our brick cottage-style home was built in 1936 and is decorated in Victorian and country style. Guest facilities include dining room, sitting room, livingroom with fireplace, and a sunroom. Our bedrooms offer queen and king beds. We offer all the amenities of a luxury hotel.

Hosts: Jim and Christine Critchley
Rooms: 3 (PB) $45-50
Full or Continental Breakfast
Credit Cards: A, B, C, D
Notes: 2, 3, 4, 5, 8, 10

Memory House

ARLINGTON

Memory House
6406 North Washington Boulevard, 22205
(703) 534-4607

---

year; 6 Pets welcome; 7 Children welcome; 8 Tennis nearby; 9 Swimming nearby; 10 Golf nearby; 11 Skiing nearby; 12 May be booked through travel agent

In a prime location is this charming, ornate, restored 1899 Victorian with period antiques, wall stenciling, prize-winning handicrafts, and collectibles. The subway, one block away, quickly takes you to the mall area of Washington, D.C. By car, it is ten minutes to the White House, museums, and monuments. Two guest rooms; air conditioning; TV; antique clawfoot tubs. Relax on wicker furniture on the porch or in double parlors. Share in old-fashioned comfort and friendship.

Hosts: John and Marlys McGrath
Rooms: 2 (1 PB; 1 SB) $70
Expanded Continental Breakfast
Credit Cards: None
Notes: 2, 5, 8, 9, 12

BASYE

Sky Chalet Country Inn and Restaurant

Route 263 West, P. O. Box 300, 22810
(703) 856-2147

A romantic hideaway in the Shenandoah Valley boasts spectacular, breathtaking, panoramic mountain and valley views. Welcoming weary travelers since 1937, Sky Chalet has rustic, homey, comfortable rooms, some with fireplaces, but no TV or phones! Enjoy mountaintop dining with the open stone fireplace, homemade breads, desserts, valley applebutter, and delicious entrees! Relax in the gazebo, hammocks, or the rocking chairs on the veranda. The mountain lovers' paradise—where every season is beautiful!

Hosts: Ken and Mona Seay
Rooms: 10 (PB) $49-59
Continental Breakfast
Credit Cards: A, B
Notes: 2, 4, 5, 6, 7, 8, 9, 10, 11, 12

CHATHAM

Sims-Mitchell House

242 Whittle Street, Southwest
P.O. Box 429, 24531-0429
(804) 432-0595; (800) 967-2867 reservations

Visit this historic 1870 home with a family atmosphere. In the raised English basement of the main house is a guest suite with two bedrooms, sitting room, bath, and private entrance. Also available is a cottage with two bedrooms, bath, sitting room, and kitchen. Located a few blocks from two preparatory schools, Chatham Hall and Hargrave Military Academy. Danville is 20 miles away; Smith Mountain Lake is 25 miles away. Your hostess is a cookbook writer, your host is a planetarium specialist.

Hosts: Henry and Patricia Mitchell
Suites: 2 (PB) $45-70
Full Breakfast
Credit Cards: A, B
Notes: 2, 7, 12

CULPEPER

Fountain Hall

609 South East Street, 22701
(703) 825-8200; (800) 476-2944

Fountain Hall is a charming 1859 Colonial Revival bed and breakfast. All of

---

NOTES: Credit cards accepted: A Master Card; B Visa; C American Express; D Discover Card; E Diners Club; F Other; 2 Personal checks accepted; 3 Lunch available; 4 Dinner available; 5 Open all

our rooms are tastefully decorated with antiques and have been individually named, making each truly unique. Three guest rooms have private porches overlooking the grounds. Fireplaces can be found in the common rooms. Fountain Hall provides easy access to Amtrak, Dulles, national, and Charlottesville airports, as well as Washington, D.C. and Fredericksburg.

Hosts: Steve and Kathi Walker
Rooms: 5 (PB) $65-95
Expanded Continental Breakfast
Credit Cards: A, B, C, D
Notes: 2, 5, 8, 10, 11

FREDERICKSBURG

Lavista Plantation
4420 Guinea Station Road, 22408
(703) 898-8444

This Classical Revival-style manor house, circa 1838, is situated on ten quiet, country acres and is surrounded by farm fields and mature trees. Stocked pond, six fireplaces, antiques, rich Civil War past, radio, phone, TV, bicycles. Fresh eggs and homemade jams are served for breakfast; air conditioned; close to historic attractions.

Hosts: Edward and Michele Schiesser
Room: 1 (PB) $63.90
Suite: 1 (PB) $79.88
Full Breakfast
Credit Cards: A, B
Notes: 5, 7

HARRISONBURG

Kingsway Bed and Breakfast
3581 Singers Glen Road, 22801
(703) 867-9696

Enjoy a view of the mountains from this modern, country home in the beautiful Shenandoah Valley. This residence reveals the carpentry and homemaking skills of your hosts who enjoy people and meeting their needs. Many house plants, outdoor flowers, and the in-ground pool make your stay restful and refreshing. Just four and one-half miles from downtown; near Skyline Drive, caverns, historic sites, antique shops, and flea markets.

Hosts: Chester and Verna Leaman
Rooms: 2 (PB) $45-55
Expanded Continental Breakfast
Credit Cards: None
Notes: 2, 5, 6, 7, 9, 10, 11, 12

LEESBURG

Carradoc Hall Hotel
1500 East Market Street, Route 7, 22075
(703) 771-9200; (800) 552-6702

Traditional hospitality in the Virginia hunt country is found on eight picturesque acres of grand, old trees and natural springs, which provide the country estate setting for the Carradoc Hall Mansion house, dating from 1773. The

---

year; 6 Pets welcome; 7 Children welcome; 8 Tennis nearby; 9 Swimming nearby; 10 Golf nearby; 11 Skiing nearby; 12 May be booked through travel agent

mansion contains four two-room suites restored to their original 18th-century elegance, and attached is a 122-guest room hotel with its own lobby, banquet rooms, and outdoor pool. Convenient to Morven Park, Waterford, Oatlands, and Dulles International Airport.

Hosts: Tony, Sam, and Freddy
Rooms: 126 (PB) $53-125
Continental Breakfast
Credit Cards: A, B, C, D, E, F
Notes: 2, 3, 4, 5, 6, 7, 8, 9, 10, 12

LURAY

Shenandoah River Roost
Route 3, Box 566, 22835
(703) 743-3467

Sit on the front porch of this two-story log home and enjoy beautiful views of the mountains and the Shenandoah River. Located three miles west of Luray Caverns, ten miles west of Skyline Drive and Shenandoah National Park. Swimming, tubing, canoeing, and golf are all nearby. No smoking.

Hosts: Rubin and Gerry McNab
Rooms: 2 (SB) $60
Full Breakfast
Credit Cards: None
Closed November 1-May 1
Notes: 2, 7 (over 12), 9, 10

MADISON HEIGHTS

Winridge Bed and Breakfast
Route 1, Box 362, 24572
(804) 384-7220

Come and share our grand, southern Colonial home on 14 acres of country meadows. Our homestay offers wonderful views of the mountains. Sit on the swing or rest in the hammock under the big shade trees. Stroll around the lawn and gardens enjoying the beauty of birds, butterflies, and flowers. Relax on two large porches. Close to Lynchburg and the Blue Ridge Parkway.

Hosts: LoisAnn and Ed Pfister
Rooms: 3 (1 PB; 2 SB) $59-69
Full Breakfast
Credit Cards: None
Notes: 2, 5, 7, 8, 10, 11

MANASSAS

Sunrise Hill Farm Bed and Breakfast
5513 Sudley Road, 22110
(703) 754-8309

Just 35 minutes from Washington, D.C., this Civil War treasure is within the heart of the Goodacre Manassas National Battlefields. An uncommonly beautiful location overlooking Bull Run Creek, it is convenient to Washington, D.C., Harpers Ferry, Antietam, Skyline Drive, Luray Caverns, numerous historic sites, and antique-filled towns. Furnished in period style, it is a haven for Civil War buffs and guests visiting Washington, D.C. and northern Virginia.

Hosts: Frank and Sue Boberek
Rooms: 3 (1 PB; 2 SB) $65
Full Breakfast

NOTES: Credit cards accepted: A Master Card; B Visa; C American Express; D Discover Card; E Diners Club; F Other; 2 Personal checks accepted; 3 Lunch available; 4 Dinner available; 5 Open all

Credit Cards: A,B
Notes: 2, 5, 7, 8, 9, 10, 11, 12

MEADOWS OF DAN

Spangler Bed and Breakfast
Route 2, Box 108, 24120
(703) 952-2454

The Spangler Bed and Breakfast borders the National Parkway at milepost 180, four miles south of Mabry Mill, elevation 3,000 feet. The farmhouse dates from 1904 with four large bedrooms, livingroom with piano, dining room, and kitchen. There is an old log cabin for one couple, and a new log cabin for two couples with shared bath. These face a three and one-half-acre lake with fishing, boating, and swimming. No smoking. Groups welcome.

Hosts: Trudy and Harold Spangler
Rooms: 7 (1 PB; 6 SB) $40-55
Full Breakfast
Credit Cards: None
Notes: 2, 5, 7, 8, 9, 10, 11

MORATTICO

Holly Point
Mailing address: Route 3, Box 410,
Lancaster, 22503
(804) 462-7759

Your hostess at this stately home claims to be related to George Washington and will be happy to direct you to local historic sites. You will enjoy the 120 acres of pine forest and views of the scenic Rappahannock River. There are opportunities for land and water sports.

Host: Mary Chilton Graham
Rooms: 3 (1 PB; 2 SB) $30-40
Continental Breakfast
Credit Cards: None
Closed November-April
Notes: 2, 6, 7, 9

NELLYSFORD

Upland Manor
Route 1, Box 375, 22958
(804) 361-1101

Between the Blue Ridge Mountains and Charlottsville, Upland Manor offers a relaxing getaway to enjoy scenic and historic areas or nearby activities of golf, tennis, swimming, canoeing, skiing, horseback riding, antiqueing, and more. Beautifully restored to its original grandeur, Upland Manor offers ten large, comfortable rooms; three have Jacuzzis.

Hosts: Karen Estey and Elena Woodard
Rooms: 10 (PB) $95-125
Expanded Continental Breakfast
Credit Cards: A, B
Notes: 8, 9, 10, 11, 12

NEW CHURCH

The Garden and the Sea Inn
Route 710, P. O. Box 275, 23415
(804) 824-0672

---

year; 6 Pets welcome; 7 Children welcome; 8 Tennis nearby; 9 Swimming nearby; 10 Golf nearby; 11 Skiing nearby; 12 May be booked through travel agent

This elegant, European-style country inn with French-style gourmet restaurant is near Chincoteague and Assateague islands. Large, luxurious rooms, beautifully designed; spacious private baths; Victorian detail; stained glass; Oriental rugs; antiques; bay windows. Beautiful beach and wildlife refuge are nearby; afternoon tea; romantic escape package; chamber music dinner concerts. Three more guest rooms are under renovation.

Hosts: Jack Betz and Victorian Olian
Rooms: 2 (PB) $75-95
Expanded Continental Breakfast
Credit Cards: A, B, C, D, E
Notes: 2, 4, 8, 9, 10, 12

PALMYRA

Palmer Country Manor
Route 2, Box 1390, 22963
(800) 253-4306

Palmer Country Manor is a gracious 1830 estate on 180 wooded acres. Each private cottage features a large living area with a fireplace and color TV, and a deck with a view. Ballooning, swimming, fishing, hiking, white water rafting, biking, historic sites, and fine dining. Packages include breakfast and dinner.

Hosts: Gregory and Kathleen Palmer
Rooms: 12 (10 PB; 2 SB) $90-125
Full Breakfast
Credit Cards: A, B, C
Notes: 2, 3, 4, 5, 7, 8, 9, 10, 12

RICHMOND

The Emmanuel Hutzler House
2036 Monument, 23220
(804) 353-6900

Designed in the Italian Renaissance style, the interior of this house has a classical, early-Renaissance appearance, with natural mohagany paneling, leaded-glass windows, and coffered ceilings with dropped beams. The large livingroom where guests can relax has a marble fireplace flanked by mohogany bookcases. Centrally located, the inn is convenient for a mid-week business trip or a lovely setting for a weekend getaway.

Host: Lyn M. Benson
Rooms: 4 (PB) $85-125
Full Breakfast
Credit Cards: A, B, C
Notes: 2, 5, 7 (over 12), 8, 9, 10, 12

The William Catlin House
2304 East Broad Street, 23223
(804) 780-3746

Richmond's first and oldest bed and breakfast features antique, canopy poster beds, and working fireplaces. A delicious full breakfast is served in the elegant dining room. Built in 1845, this richly appointed home is in the Church Hill historic district and was featured in *Colonial Homes* and *Southern Living* magazines. Directly across from St. John's Church, where Patrick Henry gave his famous "Liberty or Death"

NOTES: Credit cards accepted: A Master Card; B Visa; C American Express; D Discover Card; E Diners Club; F Other; 2 Personal checks accepted; 3 Lunch available; 4 Dinner available; 5 Open all

speech. Just five minutes from I-95 and Route 64.

Hosts: Robert and Josie Martin
Rooms: 5 (3 PB; 2 SB) $89.50
Full Breakfast
Credit Cards: A, B
Notes: 2, 5, 7, 12

SMITH MOUNTAIN LAKE

The Manor at Taylor's Store
Route 1, Box 533, 24184
(703) 721-3951

This historic 120-acre estate with an elegant manor house provides romantic accommodations in guest suites with fireplaces, antiques, canopied beds, private porches, and use of hot tub, billiards, exercise room, and guest kitchen. A separate three-bedroom, two-bath cottage is ideal for a family. Enjoy six private, spring-fed ponds for swimming, canoeing, fishing, hiking. Full hearthealthy, gourmet breakfast is served in the dining room with panoramic views of the countryside.

Hosts: Lee and Mary Lynn Tucker
Rooms: 6 (4 PB; 2 SB) $60-85
Full Breakfast
Credit Cards: A, B
Notes: 2, 3, 5, 7, 8, 9, 10, 11, 12

STAUNTON

Frederick House
Frederick and New Streets, 24401
(703) 885-4220; (800) 334-5575

A historic town house hotel in the European tradition, Frederick House is located downtown in the oldest city in the Shenandoah Valley. It is convenient to shops and restaurants; across the street from Mary Baldwin College; two blocks from Woodrow Wilson's birthplace. All rooms are furnished with TV, phone, air conditioning, and private entrance.

Hosts: Joe and Evy Harman
Rooms: 14 (PB) $45-95
Full Breakfast
Credit Cards: A, B, C, D, E
Notes: 2,, 5, 7, 8, 9, 10, 11, 12

Thornrose House at Gypsy Hill
531 Thornrose Avenue, 24401
(703) 885-7026

Outside, this turn-of-the-century Georgian residence has a wraparound veranda and Greek colonnades. Inside, a fireplace and grand piano create a formal but comfortable atmosphere. Five attractive bedrooms with private baths are on the second floor. Your hosts offer afternoon tea, refreshments, and conversation. Adjacent to a 300-acre park that is great for walking, with tennis, golf, and ponds. Other nearby attractions include the Blue Ridge National Park, natural chimneys, Skyline Drive, Woodrow Wilson's birthplace, and the Museum of American Frontier Culture.

Hosts: Suzanne and Otis Huston
Rooms: 5 (PB) $50-65
Full Breakfast

---

year; 6 Pets welcome; 7 Children welcome; 8 Tennis nearby; 9 Swimming nearby; 10 Golf nearby; 11 Skiing nearby; 12 May be booked through travel agent

Credit Cards: None
Notes: 2, 5, 7, 8, 9, 10

STRASBURG

Hotel Strasburg
201 Holliday Street, 22657
(800) 348-8327

This charming Victorian restoration is in the antique capital of Virginia. All rooms have heat and air conditioning and are furnished with period antiques. Excellent dining room, quaint pub, meeting rooms for up to 30 people, golf, skiing, horseback riding, canoeing, theater, antiques, Civil War battlefields, museums, and swimming.

Host: Gary Rutherford
Rooms: 26 (PB) $69-149
Continental Breakfast
Credit Cards: A, B, C, E
Notes: 3, 4, 5, 7 (by arrangement), 8, 9, 10, 11, 12

TANGIER ISLAND

Sunset Inn
Box 156, 23440
(804) 891-2535

Enjoy accommodations one-half block from the beach with a view of the bay. Deck, air conditioning, bike riding, nice restaurants.

Host: Grace Brown
Rooms: 9 (PB) $50 winter; $60 summer
Continental Breakfast
Credit cards: None
Notes: 2, 5, 7, 9

WASHINGTON

Caledonia Farm Bed and Breakfast
Route 1, Box 2080, Flint Hill, 22627
(703) 675-3693

Enjoy ultimate hospitality, comfort, scenery, and recreation adjacent to Virginia's Shenandoah National Park. This romantic getaway to history and nature includes outstanding full breakfast, fireplaces, air conditioning, hayride, bicycles, lawn games, VCR, and piano. World's finest dining, caves, Skyline Drive, battlefields, stables, antiqueing, hiking, and climbing are all nearby. Washington, D.C. is 68 miles away; Washington, Virginia, just four miles. A Virginia historic landmark, the farm is listed on the National Register of Historic Places.

Host: Phil Irwin
Rooms: 3 (1 PB; 2 SB) $70-100
Full Breakfast
Credit cards: A, B
Notes: 2, 3, 4, 5, 7 (over 12), 8, 9, 10, 11, 12

The Foster-Harris House Bed and Breakfast
Main Street, P.O. Box 333, 22747
(703) 675-3757; (800) 666-0153

Located in the small, historic village of Washington, The Foster-Harris House offers Victorian charm, fresh flowers, down comforters, queen beds, private baths, mountain views, and warm

---

NOTES: Credit cards accepted: A Master Card; B Visa; C American Express; D Discover Card; E Diners Club; F Other; 2 Personal checks accepted; 3 Lunch available; 4 Dinner available; 5 Open all

hospitality. Minutes from Skyline Drive, Shenandoah National Park, five-star dining, and other diversions. One room has a fireplace and whirlpool bath. Central air conditioning.

Host: Camille Harris
Rooms: 4 (3 PB; 1 SB) $70-105
Full Breakfast
Credit Cards: A, B
Notes: 2, 5, 8, 10, 11, 12

WILLIAMSBURG

Applewood Colonial Bed and Breakfast
605 Richmond Road, 23185
(804) 229-0205; (800) 899-2753

The owner's unique apple collection is evidenced throughout this restored colonial home. Four elegant guest rooms (one suite with fireplace) are conveniently located four short blocks from Colonial Williamsburg and very close to the College of William and Mary campus. Antiques complement the romantic atmosphere. The dining room has a beautiful, built-in, corner cupboard and a crystal chandelier above the pedestal table where homemade breakfast is served. Afternoon tea; no smoking.

Host: Fred Strout
Rooms: 4 (PB) $70-100
Expanded Continental Breakfast
Credit Cards: A, B
Notes. 2, 5, 7, 8, 10

Fox Grape
701 Monumental Avenue, 23185
(804) 229-6914; (800) 292-3699

Warm hospitality awaits you just a ten-minute walk north of Virginia's restored Colonial capital. Furnishings include antiques, counted cross stitch, stained glass, stenciled walls, duck decoys, and a cup and plate collection. Points of interest include Colonial Williamsburg, Carter's Grove Plantation, Jamestown, Yorktown, and the College of William and Mary.

Hosts: Pat and Bob Orendorff
Rooms: 4 (PB) $58-68
Continental Breakfast
Credit Cards: A, B
Notes: 2, 5, 7, 8, 9, 10

Hite's Bed and Breakfast
704 Monumental Avenue, 23185
(804) 229-4814

This attractive Cape Cod has large rooms furnished with antiques. Phone, TV, and coffee maker in each room. Just a ten-minute walk to Colonial Williamsburg and one-half mile to the visitors' center. Three miles to Busch Gardens, and six miles to Williamsburg pottery.

Host: Mrs. James Hite
Rooms: 2 (SB) $50; $65 for private bath
Expanded Continental Breakfast
Credit Cards: None
Notes: 2, 5, 7, 8, 10

---

year; 6 Pets welcome; 7 Children welcome; 8 Tennis nearby; 9 Swimming nearby; 10 Golf nearby; 11 Skiing nearby; 12 May be booked through travel agent

Newport House
Bed and Breakfast
710 South Henry Street, 23185-4113
(804) 229-1775

A reproduction of an important 1756 home, Newport House has museum-standard period furnishings, including canopy beds. A five-minute walk to historic area. Full breakfast with Colonial recipes; Colonial dancing in the ballroom every Tuesday evening (beginners welcome). The host is a historian/author (including a book on Christ) and former museum director. The hostess is a gardener, beekeeper, 18th-century seamstress, and former nurse. A pet rabbit entertains at breakfast. No smoking.

Hosts: John and Cathy Millar
Rooms: 2 (PB) $90-110
Full Breakfast
Credit Cards: None
Notes: 2, 5, 7, 10, 12

WOODSTOCK

Azalea House
Bed and Breakfast
551 South Main Street, 22664
(703) 459-3500

A large Victorian house built in 1892 features family antiques and stenciled ceilings. Located in the historic Shenandoah Valley, it is close to Skyline Drive and mountains. Many Civil War and Revolutionary War historic sites are within a short driving distance. This home was used as the parsonage for the church two blocks away for about 75 years.

Hosts: Price and Margaret McDonald
Rooms: 3 (1 PB; 2 SB) $45-65
Full Breakfast
Credit Cards: A, B
Closed January 1-February 1
Notes: 2, 7, 9, 11

The Country Fare
402 North Main Street, 22664
(703) 459-4828

A warm, Shenandoah-country welcome awaits you in historic Woodstock. Built in 1772, this charming bed and breakfast was the site of one of the valley's many field hospitals during the Civil War. The house is furnished with Grandmother's antiques and area pieces. Stenciled designs and country collectibles abound in the three guest rooms. Home-baked breads, fruits in season, and some of Grandmother's surprises are breakfast features. A stay will surprise and delight you.

Host: Bette Hallgren
Rooms: 3 (1 PB; 2 SB) $45-65
Continental Breakfast
Credit Cards: B
Notes: 2, 5

NOTES: Credit cards accepted: A Master Card; B Visa; C American Express; D Discover Card; E Diners Club; F Other; 2 Personal checks accepted; 3 Lunch available; 4 Dinner available; 5 Open all

Washington

ANACORTES

Albatross Bed and Breakfast
5708 Kingsway West, 98221
(206) 293-0677

Across the street from Skyline Marina, our 1927 Cape Cod-style with large view deck offers king and queen beds. Nearby are Washington Park and the ferries to the San Juan Islands and Victoria, British Columbia. The marina offers charter boats, a deli, and a fine restaurant. Free transportation to and from ferries and Anacortes airport.

Hosts: Cecil and Marilyn Short
Rooms: 4 (PB) $60-75
Full Breakfast
Credit Cards: A, B, D
Notes: 2, 5, 6 (by arrangement), 7 (by arrangement), 10, 11, 12

BELLEVUE

Bellevue Bed and Breakfast
830 100th Avenue, Southeast, 98004
(206) 453-1048

Hilltop, mountain, and city views are enjoyed from our private suite or single rooms, which feature private baths and entrance. We serve a full breakfast, gourmet coffee, and complimentary extras at reasonable rates.

Hosts: Cy and Carol Garnett
Rooms: 2 (PB) $55
Full Breakfast
Credit Cards: A, B
Notes: 2, 3, 4, 5, 7 (over 12), 8, 9, 10, 11

Petersen Bed and Breakfast
10228 Southeast Eighth Street, 98004
(206) 454-9334

We offer two rooms five minutes from Bellevue Square with wonderful shopping and one-half block from the bus line to Seattle. Rooms have down comforters, and we have a hot tub on the deck. Children are welcome. No smoking.

Hosts: Eunice and Carl Peterson
Rooms: 2 (SB) $40-45
Full Breakfast
Credit Cards: None
Notes: 2, 5, 7, 9, 10

---

year; 6 Pets welcome; 7 Children welcome; 8 Tennis nearby; 9 Swimming nearby; 10 Golf nearby; 11 Skiing nearby; 12 May be booked through travel agent

BELLINGHAM

Circle F Bed and Breakfast
2399 Mt. Baker Highway, 98226
(206) 733-2509

Circla F Bed and Breakfast is a home away from home for all our guests. The Victorian-style ranch house was built in 1892 and is located on 330 acres of pasture and woodlands. We are a working farm, and you can enjoy hiking trails and visits with the farm animals. A hearty breakfast is served by a friendly farm family who enjoys the company of all visitors.

Host: Guy J. Foster
Rooms: 4 (1 PB; 3 SB) $45-55
Full Breakfast
Credit Cards: None
Notes: 2, 5, 7

CASHMERE

Cashmere Country Inn
5801 Pioneer Drive, 98815
(509) 782-4212

Just ten minutes from Leavenworth in the heart of apple country, this 1907 farmhouse is a true find. Everything from the country and rose gardens, charming furnishings, and lavish breakfast is done with style, elegance, and attention to detail. The large livingroom features a cozy fireplace; two rooms have private baths; two share a large bath with a claw foot tub. The sunny dining room with French windows overlooks the inn's orchard, pool, and hot tub. This is a delightful getaway!

Hosts: Patti and Dale Swanson
Rooms: 4 (2 PB; 2 SB) $60-75
Full Breakfast
Credit Cards: A, B, C
Notes: 2, 4, 5, 8, 9, 10, 11

COUPEVILLE

The Colonel Crockett Farm Bed and Breakfast Inn
1012 South Fort Casey Road, 98239
(206) 678-3711

The inn offers 135 years of Victorian/Edwardian serenity in an island setting with pastoral and marine views. Period antiques enhance three large bed/sitting rooms and two smaller bedrooms. Common areas include an oak-paneled library, a wicker-furnished solarium, and a dining room that features individual tables. Separate owner's apartment. This 1855 Victorian farmhouse is on the National Register of Historic Places and has extensive grounds, walkways, and flowerbeds. No smoking.

Hosts: Robert and Beulah Whitlow
Rooms: 5 (PB) $65-95
Full Breakfast
Credit Cards: A, B
Notes: 2, 5, 7 (over 14), 10, 12

Coupeville Inn
200 Coveland Street, P. O. Box 370, 98239
(206) 678-6668

NOTES: Credit cards accepted: A Master Card; B Visa; C American Express; D Discover Card; E Diners Club; F Other; 2 Personal checks accepted; 3 Lunch available; 4 Dinner available; 5 Open all

This blue and white French mansard building has rooms with private balconies overlooking the historic seaport and Penn's Cove. Beaches, trails, lighthouse, forts, and winery are nearby. Queen beds, color TV, phones, and freshly baked continental breakfast.

Hosts: Alan and Jan Dutcher
Rooms: 24 (PB) $49.50-85
Continental Breakfast
Credit Cards: A, B, C, D, E
Notes: 2, 5, 6 (by arrangement), 7, 8, 9, 10, 12

DEER HARBOR—ORCAS ISLAND

Deer Harbor Inn
P. O. Box 142, 98243
(206) 376-4110

For more than 70 years, thousands have enjoyed the solitude and natural beauty of Deer Harbor on Orcas Island. We offer eight guest rooms in a log cabin. There are two sitting and reading rooms and two decks with views. Fine dining is available at the Deer Harbor Inn Restaurant. Sailing and fishing charters and small boat rentals are available, as well as hiking, fishing, and bird watching. Drive to the top of Mt. Constitution for a stunning view.

Hosts: Craig and Pam Carpenter
Rooms: 8 (PB) $65-85
Continental Breakfast
Credit Cards: A, B, C
Notes: 2, 4, 5

Palmer's Chart House
P. O. Box 51, 98243
(206) 376-4231

We are the oldest bed and breakfast in San Juan County, having been in operation for more than 15 years. We have been featured in national magazines. A special feature of Palmer's Chart House is our sailing yacht, *Amante*, which is available to our guests for an additional fee.

Hosts: Majean and Don Palmer
Rooms: 2 (PB) $45-60
Full Breakfast
Credit Cards: None
Notes: 2, 5, 11, 12

ELLENSBURG

Murphy's Country Bed and Breakfast
Route 1, Box 400, 98926
(509) 925-7986

Two large guest rooms in a lovely 1915 country home with a sweeping view of the valley. Full breakfast; close to fly fishing and golfing.

Host: Doris Callahan-Murphy
Rooms: 2 (S1.5B) $55
Full Breakfast
Credit Cards: B, C
Notes: 2, 5, 10

LANGLEY—WHIDBEY ISLAND

Log Castle Bed and Breakfast
3273 East Saratoga Road, 98260
(206) 321-5483

---

year; 6 Pets welcome; 7 Children welcome; 8 Tennis nearby; 9 Swimming nearby; 10 Golf nearby; 11 Skiing nearby; 12 May be booked through travel agent

A log house on a private, secluded beach features turret bedrooms, wood-burning stoves, porch swings, and panoramic views of the beach and mountains. Relax before a large stone fireplace or listen to the call of gulls as you watch for bald eagles and sea lions.

Hosts: Senator Jack and Norma Metcalf
Rooms; 4 (PB) $80-100
Full Breakfast
Credit Cards: A, B
Notes: 2, 8

Log Castle

LOPEZ

MacKaye Harbor Inn
Route 1, Box 1940, 98261
(206) 468-2253

This Victorian beachfront bed and breakfast in the San Juan Islands is an ideal getaway, full of warmth and nostalgia. There is a sandy beach and extensive grounds on a tree-lined harbor. Wildlife frequents the area. Rowboat, kayaks, and bicycles are available. Excellent for small groups of five or six couples. The kitchen is available for guest use. No smoking.

Hosts: Robin and Mike Bergstrom
Rooms: 5 (1 PB; 4 SB) $69-105
Full Breakfast
Credit Cards: A, B
Notes: 2, 5, 9, 10, 12

MAPLE VALLEY

Maple Valley Bed and Breakfast
20020 Southeast 228 Street, 98038
(206) 432-1409

Welcome to our warm cedar home in the wooded Northwest. Spacious grounds, wildlife pond, and fine feathered friends. Experience hootenany pancakes, "hot babies," and gracious, family hospitality. Crest Airpark is just minutes away. Volkswalking from our threshold. Be special; be our guest.

Hosts: Jayne and Clarke Hurlbut
Rooms: 2 (SB) $50-60
Full Breakfast
Credit Cards: None
Notes: 2, 5, 7, 8, 9, 10, 11, 12

Maple Valley Bed and Breakfast

NOTES: Credit cards accepted: A Master Card; B Visa; C American Express; D Discover Card; E Diners Club; F Other; 2 Personal checks accepted; 3 Lunch available; 4 Dinner available; 5 Open all

RANDLE

Hampton House
409 Silverbrook Road, 98377
(206) 497-2907

Country charm in a restored 1906 local landmark on one and one-half acres. Near Mt. Saint Helens and Mt. Rainier. Friendly hosts help you plan sightseeing in the area. Full breakfast features northwest fruits and berries in season. A two-hour drive from either Seattle or Portland airports. Hiking and fishing available.

Hosts: Sylvia and Jack Wasson
Rooms: 4 (2 PB; 2 SB) $55-65
Full Breakfast
Credit Cards: None
Notes: 2, 5, 8, 10, 11

SEABECK

Summer Song Bed and Breakfast
P. O. Box 82, 98380
(206) 830-5089

Summer Song, a whisper of an older time, a new breath of today, is a completely furnished cottage located on the shores of Hood Canal. A spectacular backdrop of the Olympia Mountains reflects on its moody waters. God has provided a peace and beauty in the middle of nature, and our guests are held on the tip toe of wondering, "Does the song of the sea end on the shore or in the hearts of those who listen?"

Hosts: Ron and Sharon Barney
Cottage: 1 (PB) $55-65
Full Breakfast
Credit Cards: A, B
Notes: 2, 3, 4, 5, 9, 10

Chambered Nautilus Bed and Breakfast Inn

SEATTLE

Chambered Nautilus Bed and Breakfast Inn
5005 22nd Avenue Northeast, 98105
(206) 522-2536

A gracious 1915 Georgian Colonial is nestled on a hill and furnished with a mixture of American and English antiques and fine reproductions. A touch of Mozart, Persian rugs, a grand piano, two fireplaces, four lovely porches, and nationally award-winning breakfasts help assure your special comfort. Excellent access to Seattle's theaters, restaurants, public transportation, shopping, biking and jogging trails, churches, Husky Stadium, and the University of Washington campus.

Hosts: Bill and Bunny Hagemeyer
Rooms: 6 (4 PB; 2 SB) $65-95

---

year; 6 Pets welcome; 7 Children welcome; 8 Tennis nearby; 9 Swimming nearby; 10 Golf nearby; 11 Skiing nearby; 12 May be booked through travel agent

Full Breakfast
Credit Cards: A, B, C, E, F
Notes: 2, 5, 8, 9, 10, 11, 12

Chelsea Station Bed and Breakfast Inn
4915 Linden Avenue North, 98103
(206) 547-6077

Chelsea Station consistently provides the peaceful surroundings travelers enjoy. Lace curtains, ample breakfasts, and comfy king beds share warm feelings of "Grandma's time." The nearby Seattle Rose Garden contributes beauty to the human spirit. With a cup of tea in the afternoon, Chelsea Station is a perfect place for relaxation and renewal. No smoking.

Hosts: Dick and Mary Lou Jones
Rooms: 5 (PB) $59-94
Full Breakfast
Credit Cards: A, B, C, D, E
Notes: 2, 5, 8, 9, 10, 12

SEAVIEW

Gumm's Bed and Breakfast Inn
Highway 101 and 33 Avenue South
P. O. Box 447, 98644
(206) 642-8887

This home features a large livingroom with a great stone fireplace. Four guest rooms are uniquely decorated with special thought to the guests' comfort. Sun porch, hot tub, TV. Breakfast is served in the Julie Anne room, with three French doors opening onto a spacious deck.

Host: Mickey Slack
Rooms: 4 (2 PB; 2 SB) $65-75
Full Breakfast
Credit Cards: A, B
Notes: 2, 5, 7, 8, 10

WHITE SALMON

Llama Ranch Bed and Breakfast
1980 Highway 141, 98672
(509) 395-2786; (800) 800-LAMA

Hospitality plus unforgettable delight. Jerry and Rebeka share their love of llamas on free llama walks through the woods with each guest walking a "llovable" llama. There are stunning views of both Mt. Adams and Mt. Hood. The ranch is located between the Mt. Adams wilderness area and the Columbia Gorge national scenic area with many varied activities close by. Picturesque views and photographic memories abound, along with the serenity, dignity, and beauty of llamas.

Hosts: Jerry and Rebeka Stone
Rooms: 7 (2 PB; 5 SB) $55-75
Full Breakfast
Credit Cards: A, B, D
Notes: 2, 5, 6, 7, 10, 11, 12

NOTES: Credit cards accepted: A Master Card; B Visa; C American Express; D Discover Card; E Diners Club; F Other; 2 Personal checks accepted; 3 Lunch available; 4 Dinner available; 5 Open all

West Virginia

BATH

Maria's Garden and Inn
201 Independence Street
Berkeley Springs, 25411
(304) 258-2021

Nestled in the heart of the town of Bath, you can sample a slice of American heritage, walk to the castle and famed mineral springs, partake in the Roman baths, or just relax amid nature's beauty. Maria's offers a widely varied American-Italian restaurant menu of home-cooked foods and features a little garden dedicated to Our Lady of Fatima. Maria's is a resting place for all of God's children.

Hosts: Margaret Perry, son Curtis, and daughter Alesa
Rooms: 10 (4 PB; 6 SB) $35-65
Full Breakfast
Credit Cards: A, B, C, D, E
Notes: 2, 3, 4, 5, 7, 8, 9

ELKINS

Tunnel Mountain Bed and Breakfast
Route 1, Box 59-1, 26241
(304) 636-1684

A charming, three-story fieldstone home is nestled on the side of Tunnel Mountain, four miles east of Elkins, Stuart Recreation Area exit off Route 22. Five private, wooded acres overlook scenic mountains, lush forests, and the Cheat River Valley. Three romantic guest rooms are furnished with antiques and handmade comforters. The large common room has a fireplace. Activities include hiking, cross-country and downhill skiing, fishing, hunting, rafting, canoeing, golf, antiqueing, festivals, tennis, caving, swimming.

Hosts: Anne and Paul Beardslee
Rooms: 3 (PB) $50-55
Full Breakfast
Credit Cards: None
Notes: 2, 5, 8, 9, 10, 11

Tunnel Mountain Bed and Breakfast

---

year; 6 Pets welcome; 7 Children welcome; 8 Tennis nearby; 9 Swimming nearby; 10 Golf nearby; 11 Skiing nearby; 12 May be booked through travel agent

HUTTONSVILLE

Hutton House
Route 219-250, 26273
(800) 234-6701

Meticulously restored and decorated, this Queen Anne Victorian on the National Register of Historic Places is conveniently located near Elkins, Cass Railroad, and Snowshoe ski resort. It has a wraparound porch and deck for relaxing and enjoying the view, TV, gameroom, lawn for games, and a friendly kitchen. Breakfast and afternoon refreshments are served at your leisure; other meals are available with prior reservation or good luck! Come see us!

Host: Loretta Murray
Rooms: 7 (3 PB; 4 SB) $50-70
Full Breakfast
Credit Cards: A, B, C
Notes: 2, 5, 7, 10, 11, 12

MATHIAS

Valley View Farm
Route 1, Box 467, 26812
(304) 897-5229

National Geographic's *America's Great Hideaways* calls Valley View Farm "Your home away from home," and it is just that. This cattle and sheep farm of 250 acres specializes in excellent food and friendly hosts. Lost River State Park is nearby. Horseback riding and other recreation is available in season. Craft shops. Located on Route 259 near Mathias, opposite Stone Mennonite Church.

Host: Edna Shipe
Rooms: 4 (SB) $25 per person
Full Breakfast
Credit Cards: None
Notes: 2, 3, 4, 5, 6, 7, 8, 9, 11

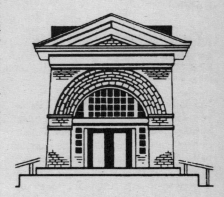

Chestnut Ridge School Bed and Breakfast

MORGANTOWN

Chestnut Ridge School Bed and Breakfast
1000 Stewartstown Road, 26505
(304) 598-2262

A 1920s elementary school is just minutes from the West Virginia University campus and medical center. Each guest room contains a queen bed and sparkling marble and brass bath. We are surrounded by scenic and recreational

---

NOTES: Credit cards accepted: A Master Card; B Visa; C American Express; D Discover Card; E Diners Club; F Other; 2 Personal checks accepted; 3 Lunch available; 4 Dinner available; 5 Open all

areas and offer hospitality, beautiful sunsets, and a smoke-free environment.

Hosts: Nancy and Sam Bonasso
Rooms: 4 (PB) $50-60
Continental Breakfast
Credit Cards: None
Notes: 2, 5, 8, 9, 10

SUMMIT POINT

Countryside
P. O. Box 57, 25446
(304) 725-2614

Countryside is a small, cozy bed and breakfast located in the quaint village of Summit Point, near historic Harpers Ferry. Tucked away on a tree-lined street, Countryside is decorated with a cheery mixture of old and new collectibles, baskets, and quilts. Old-fashioned hospitality welcomes the crowd-weary traveler.

Hosts: Lisa and Daniel Hileman
Rooms: 2 (PB) $50-60
Continental Breakfast
Credit Cards: A, B
Notes: 2, 5, 7

Wisconsin

ALBANY

Albany Guest House
405 South Mill Street, 53502
(608) 862-3636

An experience in tranquility, just 30 miles south of the capital dome in Madison. Enjoy a restored 1908 home with a flower-filled front porch, ideal for swinging or rocking, or light the fireplace in the master bedroom. The Sugar River Trail runs through town, offering biking, hiking, and cross-country skiing. Visit nearby New Glarus, America's Little Switzerland, or visit House on the Rock. Savor our full breakfast after a cozy night's rest.

Hosts: Bob and Sally Braem
Rooms: 4 (2 PB; 2 SB) $45-65
Full Breakfast
Credit Cards: None
Notes: 2, 5, 10, 11

ALGOMA

Amberwood Inn
N7136 Highway 52, Lakeshore Drive, 54201
(414) 487-3471; (602) 968-2850 off-season

Enjoy luxurious suites on Lake Michigan with private decks and double French doors that open to the beach. Sleep to the sound of the waves, awaken to a spectacular sunrise over the water. Celebrate the romance of waterfront country living at its best. Swim, golf, bike, walk, relax. Sauna available. Ten minutes to Door County galleries and shops. Handmade quilts and antiques are available for purchase. Walker Art Studio on the premises.

Host: Jan Warren
Rooms: 4 (PB) $55-75
Full Breakfast
Credit Cards: A, B
Notes: 2, 7, 8, 9, 10, 11

BARABOO

The Barrister's House
226 Ninth Avenue, 53913
(608) 356-3344

A comfortably elegant Colonial guest house has four uniquely decorated rooms. Formal dining room, library, and sitting room, all with fireplaces, provide a variety of opportunities for relaxation. A screened porch, open ve-

---

NOTES: Credit cards accepted: A Master Card; B Visa; C American Express; D Discover Card; E Diners Club; F Other; 2 Personal checks accepted; 3 Lunch available; 4 Dinner available; 5 Open all

randa, and flagstone terrace are available for those who prefer to relax outdoors. Situated on one of Baraboo's bluffs, The Barrister's House offers the perfect getaway in an all-season vacationland.

Hosts: Glen and Mary Schulz
Rooms: 4 (PB) $55-65
Continental Breakfast
Credit Cards: None
Notes: 2, 5, 7 (over 6), 8, 9, 10, 11

Mielke-Mauk House

CAMPBELLSPORT

Mielke-Mauk House

Kettle Moraine Lake, W977 Highway F, 53010
(414) 533-8602

Located in the Kettle Morraine State Forest area, 40 miles north of Milwaukee, overlooking a lake, Mielke-Mauk House offers rooms in a separate wing with kitchen of an 1800s farmhouse or 1860 Scandinavian log house. Both offer country decor, wood floors, handmade quilts, fireplaces, rowboat, skiing, skating, grills. Available privately for two or for a group.

Hosts: Richard and Faith Mauk
Rooms: 5 (4 PB; 1 SB) $60-90; $55-150 family and weekly rates
Continental Breakfast
Credit Cards: A, B
Notes: 2, 6 (by arrangement), 9, 10, 11

CEDARBURG

The Washington House Inn

W62 N 573 Washington Avenue, 53012
(414) 375-3550; (800) 369-4088

Built in 1884 and listed on the National Register of Historic Places, 29 guest rooms feature antiques, down comforters, whirlpool baths, fireplaces, and cable TV. Located in the heart of the Cedarburg historic district, within walking distance of area antique shops, fine dining, and historic Cedar Creek settlement.

Host: Wendy Porterfield
Rooms: 29 (PB) $59-139
Expanded Continental Breakfast
Credit Cards: A, B, C, D, E
Notes: 2, 5, 7, 8, 9, 10, 11

DE-PERE

R&R Homestead Bed and Breakfast

803 Morning Glory Lane, 54115
(414) 336-8244

---

year; 6 Pets welcome; 7 Children welcome; 8 Tennis nearby; 9 Swimming nearby; 10 Golf nearby; 11 Skiing nearby; 12 May be booked through travel agent

Enjoy pleasant, cozy, European atmosphere in a 23-year-old home with three guest rooms. The suite has a queen canopy bed and fireplace with electric log; second room has a wallhanging fireplace with queen cannonball bed; third room has a double bed and is nicely decorated. All rooms are wallpapered in superb taste.

Hosts: Ruth and Richard Roffers
Rooms: 3 (SB) $40-65
Full Breakfast
Credit Cards: A, B
Notes: 2, 9

ELLISON BAY

Country Woods Bed and Breakfast
520 Europe Lake Road, 54210
(414) 854-5706

Visit nature's delight at the top of Door County, Wisconsin's Cape Cod of the Midwest. Located on 50 acres of private woodlands on Europe Lake and adjacent to Newport State Park and walking distance from the shores of Lake Michigan, the inn is close to Washington Island ferry and our famous "fish boils." Hearty breakfast is served on the sun deck, and the gathering room has a stone fireplace. Great for hikers, bikers, and nature enthusiasts. Cottages also available.

Hosts: Cheryl and Carl Carlson
Rooms: 4 (2 PB; 2 SB) $65-85
Full Breakfast
Credit Cards: None
Notes: 2, 8, 9, 10, 11, 12

FISH CREEK

Thorp House Inn and Cottages
4135 Bluff Road, P. O. Box 490, 54212
(414) 868-2444

A turn-of-the-century historic home has a bay view and four romantic guest rooms, parlor with stone fireplace, and cozy library—all furnished with fine antiques and lots of authentic detail. Home-baked continental breakfast. Country antique cottages with fireplaces are also available. We are located in the village of Fish Creek, the heart of Door County, just blocks from a state park. Whirlpool room and whirlpool cottage.

Hosts: Christine and Sverre Falck-Pedersen
Rooms: 4 (PB) $70-115
Continental Breakfast
Credti Cards: None
Notes: 2, 5, 7 (cottages only), 8, 9, 10, 11

GREEN BAY

Stonewood Haus
Box 10201, 54155
(414) 499-3786

Secluded, picturesque, and just minutes from downtown Green Bay and airport, lovely Stonewood is nestled on nine acres of woods, meadows, and rippling Trout Creek. It is exquisitely unique, combining Old World charm with modern comforts. Relax on the patio, curl up in front of the fireplace, or enjoy the many scenic views. We pride ourselves on hospitality and personal

---

NOTES: Credit cards accepted: A Master Card; B Visa; C American Express; D Discover Card; E Diners Club; F Other; 2 Personal checks accepted; 3 Lunch available; 4 Dinner available; 5 Open all

attention. Your comfort is our priority. Discounts for extended stays, corporate rates, gift certificates.

Host: JoAnn Naumann King
Rooms: 5 (1 PB; 4 SB) $59-79
Full Breakfast
Credit Cards: A, B
Notes: 2, 5, 7 (by arrangement), 8, 9, 10, 11, 12

IOLA

Taylor House
210 East Iola Street, P. O. Box 101, 54945
(715) 445-2204

This turn-of-the-century Victorian has antique-furnished bedrooms and a parlor with fireplace where you are invited to socialize with other guests. You are also welcome in our family room. Breakfast is served in the dining room. For your comfort and safety, we offer air-conditioned rooms. Reservations require deposit, which is refundable with 14 days notice. No smoking.

Hosts: Crystal and Richard Anderson
Rooms: 4 (1 PB; 3 SB) $30-50
Full Breakfast
Credit Cards: None
Notes: 2, 5, 10, 11

LA FARGE

Trillium
Route 2, Box 121, 54639
(608) 625-4492

We offer a cozy, private, fully furnished guest cottage on our family farm. The cottage has two double beds, two single beds, crib, and high chair. Children under 13 stay without charge. There is a stone fireplace in the livingroom, hardwood floors throughout, and porch. Guests reserve the entire cottage, which faces out over woods, fields, garden, and orchard. Near state parks, historic sites, three major rivers, numerous smaller lakes, Wisconsin's largest Amish community, bike trails, cross-country and downhill skiing.

Hosts: Rosanne Boyett
Cottage: 1 (PB) $45-63
Full Breakfast
Credit Cards: None
Notes: 2, 5, 7, 8, 9, 10, 11

Taylor House

LIVINGSTON

Oak Hill Farm
9850 Highway 80, 53554
(608) 943-6006

A comfortable country home with a warm, hospitable atmosphere is enhanced with fireplaces, porches, and facilities for picnics. In the area, you will find state parks, museums, lakes, and the Chicago Bears' summer training camp.

Hosts: Elizabeth and Victor Johnson
Rooms: 4 (1 PB; 3 SB) $30-40
Continental Breakfast
Credit Cards: None
Notes: 2, 5, 6, 7, 8, 9, 10, 11

MADISON

Annie's Hill House
2117 Sheridan Drive, 53704
(608) 244-2224

When you want the world to go away, come to Annie's, the quiet inn on Warner Park with the beautiful view. Luxury accommodations at reasonable rates. Close to the lake and park, it is also convenient to downtown and the University of Wisconsin campus. There is a shaded terrace, pond, and a romantic gazebo surrounded by butterfly gardens. Two beautiful two-bedroom suites with double Jacuzzi.

Hosts: Anne and Larry Stuart
Suites: 2 (PB) $75-95
Full Breakfast
Credit Cards: A, B, C, D
Notes: 2, 5, 7 (by arrangement), 8, 9, 10, 11

PLAIN

Bettinger House
Bed and Breakfast
855 Wachter Avenue, Highway 23, 53577
(608) 546-2951

In this 1904 two-story, red brick home, Marie's grandmother, Elizabeth, a midwife, delivered over 300 babies. It is close to the American Players Theatre, Frank Lloyd Wright's Taliesin, and House on the Rock. Air conditioning, fully refurbished. Biking, canoeing, and downhill and cross-country skiing are nearby.

Hosts: Jim and Marie Neider
Rooms: 6 (3 PB; 3 SB) $40-50
Full Breakfast
Credit Cards: A, B
Notes: 2, 5, 7, 8, 9, 10, 11, 12

The Kraemer House
Bed and Breakfast
1190 Spruce Street, 53577
(608) 546-3161

We invite you to come and visit world-famous House on the Rock and Frank Lloyd Wright's Taliesin in Spring Green. Our rooms are lovely and bright, each with a different color and theme. A generous breakfast will temp the most particular palate. Located in an interesting area with lots of places to visit. The village of Plain is nestled among the rolling hills that will remind you of Germany.

Hosts: Duane and Gwen Kraemer
Rooms: 4 (1 PB; 3 SB) $45-65
Full Breakfast
Credit Cards: A, B
Notes: 2, 5, 8, 9, 10, 11

NOTES: Credit cards accepted: A Master Card; B Visa; C American Express; D Discover Card; E Diners Club; F Other; 2 Personal checks accepted; 3 Lunch available; 4 Dinner available; 5 Open all

SPARTA

The Franklin Victorian Bed and Breakfast
220 East Franklin Street, 54656
(608) 269-3894; (800) 845-8767

This turn-of-the-century home welcomes you to bygone elegance with small-town quiet and comfort. The four spacious bedrooms provide a perfect setting for ultimate relaxation. Full home-cooked breakfast is served before starting your day of hiking, biking, skiing, canoeing, antiqueing, or exploring this beautiful area.

Hosts: Lloyd and Jane Larson
Rooms: 4 (2 PB; 2 SB) $55-75
Full Breakfast
Credit Cards: A, B
Notes: 2, 5, 7 (over 10), 8, 9, 10, 11

SPRING GREEN

Hill Street Bed and Breakfast
353 Hill Street, 53588
(608) 588-7751

The 1900 Queen Anne Victorian has a turret room, hand-carved woodwork, queen beds, and air conditioning. Near House on the Rock, Frank Lloyd Wright's Taliesin, American Players Theatre. Biking, canoeing on the Wisconsin River, and cross-country and downhill skiing are all close by.

Host: Doris Randall
Rooms: 7 (5 PB; 2 SB) $50-70
Full Breakfast
Credit Cards: A, B
Notes: 2, 5, 7, 8, 9, 10, 11, 12

WISCONSIN DELLS

Historic Bennett House Bed and Breakfast
825 Oak Street, 53965
(608) 254-2500

The 1863 home of an honored pioneer photographer is listed on the National Register of Historic Places. We'll pamper you with elegant lace, crystal, antiques, romantic bedrooms, and luscious fireside breakfast. The private suite has a parlor, Eastlake bedroom, and shower bath. The English room has a walnut and lace canopy bed. And the garden room has a brass bed. Walk to river tours, antiques, and crafts. Minutes to hiking, biking, canoeing, four golf courses, five ski areas, five state parks, greyhound racing, bird watching, and Indian culture. Bennett, Rockwell, circus, and railroad museums are also near by. Gift certificates are available.

Hosts: Gail and Rich Obermeyer
Rooms: 4 (1 PB; 3 SB) $55-80
Full Breakfast
Credit Cards: None
Notes: 2, 5, 8, 9, 10, 11, 12

---

year; 6 Pets welcome; 7 Children welcome; 8 Tennis nearby; 9 Swimming nearby; 10 Golf nearby; 11 Skiing nearby; 12 May be booked through travel agent

Wyoming

CODY

Trout Creek Inn
Yellowstone Highway 14, 16, 20 West, 82414
(307) 587-6288

Nestled in the most beautiful 50 miles in the world, according to Teddy Roosevelt, Trout Creek Inn is part of a ranch; hence it has private trout fishing, hiking, and horseback riding not available to the public. Enjoy an all-you-can-eat country breakfast in the big dining room; large heated pool; children's playground; satelite TV. Twenty minutes to Cody's rodeos, museums, and river rafting; 30 minutes to Yellowstone National Park. Sleep in rural quiet in clean, mountain air "above the dust."

Hosts: Bert and Norma Sowerwine
Rooms: 21 (PB) $50-54
Full Breakfast
Credit Cards: A, B, C, D, F
Notes: 2, 5, 6, 7, 8, 9, 10

ENCAMPMENT

Platt's Rustic Mountain Lodge
Star Route 49, 82325
(307) 327-5539

Located 12 miles south of Encampment on Highway 230, in a beautiful, peaceful mountain setting, the rustic lodge has modern conveniences. It is set on a working ranch with horseback riding, fishing, hiking, rock hounding, photography tours, snowmobile trips, and cross-country skiing. This is an area rich in minerals, wildlife, and history. Family-owned business; by reservation only.

Hosts: Mayvon and Ron Platt
Rooms: 3 (2SB) $35 per person
Full Breakfast
Credit Cards: None
Closed holidays
Notes: 7, 8, 9

NOTES: Credit cards accepted: A Master Card; B Visa; C American Express; D Discover Card; E Diners Club; F Other; 2 Personal checks accepted; 3 Lunch available; 4 Dinner available; 5 Open all

WILSON

Teton View Bed and Breakfast
2136 Coyote Loop, P. O. Box 652, 83014
(307) 733-7954

Rooms have mountain views. The large eating area, where homemade pastries, fresh fruit, and coffee are served, connects to a private upper deck with fantastic mountain and ski resort views. Private entrance; convenient to Yellowstone and Grand Teton national parks; four miles from ski area.

Hosts: John and Joanna Engelhart
Rooms: 3 (1 PB; 2 SB) $60-80
Full Breakfast
Credit Cards: A, B
Closed January
Notes: 2, 7, 8, 9, 10, 11, 12

Alberta

NANTON

The Squire Ranch
Rural Route 1, T0L 1R0
(403) 646-5789

Welcome to our ranch in the lovely foothills of the Rocky Mountains. We have horses, cattle, goats, sheep, llamas, miniature donkeys, and bantam chickens. Yard, playground, and indoor activities are available. This is good country for riding, walking, hunting, and fishing. We have easy access to Fort MacLeod, Kananaskis, Waterton, and Banff. There is a small gift shop on the premises.

Hosts: Sam and Rosemary Squire
Rooms: 3 plus cabin (1 PB; 2 SB) $30-50
Full Breakfast
Credit Cards: None
Notes: 3, 4, 5, 7, 8, 9, 10, 11

NOTES: Credit cards accepted: A Master Card; B Visa; C American Express; D Discover Card; E Diners Club; F Other; 2 Personal checks accepted; 3 Lunch available; 4 Dinner available; 5 Open all

British Columbia

MILL BAY

Pine Lodge Farm Bed and Breakfast
3191 Muatter Road, V0R 2P0
(604) 743-4083

Our beautiful antique-filled lodge is located 25 miles north of Victoria. It is situated on a 30-acre farm overlooking ocean and islands. Arbutus trees, walking trails, farm animals, and wild deer add to the idyllic setting. Each room has en suite baths. Also, a delightful cottage with two bedrooms and baths, livingroom, dinette, kitchen, and hot tub is available. Full farm breakfast.

Hosts: Cliff and Barb Clarke
Rooms: 7 (PB) $75-85
Cottage: 1 (PB) $110-160
Full Breakfast
Credit Cards: A, B
Notes: 2, 5, 7, 8, 12

NORTH VANCOUVER

Laburnum Cottage Bed and Breakfast
1388 Terrace Avenue, V7R 1B4
(604) 988-4877

A beautiful home set in one-half acre of an award-winning English garden. Besides the three bedrooms in the home, there are two beautiful self-contained cottages that are perfect for a honeymoon. The bedrooms are all en suite. Your hostess, Delphine Masterton, is known for her gourmet breakfasts. At least seven cars can be parked off-street in the driveway. Downtown Vancouver is 12 minutes away. Within minutes is tennis, Grouse Mountain, beaches, shopping, Capilarno Suspension Bridge, and golf.

Hosts: Margot and Delphine Masterton
Rooms: 3 (PB) $95-110 Canadian
Cottages: 2
Full Breakfast
Credit Cards: A, B
Notes: 2, 5, 6, 8, 9, 10, 11

UCLUELET

Bed and Breakfast at Burley's
Box 550, 1078 Helen Road, V0R 3A0
(604) 726-4444

A waterfront home on a small "drive to" island at the harbor mouth. Watch the ducks and birds play, heron and

---

year; 6 Pets welcome; 7 Children welcome; 8 Tennis nearby; 9 Swimming nearby; 10 Golf nearby; 11 Skiing nearby; 12 May be booked through travel agent

kingfisher work, and eagles soar. In the harbor, trollers, draggers, and seiners attract the gulls. Loggers work in the distant hills. There is a view from every window, a large livingroom, fireplace, books, and recreation room with pool table.

Hosts: Run Burley and Micheline Riley
Rooms: 6 (SB) $35-50
Continental Breakfast
Credit Cards: A, B
Notes: 8, 9, 10

Bed and Breakfast at Burley's

VANCOUVER

Diana's Luxury Bed and Breakfast
1019 East 38 Avenue, V5W 1J4
(604) 321-2855; FAX (604) 321-3411

Our bed and breakfast is set in a quiet neighborhood close to shopping, golf, tennis, skiing, and downtown Vancouver. All amenities, restaurants, and sightseeing. Come, enjoy the beauty of Vancouver and the luxury of Diana's bed and breakfast

Hosts: Diana and Danny
Rooms: 7 (2 PB; 5 SB) $55-65
Continental Breakfast
Credit Cards: A, B
Notes: 5, 8, 9, 10, 11

VERNON

The Windmill House
5672 Learmouth Road
Rural Route 1, S19A, C2, V1T 6L4
(604) 549-2804

Sleep in a beautiful windmill set in the heart of the Coldstream Valley, just east of Vernon. Close to fishing, beaches, orchards, skiing on Silver Star, wineries, and gold panning. Superb breakfasts and accommodations. Hosts raise pure-bred dairy goats and are artists with many fine originals and prints for sale. Smoke-free environment; resident pets.

Hosts: Linda McKay and Jeremy Dyde
Rooms: 4 (1 PB; 3 SB) $35-55 Canadian
Full Breakfast
Credit Cards: A, B, E
Notes: 2, 5, 6, 7, 8, 9, 10, 11

VICTORIA

Battery Street Guest House
670 Battery Street, V8V 1E5
(604) 385-4632

NOTES: Credit cards accepted: A Master Card; B Visa; C American Express; D Discover Card; E Diners Club; F Other; 2 Personal checks accepted; 3 Lunch available; 4 Dinner available; 5 Open all

A comfortable guest house (1898) in downtown Victoria is in a lovely location. Beacon Hill Park and the ocean are only one block away from this very quiet area. An ample breakfast is served, and your hostess speaks Dutch as her first language. Non-smokers only.

Host: Pamela Verduyn
Rooms: 4 (2 PB; 2 SB) $55-75
Full Breakfast
Credit Cards: None
Notes: 2, 5, 6 (dog, cat)

Top O'Triangle Mountain
3442 Karger Terr, V9C 3K5
(604) 478-7853

Our home, built of solid cedar construction, boasts a spectacular view of Victoria, the Juan de Fuca Strait, and the Olympia Mountains in Washington. We are a relaxed household with a few rules, lots of hospitality, and clean, comfortable rooms. A hearty breakfast is different each morning.

Hosts: Pat and Henry Hansen
Rooms: 3 (PB) $60-85 Canadian
Full Breakfast
Credit Cards: A, B
Notes: 5, 7, 11, 12

WEST VANCOUVER

Beachside Bed and Breakfast
4208 Evergreen Avenue, V7V 1H1
(604) 922-7773; FAX (604) 926-8073

Guests are welcomed to this beautiful waterfront home with a basket of fruit and fresh flowers. Situated on a quiet cul-de-sac in an exclusive area of the city, the house, with Spanish architecture accented by antique stained-glass windows, affords a panoramic view of Vancouver's busy harbor. There are private baths, a patio leading to the beach, and a large Jacuzzi at the seashore, where you can watch seals swim by daily. Near sailing, fishing, hiking, golf, downhill skiing, and antique shopping.

Hosts: Gordon and Joan Gibbs
Rooms: 3 (PB) $80-129
Full Breakfast
Credit Cards: A, B
Notes: 2, 5, 8, 10, 11, 12, 13

---

year; 6 Pets welcome; 7 Children welcome; 8 Tennis nearby; 9 Swimming nearby; 10 Golf nearby; 11 Skiing nearby; 12 May be booked through travel agent

Manitoba

BOISSEVAIN

Dueck's Cedar Chalet
Box 362, R0K 0E0
(204) 534-6019

Large, all-cedar suite with refrigerator, coffee maker, private Jacuzzi, bath, and entrance. Honeymoon and anniversary visits are a specialty. Close to Turtle Mountain Provincial Park, International Peace Gardens, good beaches, and the United States border. Close to heated, outside pool in summer.

Hosts: Hilda and Henry Dueck
Rooms: 4 (2 PB; 2 SB) $30-50 Canadian
Full Breakfast
Credit Cards: None
Notes: 2, 3, 4, 6 (limited), 7, 8, 9, 10, 11

NOTES: Credit cards accepted: A Master Card; B Visa; C American Express; D Discover Card; E Diners Club; F Other; 2 Personal checks accepted; 3 Lunch available; 4 Dinner available; 5 Open all

Nova Scotia

DILIGENT RIVER

Confederation Farm
Rural Route 3, Parrsboro, B0M 1S0
(902) 254-3057

Confederation Farm invites you to see the beach and historic harbor of Diligent River. Hiking trails, clam digging, recent dinosaur finds, and high tides. Four rooms in the main house and four large cottages with private baths provide warm hospitality. An on-site pioneer museum displays old wagons, dairy equipment, blacksmith forge, and more.

Hosts: Bob and Julia Salter
Rooms: 4 (S2B) $40
Cottages: 4 (PB) $45
Full Breakfast in main house only
Credit Cards: None
Closed November-April
Notes: 2, 8, 9, 10

---

year; 6 Pets welcome; 7 Children welcome; 8 Tennis nearby; 9 Swimming nearby; 10 Golf nearby; 11 Skiing nearby; 12 May be booked through travel agent

Ontario

BRAESIDE

Glenroy Farm
Rural Route 1, K0A 1G0
(613) 432-6248

Beautiful, quiet farm setting just a one-hour drive from Ottawa. Situated in historic McNab township of Renfrew County in the heart of the Ottawa Valley, halfway between the towns of Renfrew and Arnprior. We live in an 1884 stone house that has been well-maintained by three generations of McGregors, the family who built the home and lived in it. We have a farming operation growing strawberries and corn and raising beef cattle. Located within driving distance of the Ottawa River raft rides, Storyland, Logos Land, Bonnechere Caves, and other attractions. Home of the 1994 International Plowing Match.

Hosts: Noreen and Steve McGregor
Rooms: 5 (1 PB; 4 SB) $35-50
Full Breakfast
Credit Cards: None
Notes: 2, 7, 9, 10, 11

LEAMINGTON

Home Suite Home Bed and Breakfast
115 Erie Street South, N8H 3B5
(519) 326-7169

Enjoy warm hospitality in one of Leamington's turn-of-the-century distinctive and spacious homes. We have tastefully restored and furnished this home with antiques and wicker and decorated with Victorian and country styles. We offer a large livingroom with TV and fireplace and an in-ground swimming pool with sundeck. Five minutes from Point Pelee National Park, famous for bird watching, butterfly migration, hiking, cycling, canoeing, fine beaches, and hawk migration. Dinner theaters and ferry trip to Pelee Island are available. A ten-minute walk to fine shops and restaurants.

Hosts: Harry and Agatha Tiessen
Rooms: 4 (2 PB; 2 SB) $50-60
Full Breakfast
Credit Cards: None
Notes: 2, 5, 7, 8, 9, 10, 12

NOTES: Credit cards accepted: A Master Card; B Visa; C American Express; D Discover Card; E Diners Club; F Other; 2 Personal checks accepted; 3 Lunch available; 4 Dinner available; 5 Open all

Point Pelee Bed and Breakfast Association
115 Erie Street South, N8H 3B5
(519) 326-7169

This reservation service at Canada's most southern point has 55 rooms and country cottage rentals available. Comfortable accommodations, convenience to area attractions (most homes within five to ten minutes of Point Pelee National Park), and friendly directions to points of interest. Enjoy this area that is world-famous for bird watching. $40-60. Agatha Tiessen, coordinator.

OTTAWA

Australis Guest House
35 Marlborough Avenue, K1N 8E6
(613) 235-8461

We are the oldest established and still operating bed and breakfast in the Ottawa area. Located on a quiet, tree-lined street one block from the Rideau River, with its ducks and swans, and Strathcona Park. We are a 20-minute walk from the parliament buildings. This period house boasts leaded-glass windows, fireplaces, oak floors, and unique eight-foot-high stained-glass windows overlooking the hall. Hearty, home-cooked breakfasts with home-baked breads and pastries. Winner of the Ottawa Hospitality Award for April 1989. Recommended by *Newsweek*, January 1990, and featured in the *Ottawa Sun* newspaper, January 1992 for our Australian bread. Baby sitting is available.

Hosts: Carol and Brian Waters
Rooms: 3 (1 PB; 2 SB) $45-65 Canadian
Full Breakfast
Credit Cards: None
Notes: 2, 5, 7, 8

STRATFORD

Burnside Guest Home
139 William Street, N5A 4X9
(519) 271-7076

Burnside is a turn-of-the-century home on the north shore of Lake Victoria, the site of the first Stratford logging mill. The home features many family heirlooms and antiques and is centrally air conditioned. Our rooms have been redecorated with light and cheery colors. Relax in the gardens overlooking the Avon River on hand-crafted furniture amid the rose, herb, herbaceous, and annual flower gardens. Within walking distance of Shakespearean theaters. Stratford is the home of a world-renowned Shakespearean festival from May 1 to November 15, 1992. Also enjoy farmers' market, Mennonite country, art and craft shops, outstanding architecture, and the outdoor Art in the Park.

Host: Lester J. Wilker
Rooms: 5 (SB) $50-55 Canadian; $55-60 in summer; $25 for students
Full Breakfast
Credit Cards: None
Notes: 2, 5, 8, 9, 10, 11

---

year; 6 Pets welcome; 7 Children welcome; 8 Tennis nearby; 9 Swimming nearby; 10 Golf nearby; 11 Skiing nearby; 12 May be booked through travel agent

Prince Edward Island

MONTAGUE

Partridge's Bed and Breakfast
Rural Route 2, Panmure Island, C0A 1R0
(902) 838-4687

A walk through the woods to our beach offers quiet relaxation. Clams and mussels can be dug, and Graham's Lobster Factory is nearby. Grocery stores and excellent restaurants are closeby. Baby sitting and cribs are available. Bicycles, a canoe, and a rowboat are free. Seal cruises, plays, tennis, golf, and horseback riding are within 20 miles.

Hosts: Gertrude and Rod Partridge
Rooms: 7 (5 PB; 2 SB) $40-50
Full Breakfast
Credit Cards: B
Notes: 5, 6, 7, 8, 9, 10, 11, 12

MURRAY RIVER

Bayberry Cliff Inn
Rural Route 4, Little Sands, C0A 1W0
(902) 962-3395

Located on the edge of a 40-foot cliff are two uniquely redecorated post-and-beam barns, antiques, and marine art. Seven rooms have double beds, three with extra sleeping lofts. One room has two single beds. The honeymoon room has a private bath. Seals, restaurants, swimming, and craft shops.

Hosts: Don and Nancy Perkins
Rooms: 8 (1 PB; 7 SB) $35-65
Full Breakfast
Credit Cards: A, B
Notes: 2, 9, 10

O'LEARY

Smallman's Bed and Breakfast
Knutsford, Rural Route 1, C0R 1V0
(902) 859-3469; (902) 859-2664

We have a split-level house with a garage on the west end and brick gate posts. We have a racetrack behind the house where some guests like to go for a walk. There are churches, stores, craft shops, tennis, golf, and beaches for relaxing. We live in a country area on Route 142 off Highway 2.

Hosts: Arnold and Eileen Smallman
Rooms: 4 (SB) $25-35
Full or Continental Breakfast
Credit Cards: None
Notes: 4 (on request), 7, 8, 9, 10, 11

NOTES: Credit cards accepted: A Master Card; B Visa; C American Express; D Discover Card; E Diners Club; F Other; 2 Personal checks accepted; 3 Lunch available; 4 Dinner available; 5 Open all

Quebec

MONTREAL

Armor Inn
151 Sherbrooke Est, H2X 1C7
(514) 285-0140

The Armor Inn is a small hotel with a typical European character. In the heart of Montreal, it offers a warm, family atmosphere and is ideally situated close to Métro, Saint Denis, and Prince Arthur streets. It is a 15-minute walk to Old Montreal, the Palais of Congress, and numerous underground shopping centers.

Host: Annick Morvan
Rooms: 15 (7 PB; 8 SB) $38-55
Continental Breakfast
Credit Cards: A, B
Notes: 5, 7, 12

Casa Bella Hotel
264 Sherbrooke West, H2X 1X9
(514) 849-2777

The same owner has operated this charming hotel for 21 years. The 100-year-old European-style house has been renovated and is located downtown, near "La Place Des Arts," U.S. Consulate, Métro, bus, and within walking distance of Old Montreal, Prince Arthur Street, and shopping center. Rooms are comfortable for a low price. Parking is available.

Rooms: 20 (14 PB; 6 SB) $43-72
Continental Breakfast
Credit Cards: A, B, E
Notes: 5, 7

Manoir Sherbrooke
157 Sherbrooke Est, H2X 1C7
(514) 845-0915

The Manoir Sherbrooke is a small hotel with a European character offering a family atmosphere. It is convenient to Métro and Saint Denis and Prince Arthur streets. It is within walking distance of Old Montreal, the Palais of Congress, and numerous shopping centers.

Host: Annick Legall
Rooms: 22 (14 PB; 8 SB) $42-70
Continental Breakfast
Credit Cards: A, B
Notes: 5, 7, 12

---

year; 6 Pets welcome; 7 Children welcome; 8 Tennis nearby; 9 Swimming nearby; 10 Golf nearby; 11 Skiing nearby; 12 May be booked through travel agent

QUEBEC

Bed and Breakfast Bonjour Québec
3765 Boulevard Monaco, G1P 3J3
(418) 527-1465

The first reservation service of Quebec represents 11 homes that were carefully selected to make your visit a genuine French experience. The Grande-Allee is reminiscent of the Champs Elysée in Paris. Historic sites, the St. Lawrence River, charming restaurants, and shops are within easy reach of every location.

Coordinators: Denise and Raymond Blanchet
Rooms: 22 (SB) $45-60 Canadian
Full Breakfast
Credit Cards: None
Closed November-April
Note: 2

ST-MARC-SUR-LE-RICHELIEU

Auberge Handfield
555 Chemin du Prince, J0L 2E0
(514) 584-2226; FAX (514) 584-3650

We are a historic Colonial country inn built in the 1800s and located 35 minutes south of Montreal by Highway 20, Exit 112, then on 223 north. In the summer, our guests relax on the terrace with a swimming pool and view yachts in our marina, or enjoy our newly contructed health club and spa. Also, there is the showboat, *l'Escale*, where you can appreciate a good theater play. In the spring, enjoy sugaring-off parties at our Cabane à Sucre.

Host: Conrad Handfield
Rooms: 55 (PB) $55-145
Full Breakfast
Credit Cards: A, B, C, E
Notes: 3, 4, 5, 7, 8, 9, 10, 11

SAINTE-PÉTRONILLE

Auberge La Goéliche Inn
22 Chemin du Quai, G0A 4C0
(418) 828-2248; FAX (418) 692-1742

Overlooking the St. Lawrence River, this castlelike inn offers a breathtaking view of Quebec City, which is only 15 minutes away. It is also close to famous Mont Ste-Anne ski center. Twenty-four rooms are warmly decorated with rustic French-Canadian style. Outdoor swimming pool and guided tours of historic surroundings are available on site.

Hosts: Janet Duplain, Andrée Marchand, Alain Turgeon
Rooms: 24 (16 PB; 8 SB) $70-115
Full Breakfast
Credit Cards: A, B
Notes: 3, 4, 5, 7, 8, 9, 10, 11, 12

NOTES: Credit cards accepted: A Master Card; B Visa; C American Express; D Discover Card; E Diners Club; F Other; 2 Personal checks accepted; 3 Lunch available; 4 Dinner available; 5 Open all

Puerto Rico

CEIBA

Ceiba Country Inn
Carr 977 KM 1.2, 00735
(809) 885-0471

Tropical setting on the east coast of Puerto Rico, in the mountains with a view of the ocean and the island of Culebra. Five marinas, Luquillo Beach, El Yunque Rain Forest close by. Continental buffet breakfast is served in a warm, sunny breakfast room or large Spanish patio. Library, dart board, board games. Operated by owners; guests are treated like family.

Host: Don Bingham and Nicki Treat
Rooms: 9 (PB) $55
Continental Breakfast
Credit Cards: A, B, C, D
Notes: 3, 5, 7, 12

SAN JUAN

Tres Palmas Guest House
2212 Park Boulevard, 00913
(809) 727-4617

Remodeled in 1990, all rooms include air conditioners, ceiling fans, color cable TV with remote control, AM/FM clock radio, small decorative refrigerators, continental breakfast. Oceanfront, beautiful sandy beach; daily maid service; newspapers; magazines; games; ocean-view sun deck; fresh beach towels and chairs. Tourist information available. Centrally located ten minutes from the airport and Old San Juan.

Hosts: Jeannette Maldonado and Elving Torres
Rooms: 9 plus 3 apartments (11 PB; 1 SB)
   $45-85; $45-60 off-season
Continental Breakfast
Credit Cards: A, B, C
Notes: 3, 4, 5, 7, 9

Ceiba Country Inn

---

year; 6 Pets welcome; 7 Children welcome; 8 Tennis nearby; 9 Swimming nearby; 10 Golf nearby; 11 Skiing nearby; 12 May be booked through travel agent

SANTURCE

La Condesa Inn
Cacique 2071 Ocean Park, 00911
(809) 727-3698; (809) 727-3900

This small and special guest house is 100 feet from the beach. Every room has a private bath, air conditioning, color cable TV, and clock radio. Pool and spa are available. A continental breakfast is served in the bar, on the patio, or in your room. Breakfast and light lunch are served daily. Complimentary drink welcomes you. Call for price information.

Host: Rey Alvares
Rooms: 15 (PB)
Continental Breakfast
Credit Cards: A, B, C
Notes: 3, 5, 6, 7, 9

NOTES: Credit cards accepted: A Master Card; B Visa; C American Express; D Discover Card; E Diners Club; F Other; 2 Personal checks accepted; 3 Lunch available; 4 Dinner available; 5 Open all

Virgin Islands

ST. THOMAS

Island View Guest House
P. O. Box 1903, 00801
(809) 774-4270; (800) 524-2023 reservations

This charming guest house is located midway between the airport and the town of Charlotte Amalie, on Crown Mountain, 545 feet above and overlooking the harbor. Beach and restaurants are close by. Rooms have king, queen, and twin accommodations, most with private bath and balcony. Fans, air conditioning, telephone in room, laundry facilities available. Kitchen available upon request.

Hosts: Norman Leader and Barbara Cooper
Rooms: 15 (13 PB; 2 SB) $63-95 winter; $45-68 summer
Continental Breakfast; Full Breakfast available
Credit Cards: A, B, C
Notes: 2, 5, 9

Mafolie Hotel
P. O. Box 1506, 00804
(809) 774-2790; (800) 225-7035
FAX (809) 774-4091

Enjoy the world-famous view 800 feet above the town and harbor. The hotel was totally renovated in 1991. Minisuites can sleep four and have TV, refrigerator, and king beds. The freshwater pool has a large deck; lunch is served all day. An excellent restaurant on the property serves seafood, steak, chicken, and pork—all grilled to perfection. Entree prices start at $13.50. Free transportation to Magen's Beach.

Host: Lyn Eden
Rooms: 18 plus 5 mini-suites (PB) $60-68 summer; $93-97 winter
Continental Breakfast
Credit Cards: A, B, C
Notes: 3, 4, 5, 7, 8, 9, 10, 12

---

year; 6 Pets welcome; 7 Children welcome; 8 Tennis nearby; 9 Swimming nearby; 10 Golf nearby; 11 Skiing nearby; 12 May be booked through travel agent

Index

Alabama 3	New Jersey 152
Alaska 4	New Mexico 157
Arizona 8	New York 159
Arkansas 10	North Carolina 174
California 13	North Dakota 183
Colorado 38	Ohio 184
Connecticut 45	Oklahoma 190
Delaware 49	Oregon 191
District of Columbia 51	Pennsylvania 195
Florida 52	Rhode Island 214
Georgia 57	South Carolina 219
Hawaii 63	South Dakota 225
Idaho 66	Tennessee 227
Illinois 68	Texas 230
Indiana 73	Utah 235
Iowa 79	Vermont 236
Kansas 83	Virginia 241
Kentucky 86	Washington 251
Louisiana 88	West Virginia 262
Maine 90	Wisconsin 266
Maryland 101	Wyoming 272
Massachusetts 106	Alberta 27
Michigan 121	British Columbia 273
Minnesota 129	Manitoba 278
Mississippi 132	Nova Scotia 279
Missouri 134	Ontario 280
Montana 139	Prince Edward Island 282
Nebraska 140	Quebec 282
Nevada 141	Puerto Rico 282
New Hampshire 142	Virgin Islands 28